Date Due

ILLO			

W9-CPP-118

OUR NEIGHBORS UPSTAIRS

THE CANADIANS

OUR
NEIGHBORS
UPSTAIRS

William Redman Duggan

THE
CANADIANS

Foreword by
Robert W. Straub
Governor of Oregon

Nelson - Hall  Chicago

Library of Congress Cataloging in Publication Data

Duggan, William Redman.
  Our neighbors upstairs, the Canadians.

  Bibliography: p.
  Includes index.
  1. Canada. I. Title.
F1008.D86   971   79-1308
ISBN 0-88229-530-6

Manufactured in the United States of America

10   9   8   7   6   5   4   3   2   1

Contents

Foreword

William Redman Duggan, the lately deceased author of this book, was my close friend. His life had been one of vigor, commitment, and concern. His friends will remember him for his good company and for his extraordinary courage.

Red had completed this manuscript just before he died and felt strongly that it would be of benefit to Americans and Canadians alike. He wrote, as he worked, for a better understanding and closer appreciation between these two great countries. He also worked and wrote for a better understanding between the Anglo-Canadian and the French-Canadian to avoid dismemberment of Canada.

After serving at two posts in Canada as an American Foreign Service Officer, he continued over the years to study and understand more of that country and to keep in close contact with his many friends there.

Three years ago, Red Duggan started writing this book, traveling the length and breadth of Canada, meeting and listening to leaders and others of all persuasions. His research was extensive and his means of keeping up-to-date phenomenal. He wrote for students, for businessmen, and for the public on both sides of the border.

Red Duggan was a man of candor and courage. In my six years of close association with him, and in my knowledge of his career of thirty years in the American Foreign Service, he always told it as it was—with no flimflam and no diplomatic double-talk.

ROBERT W. STRAUB
Governor of Oregon

Salem, Oregon

Preface

This is the story of the "kingdom" of Canada—of the people upstairs. It is a saga of Eskimos, Indians, and Norsemen. It is a tale of far-famed explorers, of political princes and provincial fiefs, of business barons and of the ordinary Canadians. It is a tale of a land hewn out of wilderness and cold by Britons, Frenchmen—and Americans.

Some have called Canada a nation that is dull and diffident. It is not. Rather it is a nation of rich historical tapestries and of magnificent natural wonders. It is a nation comprising a most complex human mosaic—ethnic, religious, cultural. It is a country too little known. It is a nation that we Americans, Europeans, Asians—even Canadians—should understand just a little bit better.

Some three decades ago, there appeared in Canada a classic book depicting the facts and foibles of Canadian life. That book, written by the British Columbian author-editor Bruce Hutchison, did not set itself up to be a dry academic study, but rather a facile and sparkling interpretation of the real Canadian character. The author accomplished his delineation with telling effect. One major theme that author Hutchison set forth was that the downstairs neighbors, the Americans, knew far too little about the upstairs neighbors, the Canadians. This contention is pointed up even in the title of his book—*The Unknown Country*.

In his analysis of his country's character and his countrymen's traits, Hutchison went on to prophesy that the
relationship between Canadians and Americans would
come to form one of the basic partnerships of global
politics, of trade and defense. His forecast stood the test of
time for thirty years, even though, as he acknowledged, the
two countries understood one another far too little and
sometimes not at all. Today, in the wake of such earth-
shaking events as the energy crisis and economic nationalism. Hutchison's characterizations demand review, for
relationships between these two important neighbors are
becoming increasingly abrasive, complex, divergent.

In his book, Hutchison paints his countrymen's quiet
reserve, complexities, even neuroses. As well he vividly
interprets Canada's past performance, present promise,
and great potential:

> No one knows my country—neither the stranger nor its
> own sons. My country is hidden in the dark and teeming
> brain of youth upon the eve of its manhood. My country
> has not found itself nor felt its power nor learned its true
> place. It is all visions and doubts and hopes and dreams.
> It is strength and weakness, despair and joy. . . .
>
> A problem for America they call us. . . . A backward
> nation they call us beside our great neighbor. This
> though [we] have produced more, earned more, subdued
> more, built more than any other [comparable nation] in
> the world. . . . A colony they have thought us, though
> . . . we have produced the British Commonwealth of
> equal nations. . . . A timid race they have called us
> because we have been slow to change. . . .
>
> They have not known Canada. Who but us can feel our
> hopes and fears and passions? How can aliens or even
> blood brothers know our inner doubts, our secret
> strengths and weaknesses. . . . Who can know our lone-
> liness in the immensity of our forests and prairies and
> sea rocks . . . and all about us lies Canada forever
> unknown? No—they could not know us for we have not
> known ourselves. . . . Now must the stuff of Canada
> take shape. . . . Now our time is come and we are
> ready. . . .

Today, some thirty-five years after Hutchison's book

first appeared, his nation—Canada—remains relatively "unknown." Yet it is now, assuredly, an economic giant with growing international repute. Still, neither Americans nor Europeans nor even Canadians themselves yet fully comprehend Canada's place and potential. Nor do they yet understand the intricacies, the doubtings, the pride, the pulls, the passions of the Canadian character and its continuing search for identity.

Despite the fact that more than 20 million Americans visit Canada each year, the country of Canada—its geography, history, flag, and people—is generally obscure to Americans. Canadians, perplexed, find Americans surprisingly uninformed about Canada.

Canada's Prime Minister Trudeau has aptly characterized his country's situation. Finding itself beside the gargantuan United States, he says, is like a mouse finding itself in bed beside an elephant. This elephant casts a massive—sometimes somber—sometimes roguish—but always vexatious—shadow across the whole landscape of Canadian life. Today, after more than a century of its own nationhood, Canada is determined to do something about it.

By taking a hard look "Inside Canada," this book seeks to sketch Canada's national profile and to capture the essence of its people's character today. This book seeks to set forth the colorful roots of Canadian history; the varied mosaic of its population; the pulls of its ethnic and regional disparities; the immense influences of its environment. It sets forth as well the peculiar problems of its proximity to the Colossus of the South.

Finally this book seeks to show what Canadian nationalism really is—what the country's capabilities and aspirations may be. The author tries, as well, to define who and what a Canadian really is. In sum, this book is written for friends—Canadians upstairs and Americans downstairs. For today—and for a longer tomorrow—we must preserve that neighborliness. But first we must understand each other.

The author wishes to give special acknowledgment and

thanks to Bruce Hutchison, author of *The Unknown Country* and *The Incredible Canadian*; to Chester and Eva Jewell of Vancouver; to Peter Newman, editor of *Maclean's*; to Senator John Connolly of Ottawa; to officials of the Canadian Government Information Office; to Ivan Lovell, Professor of History (Emeritus), Willamette University, Salem, Oregon; to George McCowen, Professor of History at Willamette; and especially to his amanuensis and wife, Bunny. Each of these, in his or her own way, knowingly or unknowingly contributed advice and help in the preparation of this book.

1
An Introduction to Our Neighbors

Once upon a time, Canada was known as a country bounded on the North by the Cold; on the West by the East; on the East by History, and on the South by Friends.

That delineation does not describe contemporary Canada. Today Canada might be said to be bounded on the north by unspoiled environment, unfathomed riches, and unpopulated miles. Off her western shores Canada, still finds the East—and, therein, new treasure troves of trade and friendship. Beyond her eastern shores, the hereditary cultural-political associations with Britain and France remain, but that long-standing pull of Canada toward Europe has now been loosened. New global pulls are replacing these traditional eastern associations, and the latter will probably continue to weaken as the European Common Market comes to maturity.

Finally, there is that ubiquitous, elephantine, and noisy neighbor to the south. This colossus—the United States of America—ranges forty-five hundred miles along Canada's southern and western borders. That dominating presence, with its continual cultural shocks beating like a giant tide against Canadian efforts to build her own nation, her own character, might long ago have submerged a less determined people. Living cheek by jowl with this superpower, Canada has not only survived as a nation but has slowly developed her individuality and reinforced her indepen-

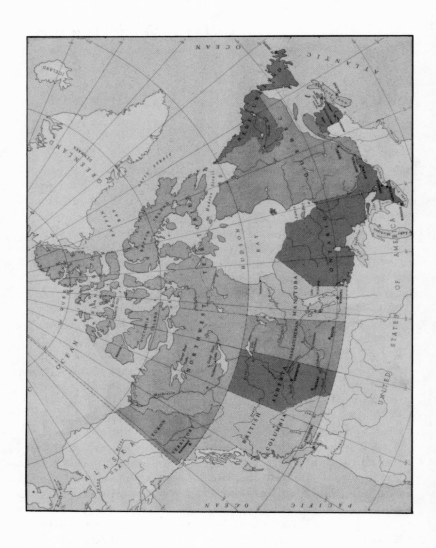

2

dence. Yet it now becomes a question whether these neighbors Canada and the United States can remain firm
friends. For there are coming into view new abrasions and
increasingly complex problems between these two nations
that inhabit the continental "bloc." Yesterday and today,
the American neighbor has wanted to borrow, and freely
use, not only the Canadian lawn mower, shovel and power
saw—but all the Canadians' tools—and the fishing rod and
the shotgun and the motorboat. Thus, day by day, the
situation between these neighbors becomes increasingly
vexing, increasingly delicate. It possesses far greater
complexity than did the simpler association of three
decades ago. These relationships demand careful and
tactful reassessment. That reassessment is all the more
imperative because Canadians today are coming to view
their southern neighbors with considerably more caution,
reserve, even trepidation, than at any time in the past
century.

And what of Canadians inside their own country? Are
they, as alleged by some, "just like the Americans"? They
are not. They have an array of problems and values—
ethnic, cultural, political, and economic—vastly different
from those of their downstairs neighbors. Let's take a look
"Inside Canada" and find out!

Possessing a land mass of 3.8 million square miles,
Canada is second in size only to the Soviet Union and
somewhat larger than China or the United States. Yet
Canada's population of 24 million is but 11 percent that of
America and equal to only 3 percent of the population of
China. Furthermore, over two-thirds of all Canadians live
in fifteen urban centers, most of these concentrated into
the southeastern corner of Canada. In fact, 80 percent of
the nation's population resides within a ribbon of urban
communities stretching from coast to coast within 100
miles of the American border. Thus, half of Canada, the so-
called Far North, is virtually uninhabited and still largely
undeveloped. This northern region is separated from cosmopolitan Canada by a band of forests and tundra and

cold. Great gulfs of water separate large portions of Canada from the continental mainland. As well, there are ethnic, religious, linguistic, and economic gulfs that are as divisive of certain regions of Canada as are the geographic barriers of distance and development.

Yet other, seemingly intractible, problems remain within Canada itself. Nearly a thousand years have passed since the first European explorers, the Vikings, are said to have come upon Canadian shores. Nearly five hundred years have elapsed since other European explorers— Portuguese, Italian, British, and French—first set foot upon those shores and, as well, intruded into the Canadian hinterland. These, in turn, were followed by permanent settlers—trappers, traders, missionaries, and soldiers who helped settle and subdue nearly half a continent. As these men and women blazed their trails through this new-found wilderness, they wrested the land from the indigenous Indian, his cousin the Eskimo, and eventually from one another.

Finally, in the mid-nineteenth century, a new confederacy was born of the exploits and the toil of those firstcomers. This new nation—Canada—rose out of the seedstock, the ethnic mosaic, of French and British and other European nations, even a few Revolutionary American "Loyalists."

While recognizing and appreciating these earlier legacies of London and Paris and Washington, the people of the new Canada insisted on creating a separateness from their forebears. They wanted and founded a nation distinctly their own. Furthermore, by creating that wholly separate and distinctive nation, the Canadians foresaw their best insurance against total domination either by their colonial progenitors or by the behemoth to the south.

A quarter-century ago, Canada was chiefly an agricultural land of small population and of only slight stature as a world power. However, she had great economic potential. Much of that potential is just now being realized. Today, Canada is highly industrialized and a giant among trading nations. She is a nation of rich natural resources. These riches are found not alone in agriculture, forests, fisheries, and minerals, but as well in major sources of manpower and of energy—precious petroleum and water power. Given these riches, Canada has become a nation of considerable repute in financial, technical, scientific, and cultural worlds. Today, Canada is a fair-haired child of international investment and multinational corporations. She holds nearly $35 billion of America's foreign investment funds and one-fifth of Britain's external investment. In recent months, Canada has become the site of new investment, commerce, or trading ties involving nations as far-flung as Japan, France, Germany, the Soviet Union, and mainland China.

Two decades ago, American firms operating on the Canadian scene numbered only a few dozen. Today, however, giant American businesses with headquarters or branches situated in Canada number upward of fifteen hundred. Today, Canada and the United States are the world's greatest trading partners. That trade now moves at the astronomical annual rate of $30 billion in each direction. Yet today—fearing unexpected surtaxes, import quotas, sudden embargoes, tariff walls, inflationary pressures—Canada has become increasingly wary of the economic activities of her southern neighbor and erstwhile friend. In retaliation, Canada seeks to impose financial controls and trade quotas of her own against the United States.

Again, for decades past, Canada and the United States have been allies in war. From the traumas of the two world wars, the two nations emerged as firm military collaborators. From those conflicts, too, the United States emerged as the military colossus of the globe. America was to hold that primacy for another two decades—then to be challenged by the Soviet Union, Canada's far northern neighbor. Prior to World War II, Canada had been a satrap of British military and naval might. However, after 1945, as Britain's world influence diminished, Canada saw herself caught, geographically and politically, between two mast-odons, the United States and the Soviet Union. She sensed the necessity of reorienting her defense ties south-ward, thus coming under the American nuclear umbrella. Out of a mutual need was thus created a North American Air Defense (NORAD). As Canada shed her traditional military ties with Britain, she also joined NATO and participated with the United Nations and the United States in important international peacekeeping opera-tions (Korea, Congo, Cyprus, Middle East, even Vietnam). At the same time, Canada sought to devise diplomatic means to lessen, if not obviate, the real danger of Canada's becoming a battleground for the superpowers. Today, with more than one-third of all her agreements with the United States in the defense realm, Canada finds herself inextri-cably entwined militarily with her southern neighbor.

Yet here too, there is trepidation. For Canada is a serious-minded and peace-loving nation. Yet, more than any other friend and ally, Canada has seen and sensed the unpalatable aspects of the Vietnam conflict. Canada has felt the poison that has permeated the American polity over that conflict. Far better than any other foreigners, Canadians have seen the wastage of manpower, of re-sources, of national pride and conscience, that America has suffered from the Vietnam War. Canada has also cautiously assumed a "Good Samaritan" role in that con-flict, a role forced on her by proximity. She has provided a refuge for more than seventy thousand American con-scientious objectors, draft dodgers, and deserters fleeing that intolerable American involvement in Asia. It is under-standable that some Canadian citizens resented their country becoming a haven for these American exiles. This problem, too, caused abrasions between the two governments.

In the light of history ranging from revolutionary inva-sion of Canada through civil war conflicts to boundary disputes and recent trade quarrels, Canadians have inevi-tably had to consider the prospect that their mighty neighbor could also some day, for reasons of presumed national interest, decide to attack Canada itself. For, during her own historical associations with America, Canada has witnessed interventions by the United States, justified or unjustified, in Mexico, Cuba, the Dominican Republic, Chile, and Vietnam among others. A recent best-selling novel in Canada titled *Ultimatum* carries the theme of a despotic American president'ᴣ decision to attack, conquer, and annex Canada.

Yet all these external concerns fade for Canada when she recalls her far more immediate and pressing internal troubles. Those concerns, ubiquitous and disquieting, center upon the pervasive problem of separatism. The separatist pulls are registered most openly in the cultural, religious, linguistic, and political conflicts, French versus English. They are present, in less violent strain, in regional and social disparities. Canada also finds herself engaged with nettling economic controversies of agricultural versus industrial sectors, of capital versus labor, of long-time settler versus new immigrant. She faces the economic disparities of rich provinces versus poor provinces, of developed lands versus neglected lands. Together, these separatist pressures both weaken and degrade the national spirit, the character and strength, of all Canada.

Even the geography of Canada works against her efforts to knit component parts into a single nation-state. The very spaciousness and sparseness of Canada provides centrifugal pressures. As noted earlier, two-thirds of all Canadians are concentrated in the nation's southeastern corner, and four-fifths of the population resides within 100 miles of the American border. Extensive regions of her Far North are virtually uninhabited. Furthermore, parts of the Maritime Provinces (Newfoundland, Nova Scotia, New Brunswick, and Prince Edward Island) are divided from the rest of Canada by great gulfs of water. For many of Canada's outlanders, the problem of communication with other parts of the nation is a constant and troublesome one. Such communication would be nearly impossible

were it not for the airplane, the radio, and, of late, the
magic of the communication satellite. This last brings to
many Canadians, for the first time, access to telephone and
television. These gigantic geographic barriers can contribute as much to the separation of the nation's body politic
as do linguistic and cultural barriers. For, lacking physical
and psychological ties, the outlanders may consider themselves victims of condescension or even complete neglect
by Ottawa.

Unlike the United States and Mexico or many another
nation recently decolonized, Canada was born without a
real revolution and has not yet experienced major civil
war. There have been disturbances, violent episodes,
moments of strife. However, none of these has been major,
long-drawn, or national in scope. Thus Canada has not yet
experienced that forced national bloodletting that so often
seems to be a necessary precursor to national cohesion, to
real unity as a nation-state. Therefore, it appears that the
cultural conflicts, ethnic differences, regional polarities,
that continue to exist in Canada today are undigested
poisons in her body politic and, as such, seriously sap her
strength as a nation.

Yet over and above all other pulls and pressures against
a unified Canada is the overriding dichotomy of the
French-Canadian Quebec versus the Anglophile-Canadian
Ontario and elsewhere. This dichotomy is measured in
terms of language, cultures, French versus English, with
both given official status. There are major religious differences, too, the French Catholic versus the Anglo Protestant. This polarization extends into education,
government, business, and social situations. The cleavage,
originally concentrated in the Quebec-Ontario area, is
spreading to other provinces and into other fields of
national life.

Only after this dichotomy is submersed and dissipated
can Canada become truly unified. If the dichotomy cannot
be healed, there could come about a dissolution of the
confederation into two weak and competing nations—or

even three. Until this question of separation is resolved, Canada's confusion over her character and her nationhood is bound to continue. Concerned observers of the Canadian scene, be they foreigners or nationals, near neighbors or far-distant friends, need to understand these pulls and their dangerous potentials. Lesser divisions than these have torn other nations asunder.

What is then the real character and composition of the Canadian nation today? What is her place on the North American scene? Will her constitutional connection with Britain, now virtually restricted to the symbolism of the scepter, continue? What is her international strength, and what are her national sinews? Is a united Canada now emerging, or are there irreparable fissures in that confederation? Finally, what are to be her future relations with her nearest North American neighbor?

Such portentous questions as to Canada's future require thoughtful examination by all concerned North Americans. In an effort to analyze these prospects, optimistic or pessimistic, this book takes a long searching look inside Canada.

2
Prehistory: The Place and the People

T he origins of the Canadian terrain have been fairly well documented by the study of its geology. The tentative theories of geologists show important mountain upheavals and glacial movements contributing to formation of the Canadian Shield; during associated ice ages and intervening temperature changes, the climate ranged from frigid to subtropical. The origins of Canada's first people, however, are even more speculative than is its geological history. The coming of the first man and woman to Canada, their origins and their travels, are only hinted at in oral tradition and given sparse certainty in anthropological assumptions.

The geological history of Canada is judged by some scientists to extend more then two billion years into the past. In those eons, there appear to have been at least four immense volcanic intrusions, these accompanied by formation of massive mountain chains. The last of these earthly revolutions was the Cenozoic, which probably occurred about four million years ago. From this great upsurge was formed the backbone of the Rockies in a band from Alaska to the Andes. Two of the major geological shifts were the Caledonian and Appalachian earth revolutions. These formed the eastern mountain bastions of North America and apparently fixed the beds and flows of the great eastern rivers of the continent, including the St. Lawrence.

After each of these upheavals, ice shields tended to level and scarify the land, then retreated to the north, leaving in their wake massive rock formations and numberless lakes and rivers. Following the last of these earthly transformations came at least four great southward surges of ice formations. The last of these ice sheets may have disappeared no more than twenty five thousand years ago. This latest ice shield covered at least two-thirds of northern and eastern Canada. It is estimated to have been as much as two miles thick. Its effect was to batter down many of the mountains into stumpy hills and uplands, stultifying also the vegetation and creating huge areas of muskeg and swampy meadows. In more temperate regions, the ice shields left forests and waterways. In the North, however, the same ice shields left only tundra, low vegetation growth, and plains of permafrost. The Canadian ice shield scraped root soil off the land and revealed much of the underlying rock formations. It has been in the oldest of these outcroppings that some of Canada's principal mining discoveries have been made—including gold, uranium, coal, nickel, iron ore.

The first explorations, the settlements, the entire early history of Canada were dominated by these peculiar geologic facts of life. The land had been left so rough, and the climate in the North was so forbidding, that permanent settlement—by Indians and by whites—took place first in the southeast, using only 10 percent of the land. Only later were exploration and settlement forced into the hinterland via the great river valleys and the Great Lakes. These waterways became corridors for exploration of the interior of the continent, with passage impeded only by the barricades of the long-lasting winter ice formations and necessary portages. Only after railways were built to span the continent east to west, providing easier transit of the mountains, did the heavy dependence on river transport and lake transport decline.

The surrounding oceans—Atlantic, Pacific and Arctic— also provided important routings for exploration, for

settlement, and for creation of the politico-economic map
of Canada. The first region developed was the Atlantic
Seaboard with its massive continental shelf bordering
Newfoundland and Nova Scotia. The fishing area there,
known as the Grand Banks, was discovered by Europeans
in the early sixteenth century. For those more intrepid of
Western European seafaring nations—Britain, France,
Spain, and Portugal—the Grand Banks became the greatest single source of edible fish on the entire globe. Associated with the early fishing expeditions was the intense
and long-lasting determination of explorers to find, some-
where along Canadian shores, the elusive northwest passage to Asia.

The remnants of the glacial ages had left little adequate
farmland in eastern Canada. Only after settlement of the
vast prairie country of the central plains and the lush
valleys of the far west did Canada actually become a major
food producer. The intense heat of summer, the intense
cold of winter and the sparse rainfall in the Prairie Provinces helped determine the kinds of crops for which Canada is famous, including wheat, rye, and barley. The heavy
moisture of east and west coasts resulted in timber growth
and helped lead to the establishment of related forestry
industries.

The values of the deep-water fisheries of both Atlantic
and Pacific coasts as major elements of the Canadian
economy are likewise self-evident and historically important. The much more recent findings of minerals (including
petroleum and other energy materials) and associated
industrialization all represent powerful influences in
changing the Canadian habitat and international position.
All these matters will be given detailed attention in pages
following.

Most knowledgeable anthropologists believe that Canada's aborigines—the Indians and their cousins the Eskimos—were not themselves indigenous to Canada. It is
now assumed that some fifteen thousand years ago the
forebears of these people migrated into North America

from Asia via the Bering Strait and Alaska. Some of them
roamed southward and settled on the islands and mainland of the Pacific coast. Others settled on the central
plains and forest lands. Others moved far into the Great
Lakes region and the St. Lawrence valley. Still others, the
Eskimos, ventured into the Far North, settling around the
shores of Hudson Bay and on the Arctic islands.

In any effort to understand Canada, it is necessary to
define what is meant by the Far North. Where does the
Canadian North begin, and what are its dimensions? Some
geographers have tried to devise responses to these questions by dividing the North into layers or belts. In truth,
however, there are no such clearly recognized boundaries
or divisions. Thus, both physically and psychologically,
most Canadians, and all foreign visitors, really enter the
Far North when they leave behind that relatively narrow
band of metropolitan life stretching along the Canadian
"Main Street" just north of the American border. Thus
there is no readily definable boundary to the Canadian
North except that which exists in one's mind.

It is generally accepted, however, that the true Canadian
North begins just above the great reaches of conifer forests
that stretch the width of middle Canada from the Yukon-
Alaskan border southeastward to Hudson Bay. The forest
belt skirts the southern shoreline of that great indentation
of salt water which itself extends eight hundred and fifty
miles north and south and six hundred miles east and
west. The forest then runs northeastward to mainland
Newfoundland (Labrador) and the Atlantic. Thus, even at
the southern tip of Hudson Bay there are to be found polar
bears, caribou, and tundra, symbols of the real Canadian
North.

All the area to the north of this great band of coniferous
forest, then, is considered to be the true Canadian North.
The North also includes the Yukon, the Northwest Territories and all the islands of the Arctic Ocean. It even
includes parts of northern Alberta and Saskatchewan,
perhaps half of Manitoba, Ontario, and Quebec, as well as
most of Labrador. It extends four thousand miles west to

east and some twenty-five hundred miles north to south, encompassing 1.7 million square miles. This represents nearly half the total land area of Canada. It is no wonder, then, that these vast reaches have had such profound influence on both Canadian character and history—and, for foreigners, have become legendary.

The Canadian nation fronts on three oceans—Atlantic, Pacific, and Arctic. In fact, it can be said that Canada dominates the Arctic, even though that dominance has not yet been tested by modern European or Asian powers. In any event, the intrusion of three continents into the Arctic makes this region a focal point of future geopolitical conflict in the Northern Hemisphere. To give further emphasis to those geopolitical implications, it must be realized that Canada is thus strategically located between the two superpowers—the United States and the Soviet Union—with tangential geographic relationships to China, Japan, and Northern Europe.

Nor, in attempting a real understanding of the Far North, can it be said simply that the region is composed of a sea of ice and a single great frozen plain of tundra and muskeg. In point of fact, the North has a much greater variety of topographic features than that. In the uptilted eastern region, there is located a great mountain range—the Arctic Highlands—which is as spectacular as the Alps. These mountains are relatively unknown, despite the fact that they are the dominant mountain range of all eastern North America.

This chain extends into the Arctic islands, forming the northern part of the Canadian Shield. On Ellesmere Island and eastward certain mountain peaks, such as the Grant-land Mountains, reach heights exceeding ten thousand feet, piercing heavy shields of permanent ice.

There is, as well, yet another great range in the west, running along the boundary of Alaska and Canada. This massif includes the stupendous Mt. Logan, 19,850 feet high. Between these two mighty mountain ranges, western and eastern, there sprawls the remnants of the Canadian Shield, with its eroded hills, multiple rivers, and lakes. In the lowlands left from the retreat of the ice shield are some of the greatest of the world's rivers—such as the Mackenzie—and some of the world's greatest and least-known lakes—such as Great Slave and Great Bear. Finally, to the north of the Canadian mainland, comprising the Arctic archipelago, there are hundreds of islands, fjords and bays—the largest of which, Hudson Bay, is bigger than any two of the Great Lakes.

A major misconception regarding the Far North appears to be the impression that its climate throughout the year is impossible for all but Eskimos and polar bears to survive. In fact, there are two seasons, winter and summer. Both are relatively dry; the summer is warm, and the winter is generally no more harsh than in Minnesota or southern Manitoba. In fact, winter winds and temperatures of the Midwestern plains can approximate or surpass in intensity the wintry blasts that blow through the Far North. Furthermore, there is likely to be more snowfall in Ontario or Michigan than in the Canadian North. In the latter area, however, there is really no transitional season—spring or fall—and the summer, while brief, is relatively pleasant. In summer, the sun stays above the horizon most of the time, and the temperature is not likely to top the seventies. Offsetting these months, however, are the long and tedious nights of winter—broken only by the luminosity of the Northern Lights and the bright moonlight.

Mention has been made of the broad range of forests along the southern reaches of this land. These forests of birch, spruce, and poplar have irregular borders that point like giant fingers into the tundra; beyond, only small birches, some bushes, and lichens survive. Thus it is that the forested areas, the taiga, merge gently into the tundra. It should be noted, as well, that there are variations in the tundra itself: the so-called Alpine tundra, fringing the mountain ranges; the shrub tundra, which borders the forest lands of the taiga and includes mosses, ferns, and bushes; and the Arctic tundra, with its stunted shrubs and lichens, which eventually fades into the polar ice cap. In summer, all of these variants of tundra are covered by myriads of small flowers.

These Arctic regions hold a great variety of wild life, dominated in summer by troublesome black flies and voracious mosquitoes. Mammal life includes lemming and caribou, musk ox, fox, wolf and reindeer. Along the Arctic shores, the polar bear, the whale, the walrus, and the seal are ever present. In northern waters are found salmon, pike and trout. Bird life varies from the Arctic tern to the far-famed Canadian geese. The North is always vividly alive.

The Eskimos, who settled onto the treeless tundra plains of the northlands, mainly ranged about the shorelines of Hudson Bay. From these waters, as well as from nearby rivers and plains, they took the main sustenance of their lives—caribou, fish, seal, walrus, whale. Certain of these—especially caribou and seal—provided the main elements of their clothing. From the fish and mammal they took their tools and their weapons of warfare. Even their fuel for warmth and light was secured from the fat of the mammals on which they lived. The bones and skin of the same animals even served as the frames for their boats and the coverings for both boats and houses. It is well-known that many of these Eskimos lived in igloos, houses formed from beveled blocks of ice and snow. Yet the majority lived in wigwams of skins.

Thus it was that the Eskimos' dependence on the animal life of their environment forced them to compete with their southerly cousins, the Indians, for access especially to the caribou. It was no wonder that the codes of their society, their traditions, their culture and religion, revolved around their life's essentials—bravery in the hunt, moon and stars and sun, rigors of winter and the long Arctic nights.

Some have said that nowhere else on earth is life more challenging than in the Arctic. Despite the demands of the environment, however, the human race has been able to enhance its existence with special kinds of art and culture, and the Eskimos too had their art, artifacts, poetry, and song.

Other cultures besides the Eskimos have learned to

adapt to, and to live successfully with, the cold and the
Arctic night. They have included, for example, the North-
men of Europe and of Asia—the Scandinavians, the Lapps,
and the Siberians. This adaptation is now being learned by
men of many nationalities in the Canadian (and the Alaskan) north.

Long before the Europeans first sighted the eastern
shores of North America, the Indians and Eskimos had
established their own, environmentally balanced way of
life on this continent. As noted earlier, the coming of the
Indian to North America and the early history of that race
on this continent continue to be shrouded by the mists of
time.

Even at the moment of the first arrival of the Europeans
on the continent, the total aboriginal population of all of
Canada numbered no more than a quarter of a million.
Today, Canada still has about a quarter of a million
Indians; the Eskimos left in the northern ranges of the
continent may number no more than twenty thousand. In
addition, there are some two hundred thousand half-
castes, or *Metis*.

The history of the aborigines merges with the story of
European settlement in eastern Canada at the beginning of
the sixteenth century. In western Canada, that historical
and cultural merging extended into the nineteenth century.
Both Indians and Eskimos taught the white man, the
European, the way to survive on this continent—in forests,
in mountains, and on the plains or tundra. By teaching
their skills in tracking, hunting, fishing, their cultivation
of Indian corn and their use of pemmican as a staple, the
Indians showed the white men how to accommodate to and
exist in harmony with their environments. Not the least of
the lessons were the use of the birchbark and the dugout
canoes, the trapping of beavers and other furred animals.

For sharing that knowledge, the aborigines of North
America were nearly exterminated from the United States.
In Canada, they were decimated, then pushed onto tribal
reserves—mere ghettoes—but they were never quite so

close to extermination as their cousins in the United States.

Along with their own civilization, the Europeans brought the Indian and Eskimo for the first time into contact with firearms and liquor, with the ravages of disease, including smallpox, measles, syphilis. In the face of these European pressures and troubles, the Indian civilizations and cultures virtually collapsed. The Indians who were left became dependent on the Europeans who had superior technology and firepower. Everywhere, except on those small tracts of lands reserved to them, the Indians forgot their own lore or had taken from them land and livelihood. They lost resources necessary to their survival, such as the fishing grounds and the vast buffalo herds. Until very recently, the ghettoes of the reserves bred further squalor and misery for their Indian inhabitants. Only in the past few years have Canadian federal and provincial governments and peoples given much better attention to the needs of the remaining aborigines.

In retrospect, it now seems certain that the penetration and full settlement of Canada would have been far more burdensome and drawn out had it not been for the fortunate combination of the aboriginal know-how with the energy of European explorers. Both groups depended on nature for food and shelter and used the many waterways—lakes and rivers—for transport into the North American hinterland. (For a fuller discussion of the modern Eskimo and Indian, see Chapter 12.)

3
From Cabot
to Captain Vancouver

About the year 1000 A. D., according to records and excavations still only partially authenticated, the Norse adventurer Leif Ericson apparently strayed off his navigational course. While en route to the Norse colony of Greenland, he came instead upon the eastern coast of Canada. In years immediately thereafter, he was reportedly followed by other Viking seafarers who established temporary camps in Newfoundland, Labrador, and Nova Scotia. It is barely possible to conclude from findings of fragmentary artifacts, including metal weapons and flints, that these Vikings or their fellows may have explored other parts of eastern Canada and New England. The nature and extent of these settlements have been under archeological scrutiny. In any event, these settlements appear to have been short-lived.

History has not yet revealed why there were apparently no real efforts at exploration or colonization of this region by Europeans until the end of the fifteenth century. But for nearly half a millennium, such exploits apparently ceased, and Europeans concentrated instead on their own continental interests. Finally, due to a combination of factors—including the development of new navigational aids, theories that the world was indeed round, and closure of European trade routes to the east by reason of Moorish conquests—Europeans were driven westward once more. European explorers of the fifteenth, sixteenth, and seventeenth centuries were all determined to give European trade new sea lanes to Asia by finding a fabled Northwest Passage. (Ironically, it was not until 1878–79 that such a passage, ice-bound and treacherous, was actually found and traversed by the Swedish explorer Nordenskjöld.)

First came the ventures of Columbus, and soon afterwards, the exploits of Cabot, Verrazano, Cortez, and Hudson. These first adventurers were followed by a second and more permanent wave of explorer-settlers— Cartier, Champlain, La Salle, Marquette, and others. It would take the combination of these explorers' efforts and more to provide Europe with the outlines and a sense of the immensity of the new continents. Meanwhile, other adventurers in other seas were finding other unknown lands— notably in Africa—and a southern sea route to Asia around the Cape of Good Hope. The names of Vasco da Gama, Cabral, and Magellan figure importantly here.

Toward the end of the fifteenth century, it became clear that both Spain and Portugal had the know-how and the munificence to support these activities. To prevent a major collision within Christendom, Pope Alexander VI in 1493 sought to divide the unknown world by awarding equal franchises to these two nations. In 1494, both parties signed the Treaty of Tordesillas. It awarded the lands lying west of a longitudinal line 370 leagues west of the Cape Verde Islands to Spain and lands east of that boundary to Portugal. Thus it was that the Portuguese concentrated on exploration of the coastlines of Africa and Brazil, while the Spanish attended to the Caribbean, to Peru and to North America.

Since their early adventurers found no gold in the North Atlantic areas, the Spanish did not seem interested in wasting their energies there. Instead they became concerned with ravaging the civilizations of Mexico and Peru, as well as carrying on their search for the fabled golden cities of Cebolla in what is now the American Southwest. Meanwhile French, English, and Dutch mariners indifferent to the Pope's decision were left to explore and, eventually, to colonize the eastern shores of North America. By the mid-sixteenth and early seventeenth centuries, the claims of these were made fairly secure.

THE ATLANTIC COAST

In 1497 there sailed out of Bristol, England, the barque *Matthew* commanded by the Italian navigator, Giovanni Caboto (John Cabot). He enjoyed the official protection of King Henry VII of England. By Cabot's official records, he reached Cape Breton Island on June 24, 1497. Later he visited Newfoundland and the coast of Labrador. These explorations by Cabot during two voyages (1497 and 1498) formed the basis for Britain's eventual claims to New-foundland and Labrador. Like Columbus, Cabot apparently believed that he had come upon the coast of Cathay. However, he and his son Sebastian did report the existence of immense shoals of fish on the continental shelf of Newfoundland, that area soon to be called the "Grand Banks." This was destined to become the most famous and richest fishing region in the known world.

Following Cabot's leads, a Portuguese navigator, Gaspar Corte-Real, in 1501 visited Labrador and Newfoundland. From there he took home to Portugal two shiploads of North American Indians to be sold into slavery. Corte-Real left clear signs of a temporary settlement in New England in 1511, but no firm records of his Canadian habitations.

Yet the search for the westerly route from Europe to the Orient continued—this search dominated by Magellan's amazing exploits in rounding Cape Horn (1521–22). That voyage was the first to give some estimate of the nature and extent of the two Americas. In addition, it proved, once and for all, the validity of the long-contested theory that the world was indeed round.

An Italian explorer, Verrazano, sailing under the flag of France, reached the western Atlantic coastline in 1523 and 1524. He touched upon sites ranging from Virginia and the present site of New York City as far north as Newfound-land. He gave the latter region the title Nova Francia (New

France). One of Verrazano's crewmen in that expedition was a young French navigator, Jacques Cartier. Neither these nor other contemporary explorers intruded far inland or established permanent settlements.

In 1534, Cartier helped lead a company of twenty-one men in a new effort to find the Northwest Passage. He entered a gulf that he named St. Lawrence, honoring the patron saint of that day, August 10, 1534. Cartier claimed those waters and surrounding lands for the king of France. Between 1534 and 1542, Cartier made several more voyages into the region, unsuccessfully attempting to establish permanent settlements there. He visited several Indian villages that later became the sites of important settlements by the French. The first of these, occupied by the Saguenay tribe, was Stadacona, now the site of Quebec City. The second was Hochelaga, near modern Montreal. However, impeded from further water ventures up the St. Lawrence by that river's rapids, Cartier failed in finding the water route to the Far East. As well, he failed to plant a lasting settlement on Canadian shores. Yet he established a pattern for future exploration and settlement of the region and gave France justification for her subsequent colonial rule of the area. For the next sixty and more years, however, the region was left to its indigenous inhabitants, the Indians. (It was not until 1608, when the explorer Champlain entered the region, that France finally succeeded in establishing permanent settlements in what is now Canada.)

Meanwhile, English explorers continued and expanded their contacts with the eastern coast of North America. In 1583, the British explorer Sir Humphrey Gilbert first visited Newfoundland. This voyage was designed to offset further colonial expansion by Spain and France. Yet, like earlier European ventures into the region, it was also designed to seek the elusive Northwest Passage. Gilbert claimed Newfoundland for his sovereign, Elizabeth I. There he sought to set up a permanent colony as a base for his further exploits. Newfoundland was thereafter considered an English colony. (It remained so until 1949, when it finally joined Canada.) Gilbert's efforts to find the Northwest Passage were as unproductive as had been other such ventures.

In the late sixteenth and early seventeenth centuries, British, French, Danish, and Dutch seamen continued to seek the waterway to the Far East. All were unsuccessful. (One such voyage is said to have provided the background for the British poet Coleridge's *Rime Of The Ancient Mariner.*) One of the strangest of these voyages was that of the Dutchman Henry Hudson, who had previously given his name to the Hudson River in New York. So far as can be ascertained from fragmentary records, about 1609 Hudson and a group of his seamen were wrecked on the shores of what is now Hudson Bay (later named in his honor). It appears that Hudson and a few of his crewmen survived the wreck but eventually perished on the shore of the bay. A mutinous group of his seamen took Hudson's ship and with it attempted to reach Europe. The vessel was wrecked off the coast of Ireland, leaving eight survivors who recounted the tragedy of Hudson's death in fragmentary form. Two centuries later, remnants of the Hudson camp were said to have been found on the shores of the bay now bearing his name.

The most famous and certainly the most successful of French explorers was Samuel Champlain. In 1604 he accompanied a group led by Sieur de Monts, serving as chief navigator and geographer. Their first organized attempt at colonization at the mouth of the Bay of Fundy (on St. Croix Island, now Dochet's Island, Maine) laid thirty-five of seventy-nine men dead of scurvy. The survivors moved the following summer to Port Royal, near the head of the Annapolis Basin in Acadia, Nova Scotia. That settlement is now called Annapolis. (In 1613 Port Royal was attacked by Englishmen from Virginia and barely survived. It became a prize that was fought over by English and French during the next two centuries.)

Champlain with his great cartographical skill still

looked for his river leading to the Pacific. The hostility of
the Indians, and the scattered coastal fur supply as compared with the St. Lawrence River area, determined Champlain and the fur merchants who supported him to return
to Canada. He arrived in the region in 1608; he explored the
coastline extensively and traveled as far as the Great
Lakes, where he built up a trade in furs with the Indians.
At that time he established his headquarters on the heights
above the Ile d'Orleans in the St. Lawrence River. This site
was destined to become Quebec City. Champlain's headquarters were Canada's first permanent French settlement
and served as the seat of French culture from that time
forward. His historic exploits won him the title "Father of
New France" and the namesake of the well-known lake in
northern New York.

British and French regimes now began laying claim to,
and carving up, the known regions of eastern Canada. In
1621 James I of England, refusing to recognize a prior
French claim, sought to take sovereignty over the entire
Gaspé Peninsula, including Port Royal. He granted the
area by charter to one Sir William Alexander, who named
the area Nova Scotia (New Scotland) in honor of his own
birthplace.

Almost continuous warfare now broke out in Europe
between Britain and France. These wars in turn were
reflected in conflict within the colonies of North
America—King William's War of 1689–1697, Queen Anne's
War of 1702–1713, King George's War of 1744–1748, and the
more decisive French and Indian War of 1754–1763.

At the conclusion of each of these conflicts, both powers
sought to regroup their colonies, rebuild their fortifications, and strengthen their lines of communication. Both
sides sought to revitalize their relationships with those
particular Indian tribes allied to their respective flags.
There were as well, at the conclusion of each of these wars,
certain geographic regroupings and shifts in political
control. One of these, in particular, has become renowned
in song and story, the literary heritage of every English-

speaking school child. This is the tale of *Evangeline* as immortalized by the New England poet Henry W. Longfellow.

The event that occasioned that famous poem followed upon the Treaty of Utrecht (1713) which concluded the war of Queen Anne. By terms of that treaty, the territory of Acadia in southern Nova Scotia reverted to Britain. The majority of inhabitants of the region were French, simple and law-abiding peasants, living along the coastline of the Bay of Fundy. They were clannish people who did not associate much with the British colonists living in central and northern Nova Scotia. These French Acadians sought to preserve their own way of life, their language and customs, their Catholic heritage. In 1755, a new British governor, Sir Charles Lawrence, arrived in Nova Scotia. In an ill-tempered effort to meld these French-speaking Acadians more firmly into the life of the colony, the new governor insisted that they take an oath of allegiance to the British crown. The Acadians refused but contended that they were both politically neutral and peacefully inclined. Their explanation did not satisfy the British governor. The situation became critical when the Acadians refused military conscription. The impetuous and harsh Governor Lawrence then ordered the Acadians deported by force. Within the next year, families were broken up and exiled to various French and British colonies to the south. Some went to Louisiana, the eventual home of Evangeline. This region is now known as "Cajun Country." Others went to the Carolinas and the Caribbean. The sad story of *Evangeline*, however, epitomizes only the beginnings of tribulations that were to grip half the North American continent for the next century.

In its first years, Quebec City had served as trading post and fortress rather than base for extending French colonial influence. The famed advisor to the court of Versailles, Cardinal Richelieu, determined that a more powerful effort had to be made to expand the colonization scheme in North America. Accordingly, some two hundred new French colonists were sent to Quebec each year, these including at least forty young, marriageable, and attractive French girls personally chosen by the king. These were known as Filles du Roi.

A few French missionary priests were also included among the settler groups sent from France. These took their work among both settlers and indigenous Indians very seriously. The Indians began to call these priests "Black Robes," and some of these became famed explorers in their own right. They concentrated their conversions and travels around the Great Lakes, and eventually in the valley of the Mississippi.

Meantime, Montreal was founded in 1642 by the French Catholic noble Sieur de Maisonneuve. The site, one hundred and sixty miles up the St. Lawrence River from Quebec City, had been the Indian village of Hochelaga, which Jacques Cartier had visited over a century before. Cartier, it will be recalled, had already given this place the name Mount Royal (Montreal). Since this location was so near to the settlements of the various constantly warring Indian tribes, especially Iroquois and Huron, the new village was not swift to attract settlers. Nevertheless, both Quebec and Montreal were combined officially into a single French Royal Colony of New France in 1663. More pronounced efforts at defense and at commercial exploitation proceeded from both locations. Richelieu's theories of colonial mercantilism thus served to revitalize French colonial aims in North America.

In this government of New France, the Catholic clergy, obviously intellectual leaders, sought to ensure their own influence. The Catholic bishop of New France was accorded a place of prestige and power just after that of the governor. The bishop was also an active member of the Governing Council, which served as both administrative directorate and judiciary. While the governor represented the French king, the bishop became the leader of the settler group, and conflict often occurred. However, Richelieu's influence in establishing the position of the church was so effective that the Catholic hierarchy remained a prime source of power in the Quebec colony and province for the following three centuries.

Méntion should be made here of the so-called seigneurial system that was instituted in this colony of New France. It was a system of land grants to the seigneurs, usually noble Frenchmen, who, in turn, rented parcels of their lands to peasants in a form of land tenancy. This was a feudal type of land grant deriving from the French chateau or manor house unit. This system, introduced into French Canada in 1598, remained in full effect until 1854. Traces of the seigneurial areas are still apparent in Quebec province today.

Within this system, large tracts of land located along beaches and waterways were awarded to members of the French nobility; the new owners in turn were expected to plant colonies and farms on the lands so awarded. They established churches and schools on the tracts; these and settler tenants' houses clustered around the manor house of the seigneur. Portions of the larger tracts were parceled out to the tenant settlers, who were to work the land and share profits with the landlord. The parcels of land so granted were thin strips that included a bit of river front, a segment of pasture land, and a piece of woodland.

The seigneurs in turn had to declare their continuing fealty to the king and had to agree to maintain manor house, school, and church on the feudal fiefdom. They also had to agree to maintain "royal forests" for the benefit of the Royal Navy and to give the profit from any mines to the royal treasury. Seigneurs also had to provide and support a *curé* or local priest for the benefit of the peasants (known as *habitants*).

The seigneurs were not so successful as one might have expected. They did not have such rigorous control of the peasant tenants as did the feudal lords of Europe. Nor were there adequate markets for the foodstuffs raised. New settlers disliked the intense winters, and many were attracted by the rich potential of the fur trade. However,

within the system, the influence of the church was profound, the local priests generally having control of the
schools. Their teaching was largely theoretical and classical rather than pragmatic and vocational, a factor that long
delayed Quebec's industrialization. Through systems of
taxation and inheritance, the church also became a major
landlord. Heavy tithes on the seigneurs and habitants, as
well as grants and inheritances, gave the church control of
nearly half the land in New France by the middle of the
eighteenth century. In these many ways did the church
exert its influence over the lives of the people of New
France. That ecclesiastical influence was not to be diminished until the middle of the twentieth century.

The Pacific Coast

Given all these developments on the Atlantic Coast,
what then was happening among explorers on the Pacific
Coast? Spain had laid claim to the entire continent of
North America, by right of Columbus' discoveries and
through the papal allocation to her of most of the Western
Hemisphere. In 1546, Spanish sailors came as far north as
present-day Oregon. However, the Spanish conquistadores and missionaries apparently never progressed much
further north than the San Francisco Bay region. In 1579
the great British sailor Sir Francis Drake, in his famous
ship *Golden Hind*, put into California bays and sailed
northward as far as the 44th parallel along the Oregon
coast. Apparently he made no land ventures in that area. It
appears from historical records that neither Spanish nor
British explorers returned to this region for nearly two
hundred years. In 1774 Spain again took interest in Pacific
North America, sending a ship captain, one Juan Perez,
northward as far as Vancouver Island. British, Spanish,
Russian, and American governments sent other travelers
into the area, claiming lands for their respective sovereign-
ties but making no firm settlements.

In 1745 the British Parliament had reinspired interest in

westward travel by offering a rich reward for the first discoverer of the Northwest Passage. Partly as a result of this offer, Captain James Cook, one of the greatest of British mariners, sailed around South America and moved northward, exploring the coastline of the Pacific Northwest as he sailed. He approached the Oregon coast, mapping the region and according names to several of its promontories (such as Cape Foul Weather). Cook anchored off Vancouver Island in March, 1778. He sailed from there to the Hawaiian Islands, where he was killed.

Yet another nation showed its flag in the Canadian Pacific region during the eighteenth century. As early as 1740, Russians had crossed the Bering Sea from Siberia, settling in the Alaskan Peninsula, which adjoins the present Canadian Pacific coast. These Russians developed highly profitable fur trade stations, taking back to Russia great catches of sea otter, seal, and beaver pelts. Russian title to these areas was not disturbed until the sale of Alaska to the United States in 1867. Even today, some remnants of Russian settlement survive in Alaskan localities such as Sitka.

In 1791 Spain surrendered all claim to lands north of the 42nd parallel in northern California. British and American traders and trappers were then left free to compete over the region of the Pacific Northwest.

In 1791 British Prime Minister George Grenville had instructed Captain George Vancouver, commander of H.M.S. *Discovery*, to proceed into the Pacific Northwestern seas to chase the Spaniards away from what is now the British Columbia coastline. The British hoped thereby to deliver the Pacific Northwest, including Oregon, to London rather than to Madrid or Washington. Grenville obviously had imperialist dreams for this region. He was attempting to overcome what he considered deficiencies of his predecessors, who had given some of the richest regions of North America (notably the upper Mississippi Valley) over to the United States in the Revolutionary War peace treaty of 1783. Grenville's instructions to Captain

Vancouver were prophetic. He told Vancouver that Britain was seeking to make Canada a nation of two-ocean frontiers and trade.

Vancouver spent three years (1792–95) in the region that is now Oregon, Washington, and British Columbia. He gave his name to Vancouver Island and discovered the mouth of the Fraser River. He also mapped the Strait of Juan de Fuca and the estuary of the Columbia River.

The task of naming that great river had already been accomplished in 1789 by the American navigator Robert Gray, who named it for his own vessel, the *Columbia*. Gray, too, visited Vancouver Island, making claim thereof for the new United States.

The Pacific Northwest became locked in problems of fur trade, the Louisiana Purchase, and the results of the Lewis and Clark expedition inspired by President Jefferson. All these events provoked a long and bitter conflict among Britain, Spain, and the United States that eventually became known as the Oregon question (a subject to be taken up in later pages of this book).

4

Conflict into Concord

O ur narrative now reverts to Eastern Canada and the seventeenth century. A spirited race both for control of the fur trade and for expansion of settlements in various parts of Canada now began in earnest between France and England. That race was to continue throughout Canada for the next two hundred years.

By 1650, the fur trade already extended far to the west beyond the Great Lakes. Both French and English traders had set up trapping stations in those hinterlands. One of the most adventurous was the Frenchman Pierre Radisson, who became one of the first Europeans to visit the upper reaches of the Mississippi. After Radisson was refused permission by French authorities to trade and trap in the Great Lakes area, he turned to the British in a fit of pique, seeking to interest the government of King Charles II in the Hudson Bay region. Radisson gained the ear of Prince Rupert, a relative and advisor of the king. Together they persuaded King Charles to finance expeditions to seek furs in the Hudson Bay area.

The first of the voyages captained by Radisson under the British flag was conducted on the vessel *Nonesuch*, which sailed into Hudson Bay in 1669. The success of that voyage impelled King Charles, in the year 1670, to charter the grant of Prince Rupert's Land to the later famous and powerful Hudson's Bay Company. This company of merchant-explorers was authorized by King Charles under the title "The Gentlemen Adventurers of England Trading in Hudson Bay." The vast area covered by this grant included parts of what are now northern Quebec, northern Ontario, Manitoba, Saskatchewan, Alberta, and even the Northwest Territories.

When King Charles awarded the Hudson's Bay grant to his cousin, Prince Rupert, the king stressed the need of continuing to seek a water passage to Asia. The concession covered both fur-trading and mineral rights. It gave sole title to the lands surrounding "Hudson Straits . . . as were not already possessed by other British subjects or by subjects of any other Christian princely state." The grant included fishing rights and mines discovered or undiscovered; all the grant was to be known as Prince Rupert's Land. In exchange for this giant fiefdom, King Charles asked only continuing allegiance from the company and, in tribute, annual rentals of "two elk and two black beavers." These skins were to be paid in deference to King Charles "whenever the King, his heirs and successors, shall happen to enter these territories." It is presumed that, to this day, such tribute is offered the British monarch and her heirs each time they visit the former Hudson's Bay territories of Canada.

King Charles also instructed officers of the Hudson's Bay group to maintain "good government" within those lands granted them. He insisted that they encourage trade, but, as well, gave permission for them to send warships, soldiers, and arms into the territory "for the security of the Same . . . if it is necessary to make peace or war with any people that are not Christians. . . ." A broad mandate it was, making officers of the Hudson's Bay Company absolute masters of the territories under their control.

By some historians, this royal charter is considered to be the most important single document in Canada's colonial history. Through it the die was cast for open competition and eventual warfare between British and French over most of Canada. For through its operations, the British-oriented Hudson's Bay Company was to extend its fiefdom, not only over its original grant, but even to the shores of the Pacific Ocean and as far south as present-day Oregon. (Those extensive fur-trade, trapping, and related land rights were not curtailed until 1870.) At that time, the company, under great pressure as a result of the creation of the Canadian Confederation in 1867, sold nearly one and a half million square miles of territory to the new Canadian government for 300,000 British pounds. From this massive block sale (one of the largest realty transactions in history) were formed several Canadian provinces or parts thereof. Even thereafter, the Hudson's Bay Company was permitted to retain certain trading, land, and mineral rights which it exercises to this day. Even now, these holdings in the prairie Provinces and the Canadian Northwest are said to exceed seven million acres. Today in Canada, this company (sometimes jocularly known as HBC—"Here Before Christ") operates a retail department store chain, continues in the fur trade, and is developing oil leases on its land holdings.

By the mid-seventeenth century, there had begun in eastern Canada and the American colonies a three-way contest for control that would range over a century and most of the continent before being resolved. This conflict involved the British and their Loyalist followers in North America; the French and their colonials in Quebec, the Maritimes and the Mississippi valley; and the American colonists of the Atlantic Seaboard.

In 1672, just two years after the founding of the Hudson's Bay Company, one Louis Comte de Frontenac became governor of New France. This was a man imperious and aggressive, though courageous and chivalrous. He sought to make peace with the troublesome Iroquois tribes, but when these efforts failed, he intimidated them. By 1697 Frontenac had managed to bring most of the Indian fighting under control. Frontenac was the first French administrator to realize that, for the present, only the fur trade was truly profitable, and agricultural settlement took second place. He drew on the rich profits from the fur trade, not only to subsidize farming and fishing, but also to pay for civil and military administration.

The richness of the fur trade, however, brought British and French settlers, trappers, and traders increasingly into open competition. While the French managed to keep control of the Great Lakes, the St. Lawrence, and the upper Mississippi, British commerce was extending its reach far westward into Prince Rupert's Land under the house flag of the Hudson's Bay Company. Here and elsewhere, the French and the British were to collide in due course.

One of the greatest names known to students of North American history is that of the French explorer and fur trader, Sieur Robert de La Salle. By 1671 he had located both Niagara Falls and the Ohio River. After failing to establish a fleet of ships designed to traverse the Great Lakes, La Salle journeyed the length of the Mississippi to its mouth in 1682. He was murdered in 1687 while trying to establish a settlement that later became New Orleans, but he had successfully claimed the Louisiana territory for his king, and by 1700 the French dominated that area.

Some word is now required concerning the fur trade that so dominated the pattern of colonial development, French and English, in Canada for more than two centuries. This trade began almost casually during the latter part of the sixteenth century. It was natural that the first French settlers in the St. Lawrence region should trade with the Indian villagers settled along the shores of that waterway. Trading in otter and especially in beaver pelts soon developed into large-scale enterprise. For those pelts, the Indians received European clothing, trinkets, garden implements, and eventually liquor and firearms.

The Canadian pelts were shipped to European capitals where fur-trimmed clothing was then in high fashion. In addition, beaver made excellent felt for men's hats when treated and trimmed. These hats being the most essential part of any modish man's costume in Europe, demand for the pelts became nearly impossible to satisfy. As a result of that insatiable demand, the French trappers sought to create a monopoly in trade of these pelts from Canada. As well, the French traders and trappers drove farther and farther into the Canadian interior to search out new sources of the beaver pelt. At the same time the French crown, hoping to keep that profitable trade in French hands, assigned monopoly rights and new franchises to specific French merchants if these agreed to establish permanent settlements in the St. Lawrence region.

The various Franco-British and Indian wars of the mid-eighteenth century created havoc with the fur trade. There were difficulties in acquiring pelts from warring Indian tribes and troubles in transporting skins to Montreal and Quebec for onward shipment to Europe. When these wars had died down, officials of the Hudson's Bay Company assumed that such difficulties would be eliminated and that its monopoly in the fur trade would be assured. This was not to be so. Almost at once a number of business venturers from the new towns now known as Montreal and Toronto came into open competition with the Rupert's Land group. French, Scottish, English, and American colonists joined in these competitive drives. None of them yet realized how vast were the land masses of Canada lying to the west of the Great Lakes and Hudson Bay proper. Most of these newcomers were called "Canadians"—this derived from the Huron word *kanatta* meaning "a collection of huts." This epithet was designed to distinguish the competitors from regular employees of the Hudson's Bay Company. Officials of the Hudson's Bay group began to realize that they must take this competition seriously and that, in order to protect their monopoly, they themselves must expand their activities westward. Thus it was that the fur trade expanded enormously in the latter part of the eighteenth century. At the same time, there began to emerge a new understanding of the geography of central and western Canada.

As trade expanded, the various Indian tribes of the region became dependent on it for their livelihood. Some appalling conditions developed as a direct result of this

dependence, namely the introduction to the Indians of
firearms and "firewater" and European diseases previously unknown among the indigenes. It is estimated that
nearly one-third of the Plains Indians perished from these
various scourges during the latter half of the eighteenth
century. The Indians became increasingly exploited, and,
after realizing the full effects of these new developments,
many tribes became belligerent. Though Hudson's Bay
officials at first refused to permit use of liquor or firearms
in the trade, even they later succumbed. As well, many
trappers took Indian women as wives or consorts. The
degradation of the Indian was swift, and there soon were a
large number of half-caste children known as Metis.

We have noted that, by the middle of the eighteenth
century, the French had extended their colonial grasp over
a massive section of North America, ranging from the
mouth of the St. Lawrence to the mouth of the Mississippi. They also ranged from the upper Great Lakes to the
shores of Hudson Bay. However, their numbers were
surprisingly few. Some historians have estimated that, by
1750, French settlers in North America numbered no more
than sixty thousand. Furthermore, most of these were
concentrated in the seigneurial establishments along the
reaches of the St. Lawrence or occupying the trading posts
of Stadacona (Quebec) and Hochelaga (Montreal).

By contrast, the British colonies to the south and east
were far more cohesive and far more numerous, especially
on the Atlantic Seaboard. Their population, including the
slaves of the Southern colonies, was said, even at that
time, to number nearly 2 million. In fact, their very
numbers brought about constant pressure for movement
westward. These moves, in turn, brought on increasing
conflict with the French and with the Indian tribes of the
plains and lakes regions. One of the more famous conflicts
between French and British forces involved a young Vir-
ginian named George Washington. In 1754, representing
his British superiors, Washington was sent to the Ohio
valley to judge and test the strength of new French fortifi-

cations in that region. After the French refused British orders to vacate one or more of these new vantage points (one of which was Fort Duquesne, site of what is now Pittsburgh), British troops from Virginia, commanded by the notorious Gen. Edward Braddock, were sent to recapture the fort and to free the area for British-American colonization. American history buffs will recall that in July, 1755, Braddock was defeated. He lost his life, despite sage advice by the young Washington as to the best method of conducting the battle. However, the die was cast. Both French and British, sensing further conflict, sent troop reinforcements into North America.

The decisive war between French and British forces (commonly known to American historians as the French and Indian War) broke out in 1756. The British had the advantage at sea, while the French, at the outset, had the military advantage on land. The French shored up their string of fortifications with first-class fighting men, chief among whom was the military commander of Quebec, Gen. Louis Montcalm. Montcalm at once strengthened his line of communications with existing French fortresses in the vicinity of the Great Lakes and the Hudson Valley. At Fort Ticonderoga on Lake Champlain, Montcalm successfully repelled British attacks. Meanwhile, the British government, under the despotic George III, sought to engage the French both in Europe and at sea. Their prime motivation, however, continued to be the capture of French colonies in North America.

The British military mounted a three-fingered assault on French bastions in North America—Niagara, Ticonderoga, and Montreal. A short time later they mounted a fourth attack—this against Quebec City. In these efforts of 1758, the British were repulsed, but they mounted a similar set of strategic attacks in 1759.

Montcalm, suffering serious shortages of supplies and manpower at Montreal, was forced to withdraw his troops to Quebec. These shortages resulted as much from British control of the seas (including the St. Lawrence estuary) as from maladministration and misjudgments of Montcalm's superiors in Paris.

In 1759, the highly capable British general James Wolfe decided to storm Quebec itself. First he blockaded the city with his naval units. Then his troops stole ashore in the darkness, climbing the heights under cover of night. The next morning, the British lined up on the Plains of Abraham, just outside the city's walls. In a now-famous fight, the British and French troops were engaged. The French suffered a decisive defeat. Quebec was occupied by the British, and both commanders, Wolfe and Montcalm, were mortally wounded. The British invaders took Montreal the following year, effectively ending French control over New France and all Canada. In 1763, by terms of the Treaty of Paris, all French possessions in North America (except a few tiny islands) were given up by France. (Even Louisiana was eventually sacrificed in 1803 to the new United States.) British power over North America was now dominant. Her dominions ranged from Hudson Bay to the Gulf of Mexico and from Atlantic to Pacific.

When the British acquired the governance of some seventy thousand widely dispersed French Canadians in that year of 1763, the lords of Westminster decided to try to carry on their rule with as few changes as possible. Their new subjects were French, Catholic and widely scattered. There were also the problems of control of the Indians (full-blood and half-caste) and of the fur traders in those regions. Many of the latter sought to maintain their loyalty to France. It would yet be some years before these groups were brought under control and eliminated as threats to frontier settlements and to trade.

With British rule established over New France, infusions of British commercial and mercantile interests began. Even the new British administrators (Sir James Murray and Guy Carleton) resented the pressures from the new British settlers in Montreal and Quebec. It was necessary to protect established trade and cultural patterns against disruption.

In 1774, the so-called Quebec Act was passed. The main

essentials of this act (sometimes called the French Canadian Magna Carta) included: (1) extension of the boundaries of Quebec Province northeastward to Labrador and westward to the Great Lakes, the Mississippi and the Ohio River valley; (2) assurance that the French Catholics would be free to practice their religion without hindrance, plus assurance that the Catholic church would be free to collect tithes; (3) continuance of the seigneurial system; (4) division of the law into two systems—civil suits to be tried under French law, criminal cases under British law. This act generally pleased the seigneurs and the clergy. The habitants and the business interests were less well-pleased. It was clear from this legislation, however, that many of the concepts of French colonialism would be retained under the banners and signatures of London.

Other results of the act were threefold: (1) it created a special position for the French language, culture, religion, even civil law; (2) it gave the province of Quebec a very special status within the Canadian confederation, which exists to this day; (3) it caused an important reaction among the American colonists to the south. In fact, the act helped propel those colonists into new demands and revolutionary activity against King George III.

The combined British policies of mercantilism, excessive taxation, and failure to provide adequate representation were fast driving the American colonies into revolution against the British crown. The Americans also resented the financial support they were forced to accord the British armed forces quartered in the colonies. Leaders of some of these thirteen colonies were of the opinion that the colonies to the north were being favored by the government in Westminster. This attitude was given further support by the special concessions to the French-Canadians set forth in the Quebec Act of 1774. In retrospect, it does not seem that the British colonial policies were so abrasive to the Canadian colonists as to their American cousins. The difference may have resulted from the fact that the Canadian settlers were still somewhat less politically advanced than their southern neighbors. Furthermore, the Canadians were still more highly dependent on British markets—especially for furs—than were the more diversified, agriculture-oriented American settlers.

As a result, it was natural that the Canadians would take a more neutralist, or even more pro-British, attitude than did the American colonists. The Canadians began to trade with both sides of the revolutionary quarrel. Furthermore, when the leaders of Quebec were invited to send representatives to the Continental Congress in Philadelphia, that invitation was declined. This refusal had momentous results, both short- and long-term.

In 1775, some rather hot-headed American revolutionaries set out to bring the Canadians of Quebec into the conflict on the American side. The Americans mounted a three-pronged attack against Niagara, Montreal, and Quebec, and succeeded on the first two of these fronts. Before the ramparts of Quebec City, however,they were decisively defeated. The American commander, Richard Montgomery, lost his life in the battle. The arrival of a British fleet in the St. Lawrence River sealed the fate of the American venture, and the invading forces withdrew from both Montreal and Quebec in the face of increasing Canadian hostility. On the other hand, when the British General Burgoyne led troops from Quebec to Saratoga in northern New York in 1777, he, too, was decisively defeated by American militia led by Gens. Philip Schuyler and Benedict Arnold.

Finally, after seven years of arduous warfare under the courageous leadership of Gen. George Washington, the Americans triumphed over the British. French and Spanish help, as well as American determination, had ensured the American victory. In 1783, the British, tired of their losses in conflict, made peace with the American colonies, which were declared independent.

In the peace settlement, both Americans and British agreed that the French should not be permitted to regain a colonial foothold in North America. The formal Canadian-

American boundary began to take shape. A line extending west from the St. Croix River and the Bay of Fundy ran south of the St. Lawrence and north of the headwaters of the Connecticut River. This line proceeded westward along the St. Lawrence and through the middle of the Great Lakes (Lakes Ontario, Erie, Huron, and Superior) to the base of the Lake of the Woods.

All the vast possessions of the Ohio and upper Mississippi valleys, so diligently developed by the French with their lines of forts, now fell to the Americans. Incorporation of these regions into the new United States provided the stepping stones for continent-wide expansion and "Manifest Destiny." Acquisition of adjacent areas following the Louisiana Purchase (1803) and the later conquests of the Mexican-American War were to ensure dominance by the Americans over the most fertile and habitable portions of North America.

As a result of the antagonisms and divided loyalties of the Revolutionary War, many sympathizers and adherents of the British cause suffered loss of property, deprivation of civil rights, even exile from the American colonies. Compensation or resettlement of these Loyalists following cessation of warfare generally failed. As a result, some Loyalists returned to England, and some went to the West Indies. Most of them, however, emigrated northward into Canada to seek new homes. Some thirty-five thousand went to Nova Scotia alone. About ten thousand more moved into Ontario, then becoming known as Upper Canada. Still others settled in New Brunswick and on Prince Edward Island. Most of the exiles to Canada were known as United Empire Loyalists, a name later to become venerated in the Anglo-Saxon Protestant society of Canada.

The movement into Canada of these many exiles from the American colonies provoked a reaction of its own within Canada. Despite their loyalties to the British crown, many of these settlers held personal theories regarding autonomy. Some began to lobby strenuously for a kind of representation and local government. London made concessions to these demands only sparingly. Under growing pressure however, in 1791, the so-called Canada Act—the first real constitutional act for the Canadian colonies—was promulgated by London. This was designed as a means of pacifying both English-speaking and French-speaking Canadians. It divided the former province of Quebec or New France into two—Upper Canada (eventually Ontario) and Lower Canada (eventually Quebec). The majority of English-speaking colonists lived in Upper Canada, French-speakers in Lower Canada.

Provincial governors were appointed and governments set up, including legislative councils of upper and lower houses. The upper house was appointed, like the British House of Lords, and the lower house was elected, like the British House of Commons. However, the governors and their executive councils still controlled the real reins of government. The British government retained the right to veto all bills.

By the same act, Upper Canada adopted the freehold land and civil justice system based on English common law. However, the seigneurial system of French civil law was established in Lower Canada; this system gave preferred status to the Catholic church. The Church of England (Anglican) was also accorded special status by a system of land grants made to its clergy.

Thus, this act gave Canadian colonists representative government but not wholly responsible government. However, it planted the seeds of Canada's present confederal system as well as her generally conservative bent.

As noted earlier, new conflicts emerged between Americans and Canadians during the 1790s and early 1800s. Part of the conflict arose over the fur trade. The Canadians had been distressed over the terms of the Treaty of Versailles (1783), which barred them from the best of the trapping area south and southwest of the Great Lakes. Trouble also originated from American failure to settle Loyalist claims against the new government. Other elements of the dispute concerned the continuing boundary question, particularly in New England and in the Detroit region. Talk grew on the American side concerning the advisability of invading Canada once more. Both British and American authorities were determined to avoid further conflict. The American Chief Justice, John Jay, was sent to London to negotiate a treaty settling these contentions and to seek avoidance of new warfare between the United States and British North America. Since Britain was now becoming immersed in new conflicts with the French, London was amenable to solutions and generally favored the American attitudes. However, the British insisted on joint access to the Great Lakes. The situation again became tense when the Canadians reentered the Mississippi valley but were forced out from there in 1808. Most of the Canadians now moved westward and northward.

In the 1780s, a group of Montreal fur traders had formed the Northwest and XY Companies, designed to challenge the supremacy of the Hudson's Bay Company in the fur trade of western Canada. By the early 1800s, both the Hudson's Bay group and the so-called pedlars of the Northwest and XY Companies had moved far afield. Coming into the Pacific Northwest and the newly found Oregon territory at the mouth of the Columbia River, Canadians and Americans fell into open competition and conflict.

The so-called Northwesters included some of the most famous explorers of western Canada, whose names are still revered by geographic title and heritage. One of these was Alexander Mackenzie, discoverer of the famous northern river that bears his name. He was also the first European to reach the Pacific Coast via the Continental Divide and the Canadian Rockies. A colleague, Simon Fraser, followed Mackenzie into what is now British Columbia, and it was for him that the Fraser River was named. (Fraser mistook the Fraser River for the Columbia River, which lay farther south.) It was a third Northwester, David Thompson, who traced the entire route of the Columbia. One of the most famous geographers of the time, Thompson had served with both the Hudson's Bay Company and the Northwesters. He also aided in surveying the United States–Canadian boundary between Quebec and Lake of the Woods. Thompson was the first Canadian to come upon the famous fur settlement of Astoria at the mouth of the Columbia River. This fort and trading post, established in 1811 by the wealthy New York tycoon John Jacob Astor, was the western terminus for his American Fur Company.

As a background to the Oregon question, attention must once more be given to the situation that developed in the West just before and after the War of 1812. In 1793, Alexander Mackenzie had journeyed down the Arctic river that now bears his name. Several years later, he traveled across the Rockies to the Pacific coast exploring the Columbia and Fraser River watersheds. After returning east, he wrote a book about his travels. In it he strongly urged Great Britain to take title to the Columbia River basin. To support this claim, Mackenzie advised setting up a chain of outposts and permanent settlements in the region.

The then President of the United States, Thomas Jefferson, read Mackenzie's book and became troubled at the thought of a new British intrusion into lands that Jefferson believed must eventually become American property. He therefore decided to finance an expedition to reinforce Captain Gray's earlier claim to the Columbia River territory. After Jefferson concluded the purchase of the Louisiana Territory for the "princely sum" of $15 million, he sent the expedition on its way.

Meriwether Lewis, who had for several years been Jefferson's personal secretary, and William Clark, a genius at dealing with the Indians, were placed in joint charge of the expedition. They began their long journey across the continent in May, 1804. In November, 1805, the Lewis and Clark expedition finally reached the Pacific Ocean near Astoria, Oregon. Thereby they reinforced American claims to the Oregon Territory, though it would still be more than forty years before the American title to the area was placed beyond dispute.

Meantime, Canadian explorers and trappers had expanded their activities in the Pacific Northwest. By 1805, Simon Fraser had built trading posts on his namesake Fraser River in British Columbia and had visited Puget Sound. David Thompson, who had now joined the Northwest Company, had mapped the Missouri River basin. He also traced the full route of the Columbia River and established Fort Vancouver, the site of Vancouver, Washington, today.

By 1811, the American Fur Company, headed by the New York tycoon John Jacob Astor, had established a string of forts and fur-trading stations as far west as Astoria. Astor, fearing the results of the War of 1812, decided to terminate his activities in that region. He sold out to the Northwesters in October, 1812. The Hudson's Bay Company took over and so controlled Oregon trade and territory. Thus, when a British fleet arrived, it found the fort at Astoria already in British hands. John McLoughlin, who lived on the site today known as Oregon City, Oregon, became the territorial governor, acting as representative of Hudson's Bay Company. Titled the "chief factor" of Hudson's Bay Company, he ruled over the territory like an emperor.

The War of 1812 was, to some degree, caused by Anglo-American competition in the fur trade. It was caused, as well, by British impressment of American seamen and harassment of American ships. Furthermore, the American frontier was advancing—imposing itself on the earlier domains of British trade and trapping. It was also pushing back the Indian tribes in the regions of the Great Lakes and the Great Plains. Under the Jay Treaty of 1794, Great Britain had presumably surrendered her right to these areas. The residents of British North America, however, were not happy over that agreement.

In some respects, then, the War of 1812 was fought to determine whether or not parts of Canada would yet fall under the American flag. In other respects, however, the War of 1812 proved to be a nonstarter. Apart from such isolated and spectacular incidents as the British capture of Washington and the defeat of the British at New Orleans, it proved essentially a stalemate. Few concessions were made by either of the foes. Yet, the war further widened the gap between the British North American colonists and their American cousins to the south.

The movement of Loyalists into Canada from the new United States had a highly important influence on both Canadian history and later Canadian–United States relationships. For these Loyalists and their heirs planted the first seeds of anti-Americanism in British North American hearts and minds. Most of the subsequent major historical events—ranging from the War of 1812 through the Oregon Territory dispute and the American Civil War—helped this spirit of anti-Americanism spread to the point where the two nations could never be brought together as one. (The Civil War and confederation were the final determinants in assuring that two English-speaking nations rather than one would arise in North America.)

The War of 1812 had again brought about efforts by Americans to invade Canada. Fighting was particularly intense on the Great Lakes and along the northern border of New York State. Conclusion of that War in December, 1814, brought restoration of the prewar border between the two North American nations. The Rush-Bagot Agreement of 1817 limited the number of naval vessels that both nations could retain on the Great Lakes. That treaty reconfirmed most of the border arrangements concluded in 1783 and 1794. In the East, only the Maine–New Brunswick borderline remained in question. (This was settled later by the Webster-Ashburton Treaty of 1842.) Boundaries in the West, to and beyond the Lake of the Woods, remained in doubt until settlement of the Oregon question in 1846.

As noted, the Treaty of Ghent, which concluded the War of 1812, did not settle ownership of the Pacific Northwest. Therefore, after that war, the United States and Britain agreed to a joint occupation of the Oregon Territory for a period of ten years. That agreement was extended. Furthermore, when the Russians tried to move their Alaskan boundary southward, the United States and Britain jointly intervened to prevent that move.

The first American government on the Pacific Coast was authorized by the people of the Willamette valley, at Champoeg, May 2, 1843. This meeting was attended by Americans and Britons. After much discussion, fifty-two voted for the motion, and fifty opposed it. It has been said the French-Canadian settlers in the area cast the deciding votes against the British.

In the first decades of the 1800s, the United States government had four times offered to divide the controversial Oregon Territory with Britain by cutting that region in two at the forty-ninth parallel. Each time, however, the British had refused. This question again arose when the Webster-Ashburton Treaty was being concluded. Once again the British rejected the idea. By 1845–46, however, under continuing congressional pressure, the issue was forcing Britain and the United States towards open warfare over Oregon.

The area in conflict was now considered to include all the lands ranging from northern California to Alaska and from the Pacific to the western ridges of the Rockies. There was even pressure in the American West for annexation of all the questioned Oregon Territory up to the Alaskan border and the latitude of 50° 40′ north. Two factors now affecting the question of the Oregon region were beginning to weaken the British claim thereto. American settlements, both north and south of the Columbia River, were growing quickly, and the economy was being redirected into agriculture and timber, with resulting decline in fur trade. As a result of this economic shift, the Hudson's Bay Company had moved its headquarters from Fort Vancouver on the Columbia to Fort Victoria on Vancouver Island. This move occurred in 1845.

In 1846, the issue was finally forced to a head. President James K. Polk's administration wished to be freed of the problem of the Oregon Territory in order to put its energies into fighting the Mexican War in the American Southwest. President Polk insisted on having the Oregon question arbitrated.

Under the Oregon Agreement, Great Britain received clear title to the whole of British Columbia from the forty-

ninth parallel to the Alaskan border and including Van-
couver Island. In 1853, the American sector of the Oregon
Territory was divided, and from it came the two states of
Washington and Oregon.

The Oregon question had attested to one important fact—
namely, that if the lands in the Canadian West were not
effectively and usefully occupied by adequate numbers of
settlers, they would be overrun instead by the Americans
determined to fulfill their "Manifest Destiny." That
"destiny" meant simply domination of all North America.

After settlement of the Oregon question, it was imperative for development of the British Columbia area to
proceed. By 1849, Vancouver Island had become a Crown
Colony. In 1858, jurisdiction of that colony was extended to
the British Columbia mainland. Meantime, in the wake of
the California gold rush and the building of railroads in the
American West, the American expansion was swift. State
after new state entered the American union.

The Canadians realized the need of quickly populating
their own Western plains to offset this expansion. By 1850
Fort Garry, the site of modern Winnipeg, was established
on the Red River, and soon thereafter other settlements
sprang up in the present provinces of Manitoba, Saskatchewan, and Alberta.

Following the end of the War of 1812 and especially
during the decades from 1820 onward, there had been a
great influx of British settlers onto the North American
continent. This migration stemmed largely from the economic conditions prevailing in England, Scotland, and
Ireland—notably the effects of the industrial revolution
and the Irish potato famine of 1845. The total population of
British North America in 1820 had been only seven
hundred and fifty thousand—but by 1850 it had reached
two and a half million—two-thirds of these living in the
regions surrounding the St. Lawrence River and the Great
Lakes. Nova Scotia and New Brunswick as well as Upper
and Lower Canada profited from this migration. British
philanthropies and various commercial-agricultural settle-

ment schemes supported many of the migrants who settled in the central interior. Timber, fur, and fisheries, trade and agriculture continued to be the basis of the economy.

Throughout the nineteenth century, the Canadian provinces depended heavily on their British trading connections, continuing to supply staples and prime products to the motherland. By the 1830s, secondary industry began to develop, including flour mills, paper mills, and iron foundries. Lumber in various forms was the chief export, followed by fish. Shipbuilding, too, using the available timber, was highly important. Fur trading was at last beginning to decline. Commerce, including import and retail trade as well as banking, began to assume major proportions. Montreal and Quebec City continued to grow. York (later named Toronto) and Bytown (later named Ottawa) were founded and quickly expanded. Halifax, Nova Scotia, and Saint John, New Brunswick, as well as St. John's, Newfoundland, were also becoming settlements of consequence.

Various efforts at trade treaties with the United States had already begun so as to offset losses of markets in Europe. Many of the colonial leaders, however, saw these proposals as traps designed to draw the whole of Canada into the hands of the southern neighbor. This suspicion had become particularly acute during the Civil War. The assumption in Canada at that time was that the American North would seek to replace the seceding Southern states with the British colonies of Canada. The only alternative that appeared to offset these imperialist and economic dangers was to hasten Canadian effort at confederation and Canadian settlement westward. This latter need was further speeded by the Canadian determination to expand into the lands now held by the Hudson's Bay Company in the northwest. As the company's monopoly over the northwest areas was soon due to expire, the situation became even more troubling. An investigative commission recommended creation of new provinces in the prairie area that now comprises Manitoba, Saskatchewan, and Alberta.

Development of Canada's economy had long been impeded by lack of adequate transport. Travel had been almost wholly dependent on waterways. The "Age of the Canals" in the mid-1800s was of considerable benefit to Canada because canal building provided access to routes previously closed by rapids and falls such as Niagara. The Welland Canal was built across the Niagara peninsula in 1829. By 1832, the Rideau Canal linked Bytown (Ottawa) and Kingston on Lake Ontario.

Real expansion was to come later with the development of the major transcontinental railways. (This subject will be discussed in detail at a later stage.) However, the existence of the canal system helped much to extend the fur trade and to give great economic benefit to both Upper Canada and the northwest regions.

The Roman Catholic religion was firmly entrenched in Lower Canada, and the dominant Anglican faith had become the de facto established religion of Upper Canada. There were moves now for recognition of various other important Protestant sects, such as the Scottish Presbyterians, now strong in Upper Canada and the Maritimes. Education had been the responsibility either of the pioneer home or of the church, but now came demands for organized, community-wide, public-supported educational systems. The condition of education in Lower Canada had been seriously harmed by the banning of the Jesuit order from that region between 1774 and 1842. That situation did not improve until the Jesuits returned to Quebec and nearby communities. Throughout the period, however, the French-speaking habitants continued to guard against secular incursions into their families' education in the belief that, thereby, the English were seeking to undermine the French position.

Despite these conflicts, the churches provided both elementary and higher education. The University of New Brunswick at Fredericton, founded in 1785, was the first university established in British North America. It was soon followed by King's College (now the University of

Nova Scotia at Halifax), established in 1789. There followed establishment of Dalhousie University, also in Nova Scotia, in 1818; McGill University in Montreal, Quebec, in 1821; the University of Toronto in 1827; Queen's College (now University) in Kingston, Ontario, in 1841. Laval University was founded as a Catholic seminary and did not become a full-scale university until 1852.

As a result of the new immigration, pressure for lessening colonial ties with Britain was growing apace in Canada. Much of this new drive for self-government was inspired by massive new waves of immigration into Canada from Scotland and Ireland. The demands for political reform stimulated two separate revolts, both abortive, in the 1830s. One, led by Joseph Papineau, took place in Lower Canada. His group contended that French Canada was being treated unfairly. The second abortive revolt, in 1837, was led by one William Lyon Mackenzie and was directed against the provincial government in Toronto. After that revolt misfired, Mackenzie fled to the United States, where he was later imprisoned for incitement to riot against the colonial rulers of Canada. More important than his actions, however, was the fact that Mackenzie provided major inspiration for his grandson, William Lyon Mackenzie King, who became one of Canada's most famous prime ministers. (See Chapter 6.)

Political discontent was widespread in both Upper and Lower Canada in the late 1830s. In some settlements, the populace broke into open rebellion and riots. Inept local and provincial administration, a budding spirit of economic nationalism, and pressures for independence all contributed to the mood of the time. The British Colonial Office, realizing the advisability of a thorough investigation of the conditions of the colonies, sent the Earl of Durham to Canada to make this appraisal.

Durham's report of the colonies' conditions and needs became the basic document leading to the eventual independence of Canada. That report was presented to the British Parliament on February 11, 1839. It advocated (1) immediate union of Upper and Lower Canada and the eventual union and independence of all colonies of British North America; (2) British control of Canadian foreign affairs, defense, foreign trade, and public lands even after the colonies gained responsible government; (3) provincial control over all other matters, including municipal affairs; (4) that provincial financial acts be initiated by the governor and approved by the legislature; (5) that executive councils be chosen from the majority party of the legislative assembly and that such councils be made responsive to the legislative assembly rather than the crown; (6) that the French-Canadians should eventually be Anglicized.

The British North American colonies had achieved a kind of responsible government by 1848, but this was not self-government. The next two decades saw a push for further autonomy by each of the individual colonies. As well, there was an effort at concord among those colonies, which ended in confederation.

The concept of Canadian union, later called confederation, had been discussed for over a century before it was finally realized. In 1858, it first appeared to be a practical possibility. At the Charlottetown, Prince Edward Island, Conference of 1864, the various leaders of the movement for unification persuaded leaders of the Maritime Provinces to abandon their own ideas of a Maritime Union only and, instead, to discuss a broader confederation.

Two immediate determinants in pushing Canada toward nationhood were the American Civil War (1861-65) and the American purchase of Alaska from Russia (1867). Both of these events threatened British North American security, resources, and markets — even her cohesion. The beginnings of the American Civil War forced the pace. For many years, some of the Canadian provinces had been havens for escaped American Negro slaves. (Slavery had been abolished in Canada in 1793.) There was distinct Canadian sympathy for the Northern cause. The situation of Canada as a safe haven for the slaves was offset, however, by British sympathy for the South. In the midst of the Civil War, some ten thousand British troops were sent into Canada to protect the provinces from military onslaught from the United States. Thus it was that both social and political attitudes contributed to the Canadian view that they must remain aloof from the American conflict and, in so doing, must protect themselves. To this end, they saw their best defense in independence and full self-government. This was a time when both Britain and the United States began to realize that there was a new force on the North American continent that had to be reckoned with. Bilateral solutions between London and Washington would no longer suffice.

The British North America Act of 1867, promulgated by the British Parliament, created a union of four provinces—Ontario, Quebec, Nova Scotia, and New Brunswick. In its precepts of government, the act combined some parts of the British parliamentary system with portions of the American federal-state system. In short, the new Canada was a confederal parliamentary government with the British monarch as head of state. (This system of government will be described in detail in the following chapter.) With certain amendments, the British North America Act has remained the constitution of Canada until the present day.

Fortunately, Canada's independence had been achieved through evolution and not by revolution. However, the new country was not a single nation-state, but rather a series of disparate parts spread the width of the continent. It would take considerable diplomacy and the building of a railroad before those parts were to be made relatively cohesive. It would also take sagacious statesmanship to protect against further encroachment, now mainly economic and cultural, by the giant neighbor to the south.

5
Kingdom and Confederacy

*I*n the face of the pressures of the American giant, how did it happen that another nation, primarily English-speaking, was able to emerge on the North American continent? How was it, too, that the northern neighbor, despite beginnings similar to those of the United States—exploration and colonialism, Indian wars and independence traumas—ended up as a kingdom and confederation rather than a presidential republic? How does Canada still maintain a highly traditional and relatively conservative culture rather than a highly ideological and individualistic "California" culture? In general, too, is Canada not by constrast with the United States a solid bourgeois society rather than a brash combination of liberal versus conservative pulls?

As with the Americans, there were for the Canadians the years of great exploration. History's pages, maps, and geographic locations of present-day Canada bear the names of the same great explorers. Canada's colonial settlements had the same European roots as did the eastern United States. York, Montreal, Quebec City, and Halifax match the beginnings, in time and tradition, of Williamsburg, Charleston, New Amsterdam, and Boston. As well, there were the antecedents to revolution for both infant nations. That process was more violent and determinative for the Americans, less turbulent and demonstrably less radical for the Canadians. The Americans sought and gained total independence from Britain. Canadian national interest resided in fealty to the British crown.

After the union of the American Colonies in 1776 and in the next century, after confederation of the Canadian Provinces (1867), there were again great and surprising similarities in the stories of the two nations. Expansion westward to Pacific shores came for both. Development of transcontinental railroads was a parallel necessity for each. Fights with Plains Indians had much the same result in both countries—destruction or decimation of the indigenes. There were even comparable gold rushes and land grabs.

Yet in that long sweep of history, there were tensions and conflicts and boundary disputes between the giant older brother and the courageous, determined younger brother. The latter was resolved not to be bullied or deflected from an entirely different cast of government, of national character, of nationhood itself. And the Canada of today is different from the United States of America.

Canada's vital interests have been predicated in large part upon her geography and history. Her actions from the time of formation as a nation in 1867—indeed, even before that time—had constantly to ensure the protection of her individuality as a nation from domination and absorption by the mammoth presence to the south. From the time of the Durhan Commission of 1838–40, it was apparent to most Canadians that they must devise a distinctive format for government of their incipient nation. This format must provide adequate defense against expansion from the south. It must permit a reasonable, but not too dependent, association with the mother country, Britain. It must also bind together, firmly but peaceably, Canada's two major and diverse ethnic groupings, British and French. It was also essential that the format of the new nation take cognizance of the great disparities and vast distances that comprise the Canadian land mass.

The British North America Act of 1867 created a largely autonomous Dominion of Canada. The act was based on the recommendations of the Durham Commission and the specific requests of the four colonies that originally composed the dominion—Quebec, Ontario, New Brunswick, and Nova Scotia. The British North America Act accorded this new nation full internal autonomy under nominal direction of the British monarch; however, full sovereignty with respect to external defense and foreign affairs was not to come for some years. Britain did not relinquish her control over Canada's foreign affairs and defense until the third decade of the twentieth century. Furthermore, even today the French-Canadians have not been Anglicized. Instead, the bilingual, bicultural nature of Canada has been reinforced by legislation and by tradition.

The four provinces that originally formed the confederation were eventually joined by Manitoba in 1870; British Columbia in 1871; Prince Edward Island in 1873; Saskatchewan and Alberta in 1905; and Newfoundland in 1949.

The formula of confederation provided by the British North America Act appears to have been only partially successful in meeting Canada's national objectives. The unfortified 5,500-mile border between the United States and Canada, recognized over a span of more than a century, attests to some success in one aim—that of guarding against major political or military invasion from the south. However, intrusion from the south has taken other, and largely unexpected, forms—financial and cultural. It can be said that Canadians have been somewhat more successful in keeping the trappings but not the overburdening domination of the motherland, Great Britain. In fact, Canadians were primarily responsible for creation of a unique form of association with that motherland. They first developed the semiautonomous "dominion" relationship and, later, the imaginative and looser "commonwealth" association of ex–British colonies with that motherland. This somewhat intangible role has provided Canada with an unusual and constant influence with those sister ex-colonies. Whether Canada has succeeded in the last defined of her original objectives—the subjection and elimination of seperatist influence—French versus Anglo, federal versus provincial, East versus West—remains a highly debatable and troubling question.

Perhaps a fuller understanding of these attainments and failures in meeting her national objectives can best be reached through a more detailed examination of the British North American Act. Just what did that act provide, and what did it withhold?

Although Canada is today considered to be a fully sovereign state, a few, but highly significant, requirements for constitutional change are still reserved to the British Parliament and can be made only by that body. Such limitations on Canadian sovereignty are more nominal than real, since the British Parliament ordinarily passes without question all amendments sought by the Canadian Parliament. However, that latent power still resides with the British crown. The reason why the full authority for amendment has not been passed to Ottawa from London is that the Canadians themselves have not been able to agree on machinery and formulae for constitutional change. For this reason, the largely nominal sovereignty and constitutional authority of the British monarch as head of state of Canada is continued.

The British North America Act accorded to the central government at Ottawa certain specified powers not accorded to, or retained by, the governments of the various provinces. The original act gave to the federal government control of defense (but not external affairs); regulation of trade and navigation; control of money and banking; postal services; control of taxation (within limits); regulation of patents and copyrights; and supervision of marriage, divorce, and criminal laws and procedures. General powers on matters relating to internal security, agriculture, and immigration were given to the central government and not to the provincial legislatures. The central government was also accorded control of interprovincial and international transportation as well as supervision of those internal economic, political, and social needs that were considered to be for the general good of Canada.

Jurisdiction over amendments of the constitution and rulings on disputes between provinces and central governments was retained by the British crown. Also retained by the crown was the right to determine constitutional protection of, and extension of, the use of French and English languages. Retained also by Westminster were constitutional guarantees to certain religious and educational groups as well as requirements specifying times and duration of parliamentary sessions.

Only after 1926 were these and related powers ranging from external affairs to telecommunications modified. Only then was Ottawa's federal authority made firm in those fields. However, in areas of federal-provincial or interprovincial conflict, the British Privy Council was left as the main court of appeal.

The British North America Act established, and partially spelled out, the highly controversial matter of bilingualism —usage of English and French. It established the principle of bilingualism in official government activities. It provided that parliamentary debate might be in either language and that official publications of parliament must be in both languages. Today these bilingual requirements have been extended further. French is now reinstated as the single official language within the Province of Quebec. Except in Quebec, either or both languages may be used today for commission hearings and for court actions. Furthermore, the whole of the central government bureaucracy and the various provincial administrations are now being thoroughly bilingualized.

Under the British North America Act as originally promulgated and as since amended, there is no spelling out of individual civil rights other than the specified linguistic, religious, and educational rights. There are, for example, no specific protections provided for such basic rights as freedom of press, of speech, of assembly. These rights are accorded or indirectly defined only by common law or by tradition. However, in practice, individual civil rights can be regulated either by the central Parliament or by provincial legislatures. In 1960, the Parliament in Ottawa adopted a Bill of Rights, and the central government has proposed a constitutional amendment placing all such rights beyond modification by either parliamentary or provincial action. As yet, however, no final action has been taken on this proposal.

Each provincial assembly has the power of amendment over its own constitution in all realms except those specifically reserved to the central government at Ottawa or those few powers reserved to the British crown. Particular powers are accorded provincial governments in such areas as control of natural resources; taxation for provincial needs; education; property laws; social welfare programs including hospitals and penitentiaries; public works; licensing of businesses; control of vital statistics; and supervision over municipalities. There are also specified areas of provincial responsibility in administration of the courts and in control of certain fields of education and of religious activity. These last-named powers, however, are limited by constitutional safeguards for linguistic or denominational groups.

It is clear from the foregoing that the British North America Act provided only a framework for both the central Parliament and provincial assemblies. The rest was to be filled out by parliamentary accord, by action of the various provincial legislatures, and by development of common law and tradition. Judicial interpretation of laws thus becomes extremely important, as did custom and convention.

The monarchical aspects of the British North America Act are not autocratic, but are rather brought into being or extended by tradition and usage. Thus, there has developed, from the base of the British common law, a body of customary Canadian common law. Custom and convention, usage and understanding, have given to Canada a working parliamentary democracy rather than a constitutional monarchy. Out of this parliamentary "mix" there has come a set of similarities and contrasts between the governments of Britain and of the United States.

The Canada of today possesses some 8 million persons of French extraction and perhaps 11 million of Anglo-Saxon origin. (The remainder, approximately 5 million, includes Central Europeans, Asians, Americans, Amerindians and Eskimos.) Even at the time of confederation in 1867, this variety of ethnic roots existed. Thus, when the new Canadian nation was founded, some 35 percent of its citizenry was of French extraction and about 40 percent was of British origin. Then as now, more than 45 percent of the populace has been Roman Catholic, with about 50 percent Protestant. (The remainder are mainly Jewish, Hindu, Buddhist, or animist.)

It has already been pointed out that these major groups—political, cultural, linguistic, religious—were the heritage of the competing colonizations and the historic rivalries of the two major Western European powers, Britain and France. It has been two centuries since these traditional antagonists faced each other in open battle on the North American continent. Yet even today, that competition continues in parliament and legislature. The rivalries of Versailles and Windsor, of the Vatican and Lambeth, have not been stilled in Canada. All Canadian constitutional action (even as far back as the Act of 1791, which created the British-oriented Upper Canada and the French-oriented Lower Canada) recognized these divided loyalties and the need of counterbalancing them. The Earl of Durham's recommendations of 1839 (advising union of Upper and Lower Canada and that all British North America be made united and self-governing) further cemented such seperation into place. Finally, the British North America Act of 1867 both formalized and finalized these ethnic and political divisions.

There remain, as well, other expanding problems of separatism. These now have regional as well as ethnic overtones. They embody not only challenges to the central government from political dukedoms, but also challenges to the provinces from big-business baronies. These are all parts of a continuing task of threading together political, economic, social, and cultural components of Canada's populace to ensure emergence of a national individuality—a composite "Canadian" character.

Since Canada's major governmental institutions constitute the wellsprings of both political authority and of bureaucratic control, it is important that they be understood. At the federal level, the governor-general is the personal representative of the British monarch. The Federal Parliament is bicameral, comprising an appointed Senate and an elected House of Commons. The prime minister and his cabinet ministers must come from the elected membership of the House of Commons. The unicameral legislatures in the various provinces are elective, with premiers and their cabinet members holding seats therein. These provincial bodies are called legislative assemblies except in Quebec, where the term National Assembly is applied. Personal representatives of the governor-general are appointed in each province. They are called lieutenant-governors; their posts are mainly ceremonial.

In certain respects, the Canadian system provides a unique combination of the institutions of Westminster and of Washington. The federal Parliament and the provincial legislatures are primarily fashioned after Westminster. But the limited autonomy of the provincial governments and their legislatures resembles, in some aspects, that of the American states. Canada has ten provinces and two territories. However, provincial relationships to the central government at Ottawa differ materially from those between American state governments and Washington. In fact, the provinces have considerably more autonomy in certain fields, such as control of natural resources and municipalities within their borders. Jurisdictional disputes between provinces and central government (referred to the British Privy Council until legislation in 1949 terminated appeals to that council) are now resolved by Canada's own Supreme Court.

As mentioned previously, the original British North America Act provided a skeletal constitution only. The larger part of Canada's parliamentary and political action is based on unwritten custom and precedents of law. Powers specifically granted to Ottawa or reserved to provincial authorities have been delineated in pages preceding.

The British monarch (presently personified by Queen Elizabeth II) is sovereign head of Canada. Her majesty is considered to be symbolic both of unity and of free association with the motherland—relationships that today are characterized by membership in the British Commonwealth. The queen's personal representative in Canada is the governor-general, whom the queen appoints on recommendation of the Canadian prime minister. Ordinarily the governor-general serves for a five-year term, though reappointment to the post is common. The position may be held by a British or Commonwealth national, but today it is held by a Canadian.

The recent governor-general of Canada is Jules Leger, a former Canadian diplomat. Many eminent personages of the British nobility have earlier held the post. Most prominent among these were Viscount Alexander of Tunis and Lord Tweedsmuir. In late 1978, Prime Minister Trudeau requested, and was granted by the Queen, a new appointment in Edward Schreyer (see page 169 for background).

Given the British monarch's sovereignty over Canada, it might be argued that Canada is a constitutional monarchy. Executive authority is vested in the Queen of (Great Britain and) Canada. Theoretically it might be said that the powers of the monarch are extensive. In fact, however, they are brought to bear only upon the advice of the Canadian Parliament, cabinet, and prime minister, all these being responsible to the Canadian electorate.

The Canadian Parliament consists of a Senate (102 members) and a House of Commons (264 members). (Electoral boundary changes that came into effect June 11, 1977, mean membership in the Commons will swell by 18, to 282, after the next federal election.)

Members of the Senate are appointed by the governor-general acting on advice of the prime minister. The Senate is less powerful and less representative than is the House of Commons. The British North America Act gave to the Senate much the same legislative capacity as the British House of Lords. Powers of the Canadian House of Commons approximate those of the British House of Commons. In addition to its legislative functions, the Senate has special committees to develop legislative recommendations to meet imperative national problems. Senators originally held office for life. Now they must retire at seventy-five. Appointments to the Senate usually go to distinguished citizens, including former ministers or important provincial personalities. Present composition of the Senate by province is as follows: Ontario and Quebec, each twenty-four; New Brunswick and Nova Scotia, each ten; Alberta, British Columbia, Manitoba, Newfoundland, and Saskatchewan, each six; Prince Edward Island, four.

As in Britain, the House of Commons is the real seat of power. Election thereto, from the various provincial 'ridings' (similar to American federal legislative districts), must be held every five years or earlier at the direction of the governor-general. Acting on the official request of the prime minister, the governor-general dissolves the existing House of Commons and calls new elections. Within reason, dissolution can be sought by the prime minister at any time. Membership in the House of Commons, based proportionately on results of decennial censuses, are today as follows: Ontario, 88; Quebec, 74; British Columbia, 23; Alberta, 19; Manitoba and Saskatchewan, each 13; Nova Scotia, 11; New Brunswick, 10; Newfoundland, 7; Prince Edward Island, 4; and Yukon and Northwest Territories, each 1. This makes a total of 264 members.

October 17, 1977, the Canadian Commons opened its doors for the first time to television coverage for its proceedings. It is carried all or in part, gavel-to-gavel, by four networks, two independent stations, and forty-five cable firms.

The membership of the House of Commons as determined by the October 16, 1978, federal by-election is as follows:

Liberal Party, 136 seats; Progressive Conservative Party 97 seats; New Democratic Party (NDP), 17 seats; Social Credit Party of Canada, 9 seats; and Independent, 5 seats.

Though Canada is by no means a two-party nation, it has been a fact that, during most of its 110-year history, Canada has been ruled by one or the other of two major parties. These have been the Liberals and the Progressive Conservatives. There are, however, other important parties, such as the rising prosocialist NDP and the currently weaker Social Credit party. The present Creditistes party of Quebec is an offshoot of the latter. Membership in all parties has ebbed and flowed considerably over the years, some of the parties being amalgams of earlier political groupings. From the beginning of World War II, with the exception only of the period 1957–63 (when the Conservatives held control), the Liberal party has dominated Canadian federal politics. However, since 1963, the Liberals have sometimes been forced to govern Canada as a minority party. Today the Liberals hold a majority of seats in the House of Commons under the leadership of Prime Minister Pierre E. Trudeau.

In the political spectrum of Western democracies, the Liberals would be classed as slightly left of center. Thus they would be comparable to the British Liberal party or the "middle-of-the-road" American Democrats. The Progressive Conservatives, presently led by Joe Clark of Alberta, are somewhat to the right of center. Thus they are comparable to moderate Republicans in the United States or the progressive wing of the British Conservative Party. The Progressive Conservative party is the officially designated 'Opposition' and its leadership is given special parliamentary perquisites as in Britain.

The NDP, presently led by Ed Broadbent of Ontario, was formed in 1961. It merged the farm-based "prairie party," the Cooperative Commonwealth Federation (CCF), with portions of the Canadian Labour Congress. The NDP is slanted leftward, with programs sometimes labeled socialist and sometimes even Marxist by its critics. Its power rests in the provinces of Manitoba, Saskatchewan, British Columbia, and, to a lesser extent, Ontario.

The Social Credit party was led by André Fortin of Quebec until his untimely death in June, 1977. This party originated from populist roots in the Prairie Provinces during the depression years, but it now has a rather conservative stance. It has power mainly in British Columbia and Quebac. After Fortin's death. Lorne Reznowsky was appointed to head his party; however, he has failed to win a Parliamentary seat. That leadership again goes to convention. The French-speaking part of SOCREDS is Ralliement des Creditistes founded by Real Caouette in 1958. Finally, it should be said that the Communist party, though still legal in Canada, holds no seats today in either national Parliament or provincial legislatures.

The governor-general chooses the prime minister from the leading or "majority" party in the House of Commons. The prime minister, who is the recognized leader of his party, in turn chooses the membership of his cabinet, mainly from among members of his own party elected to the House of Commons. As in Britain, prime minister and cabinet hold office so long as they can maintain the confidence (majority support) of the House of Commons on major issues. Ordinarily, the prime minister decides when parliament is called into session, when it is prorogued (adjourned), and when new elections are to be held. As noted elsewhere, new elections must be held within a span of five years unless war or major catastrophe makes that impossible. The prime minister and cabinet choose new members of the Senate; make major judicial and administrative appointments; choose ambassadors and select lieutenant-governors (provincial representatives of the queen); propose government legislation; and, with parliamentary approval, declare war.

The cabinet, acting through its parliamentary majority in the House of Commons, can annul most provincial laws within one year of passage. However, these annulments may later be subject to judicial challenge or to further parliamentary action. The cabinet, through appropriate members thereof, controls the armed forces, ratifies treaties and conventions, holds power of pardon of criminals, and appoints principal public servants and department heads. It is noteworthy, however, that the specific powers, or limitations of powers, of the cabinet are not spelled out in the British North America Act. That act spells out in very general terms only the powers and privileges of the Privy Council, an honorific group appointed by the governor-general. In point of fact, however, the Privy Council, as such, has no real power. Numbering about a hundred, it consists of all present and former cabinet ministers, speakers of both houses of Parliament, chief justices and ex–chief justices, and a few distinguished Britons such as Prince Philip. Although a minister is a privy councillor for life, he remains a minister only at the discretion of the prime minister. Thus the cabinet is the only, the real, committee of rule.

As noted, the prime minister alone chooses the ministers of his cabinet. These either head a major governmental department or serve 'without portfolio' (without a specific department to head). Today, the cabinet of Canada is composed of thirty-one ministers, of whom twenty-six are heads of departments and five are 'without portfolio'. By custom, one or more senators holds a seat in the cabinet. Unlike members of the U.S. cabinet, all Canadian cabinet ministers must hold seats in one house or the other or be assured of election thereto. Members of the cabinet (as in Britain and the United States) have no fixed terms but hold office at the pleasure of the prime minister and subject to the vicissitudes of electoral defeat. Some Canadian cabinets have had notably long lives. Sir Wilfrid Laurier's cabinet (with substitutions and additions) held office for fifteen years. The second cabinet of Sir John A. Macdonald lasted for some thirteen years.

If the Opposition party wins a numerical majority or a plurality in new elections, the existing prime minister must step down with his cabinet. The leader of the victorious party then, as in Britain, forms the new government. As the new prime minister, he chooses the cabinet from the commons members of his own party. Normally efforts are made to choose at least one minister from each province, though the heaviest ministerial groupings have invariably come from Ontario and Quebec. Here again is seen the political necessity of counterbalancing the powers of French-speaking and English-speaking groups. Unfortunately, however, in recent years this heavy preponderance of cabinet members named from Ontario and Quebec has accentuated the problems of East-West disparities.

The nature of Canada's government during its first century as a nation, together with an exposition of the character of its federal and provincial leadership, will be discussed in chapters following.

6
Princes of the Realm: The Prime Ministers

Canada is a country that has few national heroes. On the pages of its history there are no charismatic statesmen quite so venerated as were Churchill in Britain, De Gaulle in France, or Lincoln in the United States. Nor, indeed, are there to be found in Canada, pre- or post-confederation, military leaders as respected as were the Americans George Marshall, Dwight Eisenhower, Robert E. Lee, and Andrew Jackson.

Canadian painters, actors, and authors generally have only a regional reputation, or else they acquire an international reputation in the United States and Europe. There the rewards and the applause are greater. Even such diverse talents as those possessed by Stephen Leacock, Sir William Osler, Mazo de la Roche, Raymond Massey, Barbara Ann Scott, and Sir Frederick Banting have first found fame and fortune elsewhere and only afterwards have basked in well-earned glory in their native Canada.

Perhaps this lack of truly national heroes in Canada—whether soldiers or statesmen, scientists or artists—derives partly from the Hydra-headed problem of a bicultural society. For, if the great French general Montcalm is venerated in Quebec, it is likely to be his conqueror, the British general James Wolfe, who wears a halo in Ontario or New Brunswick. Furthermore, given the breadth of Canada, a personality dubbed a hero of sorts in British Columbia may find it difficult to become well known in Nova Scotia.

In addition to the immense breadth of Canada itself, there is likely to impinge upon the national acceptance and hero worship of any Canadian personality the pervasive presences of the American media. These instruments blanket much of Canada so constantly and so completely as to defeat attempts at creation of truly national Canadian "greats."

Nonetheless, in the story of Canada since confederation in 1867, there have emerged a few very special personalities who seem to be slowly growing in esteem among their countrymen. Certain of these personalitites have been among Canada's foremost politicians—her princes of the realm—her prime ministers. In coming decades, a few of these men are likely to attain consensus as national heroes.

Not surprisingly, the lives of these personalitites, these prime ministers, seem to evoke most clearly Canada's own story from confederation to the present. These "heroes"— present or potential—are the seven men whom the author believes to have been Canada's most outstanding or controversial prime ministers. They comprise Sir John A. Macdonald, Canada's father figure and first prime minister; Sir Wilfrid Laurier, the country's first French-Canadian prime minister; Mackenzie King, Canada's longest-serving prime minister; Louis St. Laurent, proponent of Canada's domestic and international expansion; John Diefenbaker, the only populist premier; Lester Pearson, Canada's real internationalist; and Pierre Trudeau, Canada's colorful present leader of government. In the actions of these men, whether they be considered only controversial or truly great, is to be found the essence of Canada's history.

Have these men attained places in Canada's Hall of Valour? Do they bear the hallmarks of both national and international repute? Were their deeds in behalf of their country lasting? Will they meet the tests of time and be recognized as Canadian heroes a century hence? Perhaps so. In any event, the lives and deeds of these men so fully and vividly reflect the development of Canadian nationhood that the author now attempts to set forth the century and more of Canada's own history in their stories.

Sir John Macdonald

Sir John A. Macdonald was a central figure in bringing about Canada's confederation, and he served as the country's first prime minister. A member of the Conservative (Tory) party, he governed from 1867 to 1873 and from 1878 to 1891.

In two respects, he was probably the most important of all Canadian prime ministers. He is considered both 'Father of Confederation' and 'Father of the Canadian Railways.' Thus, in a sense, he is a combination of George Washington and James J. Hill, with a tinge of rowdyism and cronyism added. As father-founder of his nation, he brought discordant provincial leaders together into the beginnings of confederation. The second role, that of imaginatively pushing construction of Canada's first transcontinental railway, the Canadian Pacific, served to weld disparate parts of his country together by means of the steel rail bands. From the Rupert's Land holdings that Macdonald judiciously purchased from the Hudson's Bay Company in 1869 for the equivalent of $1.5 million, there were created several new provinces.

Macdonald was born January 11, 1815, in Glasgow, Scotland. Soon thereafter, he emigrated to Canada with his parents, settling in Upper Canada. He was called to the bar in 1836. He was elected to the colonial legislature in 1844, representing Kingston, Ontario. In 1847 he became a member of the ruling executive council. In 1854 he helped bring about a conservative political coalition. Out of this coalition developed the Conservative political party with Macdonald its recognized leader. As a result, in 1857, Macdonald became leader of the "responsible," semi-autonomous government of Upper and Lower Canada. During all these years in government, Macdonald worked unceasingly to retain ties with Great Britain while achieving more autonomy for British North America.

In 1858, in company with other leaders of his Conservative party, Macdonald began the process of confederating the whole of British North America. In this effort he was joined by Sir George Etienne Cartier, conservative leader of Quebec (Lower Canada) and a rival, George Brown, leader of Ontario (Upper Canada). Their joint ideas of confederation had slow beginnings. The first breakthrough came at the Charlottetown, Prince Edward Island, Conference of 1864. This meeting had originally been called to achieve consolidation of the several Maritime Provinces. However, under Macdonald's leadership, that idea was expanded to encompass the concept of a broader union of the Maritimes with Upper and Lower Canada. Macdonald and his confreres pushed successfully for attainment of that wider federal union. Macdonald was also the source of inspiration for a parliamentary-type confederation and for continued association of that eventually independent union with the British crown.

After conferences in Charlottetown, Quebec City, and London, the British North America Act was passed by the British Parliament. That act resulted in the creation of a new nation—the Dominion of Canada—which came into being on July 1, 1867.

At the outset, this new nation comprised Ontario (Upper Canada), Quebec (Lower Canada), New Brunswick, and Nova Scotia. As a result of Macdonald's subsequent wise purchase of the Hudson's Bay Company's properties in central and northwest Canada, accession of several western provinces to this confederacy was to follow. (Manitoba joined in 1870, Prince Edward Island in 1873, Saskatchewan and Alberta in 1905. British Columbia agreed to enter the confederation in 1871, following federal promises to build a transcontinental railway to the Pacific coast. With the entry of Newfoundland into the confederation in 1949, the continental limits of Canada were finally set. The Yukon and Northwest Territories remained special non–self-governing provinces just as they are today.)

Realizing that it was essential to tie together the western and eastern provinces for economic as well as political reasons, Macdonald, from 1870 onward, pushed for completion of a transcontinental railway. He placed all his new nation's resources behind that effort—as well as his own political prestige. He hoped, however, that the job could be completed by a private company rather than by the government. In the process of awarding construction contracts and conveying land titles for the project, several of Macdonald's political cronies, especially his ally, George Cartier, were accused, and judged guilty, of taking bribes and kickbacks. Macdonald himself was involved, as the railway contractors had agreed to provide $60,000 in election expenses to leaders of the ruling Conservative party in exchange for a monopoly position and full government backing. This trouble was to become known as the Great Pacific Scandal. In defending his government's actions in the Canadian Parliament, Macdonald is said to have made the best speech of his political career, stating dramatically, "These hands are clean. . . . "However, loss of confidence in the Conservative government was so deep, and the opposition attack so broad, that Macdonald and his government were forced to resign in 1873. The Liberal Opposition leader, A. L. Mackenzie, then took over the office of prime minister, remaining therein five years.

Sir John A. Macdonald continued to be considered the most able leader in all Canada, even by his opponents. Defeat of his government had also meant that the railway across the continent was stalled in Ontario. For the Liberal government insisted on so modifying and restricting the terms of the railway charter that it went nowhere. The Canadian populace, weary of vacillation and a do-nothing policy under Mackenzie's Liberal regime, in 1878 voted the Liberals out and Macdonald's Conservative party in.

Macdonald was returned to office as prime minister and he served until his death in 1891. Immediately after regaining office, he pushed again for completion of the railroad to the Pacific coast. He contended properly that "until this great work is completed, our Dominion is little more than a geographical expression. . . . " Financiers and contractors from several countries competed for the charter to complete the new railway to the West. Macdonald insisted on a group of vision, high principles, and determination. Thus it was that a consortium of various groups, including British and Canadian financing and American engineering, came into being. The Canadian Pacific Railway, headed by a Canadian, George Stephen, and utilizing the services of a famous American engineer, William Van Horne, at last became a reality. (Van Horne later became a Canadian, stating that the great experience of building that railroad "would have made a Canadian citizen even of the German Emperor.")

While the trackage was going down, Macdonald sought to encourage settlement along the rail right-of-way to foster trade and markets. At the same time, he realized the need to create full-scale provinces in the vast areas of land that the government-inspired railway was now crossing. It has already been noted that Macdonald had begun this move in his first administration by taking over the land concessions held by the Hudson's Bay Company. He realized, as well, that Indian land claims needed to be settled and fractious tribes subdued. Despite growing criticism in and out of Parliament, Macdonald remained true to his dream of spanning the continent with the railroad. He remained sanguine that his dreams of real confederation—real nationhood—were moving toward success along this very rail route. That vision would assure that the nation would be united finally and firmly. Macdonald's strong and optimistic spirit, coupled with his government's immigration and economic policies, made Canada's own spirit buoyant and the country increasingly prosperous.

The rail line was at last completed in October, 1886. Prime Minister Macdonald and his wife triumphantly rode the inaugural train across the country with a group of VIPs. Together they shared the excitement of driving the last spike uniting western and eastern sections of the rail line at Craigellachie, British Columbia. Then Mrs. Macdonald and her husband, with great aplomb and spirit, rode the cowcatcher of the engine triumphantly down the western side of the Rockies and into the western terminus of the line at Port Moody near present-day Vancouver. This and related incidents have been depicted in a recent Canadian television documentary based on two books by the Canadian author Pierre Berton. These colorful books are entitled *The Last Spike* and *The National Dream*.

Macdonald's halcyon days started to fade in the wake of troubled economic times. Canada's political, financial, and social problems began to deepen. Macdonald, who had attained the age of seventy-five in 1890, desired retirement but could find no satisfactory political heir. His "old guard," who had helped bring confederation and the railway into being, had disappeared. His cabinet veterans and early political allies were gone. Macdonald, alone in political stature, held on. He was kept in power now only because the Liberal Opposition, as well as his own Conservative party, could not yet find an adequate replacement.

Sir John A. Macdonald had proved to be a lion—the king of the political jungle. Furthermore, he had outlasted a whole political generation. Yet his failure was that he had been unable to get good help in his later years. He had developed no crown prince. Yet he could not persuade himself to leave office until death took him on June 6, 1891.

He had successfully led Canada into confederation and through the important stages of national puberty and adolescence. He was accused by some of being devious and unscrupulous, full of political skulduggery. Yet all had to admire his perspicacity, his vision, and his political skills. Sir John A. Macdonald must be remembered for his great achievements.

In February, 1887, Prime Minister Macdonald, faced with increasing economic difficulties, had "gone to the country" for a new electoral mandate. Once again he achieved a victory, which was to keep him in power four more years. However, out of this 1887 electoral defeat of the Liberal party by Macdonald and his Conservatives emerged a highly important new national figure. This was the new Liberal leader and future long-term prime minister of

Canada, Wilfrid Laurier. Between the election of 1887 and the passing of Macdonald in 1891 there also emerged new political frictions, corruption, and economic tensions. There were, as well, tough new controversies with the neighboring United States. The American secretary of state at that time, the chauvinistic James G. Blaine, considered Canada merely a continuing colonial appendage of the British Empire and unimportant in its own right. Blaine refused to consider Canada as a sovereign nation. When Canada attempted to negotiate with the United States government through Blaine on matters of trade and tariffs, the Canadians came off the losers. Relations between the two nations continued to deteriorate, and Macdonald, now aging fast, took the psychological and economic defeats hard. The high hopes of the confederation seemed in real danger. Canada even faced the possibility of dissolution and annexation by the increasingly powerful southern neighbor. Macdonald realized his country and his party were endangered. Once again, in 1890, he brought his party to victory at the polls through the sheer force of his leadership as The Old Chief. However, the Liberals were now making the most of Canada's political and economic difficulties. The working classes in Canada were gradually becoming disaffected and pulling away from the Conservative banners. However, despite his passing from the scene through death, Macdonald's influence was so great that his party remained in power for five more years.

Perhaps the most important heritage left by the Macdonald administration was the beginning of a "National Polity." In essence this was Macdonald's program to encourage and protect Canada, by tariff and transport development, against expansion and trade pressures of the United States of America. It sought to create home industries and to export home resources. It forced a recasting of United States–Canadian economic relationships by reorienting the trade axis east and west rather than north and south. Thus, by means of his preferential tariff arrangements with Britain; by his building of barriers against United States imports; by his encouragement of indigenous manufacturers; and by his creation of the transcontinental railroad system, Prime Minister Macdonald really began melding the Canadian confederation into a nation.

Following Macdonald's demise, there ensued a series of inconsequential Tory Conservative prime ministers: Sir John C. Abbott (1891–1892); Sir John S. D. Thompson (1892–1894); Sir Mackenzie Bowell (1894–1896); and Sir Charles Tupper (1896).

SIR WILFRID LAURIER

Sir Wilfrid Laurier, leader of the rising Opposition Liberal party, won election and appointment as prime minister of Canada in 1896. He was to remain in that post until 1911. He was a man greatly different in background, in character, and in political nature from Macdonald. It was his great task to bring his land into real international repute, to solidify Canada's relationships with both Britain and the United States, and to prepare Canada for the crisis of World War I.

Domestically, his personal inspiration and political acumen helped keep Canada both a bilingual and a bicultural entity. He sought to bring his countrymen together on such diverse issues as church-state relations and ethnic divisions. He did this largely by personal example, demonstrating aptly that it was possible for a member of one culture, the French-Canadian, to break through the barrier of another culture, the Anglo-Canadian, and to lead both groups. During his tenure in office, he also pursued policies designed to help the country industrialize, to help develop the Canadian West, and to improve the nation's transportation system. In addition, he protected Canadian autonomy from attempted British encroachment. In all this lay his greatness.

Sir Wilfrid Laurier was born November 20, 1841, in St. Lin, Quebec. His family had deep roots in Canada, one ancestor, a Norman soldier, having helped found Montreal.

As a youth he received a classical education in both French and English schools. After studying law in Montreal, he became a member of the bar in 1864; shortly thereafter, he entered politics. Elected to the House of Commons in 1874, he became leader of his Liberal party in 1889 and held the post for twenty-four years. For the first fifteen of those years, he was prime minister of Canada. The Liberal party lost its parliamentary majority in 1911, but Laurier remained in Parliament until his death on February 17, 1919.

Laurier helped his party to power and became prime minister, in 1896, by concentrating on economic problems. (North America was then just pulling out of the depression of 1893.) He sought, as well, to remove problems of race and religion from the Liberal party platform and from governmental activity. He gave particular attention to Canadian-United States relations so as to override his political opponents' contention that the Liberals actually wanted to have Canada annexed to the United States. Laurier gave his programs the interesting appellation "sunny days," seeking to make his rule upbeat and optimistic. He encouraged financial interests. He dampened the fires of religious differences.

Laurier developed a rapport with many moderate Conservatives, most of these Anglo-Protestants. In turn, because of this very racial/religious tolerance toward Anglo-Protestants, he had real difficulties with his own, far more conservative, French-Canadian Catholics. He had especially serious problems with the French-Canadian clergy and with those determined to make provincial rights inviolate against the central government. However, Laurier did not let the criticism and pressures of either of these groups sway him from truly tolerant, and truly federal, stands.

"Our great weakness," the young Laurier had told a friend in 1874, "is the everlasting one—the hostility of the priests." Laurier took it upon himself to bring the running battle between clergy and Liberal politicians to an end.

However, he had constant difficulty in attempting to convince the Catholic clergy that the Liberals had nothing in common with revolutionaries.

In 1877, he made a brilliant speech denying the charges made by the Catholic clergy against his party. In this speech, he emphasized that Canadian Liberals were more akin to British social reformers than to the radical anti-clerical liberals of Europe. He emphasized that the Catholic church and any other religious body had nothing to fear from his party, though the clergy had no right to impose their political opinions on their parishioners. He attested that it would be unwise, even dangerous, to form a strictly Catholic party in Canada. This, in turn, would be bound to create a Protestant party and would open the country to religious warfare—the most terrible kind of war.

This kind of opposition to religious parties and to political domination by the clergy formed a set of views that Laurier held consistently throughout his long and brilliant career. Even an envoy from the Vatican, one Bishop Conroy, sent by Pope Leo XIII to examine the church controversy in Quebec, agreed with Laurier that church interference in the politics of Canada was unwise; the bishop accepted Laurier's interpretation of liberalism in Canada. Thus, from the time he became prime minister, Laurier continued to deny the church's right to interfere in politics.

From the time of his first reelection, in 1900, Laurier persuasively lobbied for increased immigration. He was particularly anxious to expand settlement in the Prairie Provinces. He also pushed for the "recolonization" of Quebec and northern Ontario along the route of the new Canadian National rail line. In all this he was seeking a better economic distribution of the population with resulting political benefits. He was also working to shore up his country's bastion against any possible "imperialist" intrusions from the United States in the jingoistic days of Presidents William McKinley and Teddy Roosevelt.

Both Prime Ministers Macdonald and Laurier had

realized that Canada, like other small nations, had to depend on outside support if it really wished to preserve its independence. Thus it was essential to associate with Britain—and to play her off against the powerful southern neighbor, the United States. Said Laurier in 1903, "I have often regretted that we are living beside a great neighbor, whose people, I believe, are very grasping in their national actions . . . and who are determined to get the best in every agreement that they make. . . . "

Laurier refused to let his country slip further under the domination of the United States; thus, as much as possible, he turned to Britain for economic and military help. He would not, however, let Britain dominate Canada. Laurier, of course, came to office when the great powers of Europe were competing mightily with one another and would soon take that competition into war. It was natural, then, that he did not wish to come so close to Britain as to become greatly involved in Europe.

Laurier and other government leaders had special difficulties with the French-Canadians over preparations for fighting World War I and with the general conscription issue involved in that effort. The French-Canadians, believing the coming war to be merely a British involvement, refused to be conscripted. They had successfully resisted furnishing aid to Britain in the Boer War; so why, they argued, was it necessary for them to help the Western European Allies in the upcoming conflict? French-Canadian resistance on this point was successful. No conscription of this group occurred during all of World War I, despite the constant pleas of politicians, including their own French-Canadian leader and former prime minister.

During the decade prior to the opening of World War I, Laurier's government had been under heavy pressure to create an independent Canadian navy. This was, of course, designed to help the British fend off the imminent German military threat. Thus, in 1909–11, Laurier, who appreciated the dangers of German armed might, directed the establishment of an independent Canadian navy. He also arranged that it could be integrated, in war, with the British navy. Thereby he sought to insure both Canada's interest in the British Empire and Canada's own right to autonomy. French-Canadian liberals agreed with him, but Anglo conservatives did not.

In the election campaign of 1911, Laurier had emphasized that, the day British naval supremacy at sea was gone, then Canada's freedom—including that of French-Canada—would be truly endangered. To illustrate his oratorical qualities and his political perceptions, one magnificent address delivered in Saint John, New Brunswick, stands out:

> I am branded in Quebec as a traitor to the French, in Ontario as a traitor to the English. In Quebec I am attacked as a jingo, in Ontario as a separatist. In Quebec I am branded as imperialist, in Ontario as anti-imperialist. I am neither. I am a Canadian. Canada has been the inspiration of my life. I have had before me as a pillar of fire by night and a pillar of cloud by day a policy of true Canadianism, of conciliation, of moderation. I now appeal with confidence to the whole Canadian people to uphold me in this policy of sound Canadianism which makes for our country and of the Empire. . . .

The election of 1911 had been fought on a quadruple issue: the possibility of a European war and of Canadian participation therein; the need of conscripting Canadians (including French-Canadians) into the armed forces; the need of a Canadian navy or, at least, of help to the British navy; and the Liberal policy of reciprocity in trading relations with the United States. This election forced replacement of Laurier, the Liberal leader, with the Conservative, Sir Robert L. Borden.

The Conservatives' victory in the election of 1911 was massive. Laurier's heavy majority of just three years before was precisely reversed. The House of Commons seating as a result of the election of 1908 had been 132 Liberals, 85 Conservatives, 3 Independents. The results of the election of 1911 gave 133 seats to the Conservatives and Nationalists, 88 to the Liberals. Though Laurier held his own seat, many of his ministers fell by the wayside.

The defeat was especially pronounced in both Ontario and Quebec. Yet outside Ontario, the popular vote was generally in favor of the Liberals.

Laurier took the fortunes of the political wars philosophically after his resignation as prime minister on October 6, 1911. Sir Wilfrid Laurier, Leader of His Majesty's Government for fifteen years, now assumed the post of Leader of His Majesty's Loyal Opposition. This post and his parliamentary seat he would hold until his death in 1919. Laurier had offered to resign as his party's leader, He had now spent thirty-eight years in the House of Commons and had led his group for more than two decades. His followers refused, still believing there was no other man so well able to hold the post.

Laurier, leader of his party throughout the catastrophic years of World War I, put patriotism above party. Sir Robert Borden was now prime minister, and his Conservative leadership would last throughout the war (and until 1920). To him Laurier gave active support, working hard against national disunity or disruption.

At the outset of World War I, Borden, the Conservative leader, had proposed formation of a coalition government. Laurier refused. The main reason for Borden's suggestion had been to overcome the problem of French-Canadian conscription. Laurier supported the war effort and asked his countrymen to volunteer. He insisted, however, that he would oppose conscription. He realized that, if he joined a coalition government and thus supported conscription, that move would give control of Quebec to the separatists and would undoubtedly split the country. The end of the war was to bring new political divisions, sectionalism, and severe economic dislocations, which an aging Laurier could neither foresee nor help to fend off. That would be the task of a new generation of politicians.

In retrospect, it now seems that Laurier's chief claim to fame must rest on his laying foundations for real independence of Canada from British imperialism, while forging new pre-Commonwealth ties to that motherland. He was also able to perform political acrobatics on the hot issue of biculturalism—living through ciriticism from the French that he was too English and from the English that he was too French.

Canada was now held in high repute among the nations of the world. Canadian nationhood had grown strong. The country was coming into its own. Yet it was probably now all for the best that Laurier had vacated the prime minister's chair after two full decades of power. By regrouping, the Liberal party would be able to make fundamental changes in policy that would carry it forward to success after political success during the next five decades.

Biographers indicate that, when Laurier first took office, many observers believed his regime would be short lived and that he would be only titular head of the government. Both his health and his character seemed to be against him. Both his critics and his friends believed that a man so genteel, so innately courteous, could never be sufficiently firm for the tasks of the job. The prophets were wrong. Laurier possessed the qualities needed for leadership. In fact, his very gentility and tact helped make him an exemplary leader at a time when another type of leadership could have proved ruinous.

As prime minister, Laurier proved to be a skilled negotiator, objective and impartial. He delegated authority well and did not involve himself in detail. He was tolerant and scrupulous in dealings with others—neither arbitrary nor dictatorial. High principled, he would compromise only on means, not on ends. He preferred to govern too little rather than too much.

Sir Wilfrid Laurier has now in fact become a national institution, a national heritage. If not a hero, he was surely one of Canada's finest men—a "political great." He died February 22, 1919, with the simple words on his lips, "C'est finis!"

Following Laurier's death, political attitudes in Canada changed in reflection of the massive effects of World War I. The Liberal party, convening in Ottawa in August, 1919, selected as its new leader William Lyon Mackenzie King. King had been an ardent disciple of Laurier and had served as his minister of labour. In 1920, the refurbished Conservative party was led by Arthur Meighen who replaced Sir Robert Borden. In the 1921 elections King's Liberals won 117 seats—nearly half of these in Quebec. Meighen's conservatives won only 50 seats, and the National Progressive party took 65.

MACKENZIE KING

On the 100th anniversary of the late Prime Minister King's birth, December 17, 1974, Prime Minister Trudeau addressed the House of Commons in Ottawa:

> I would like to talk about the centennial of the birth of one of the greatest politicians of this century, William Lyon Mackenzie King. Not only does he deserve the title of "Great Canadian" but also the period during which he lived and gave his services to Canada including twenty-two years as Prime Minister, is itself incredible. . . .
> During and after the first World War, Mr. King was at the center of the tumult and anxiety which stretched the cohesion of the nation and its political parties almost to the breaking point. He devoted his energies toward easing those tensions. He was plunged into the realities of international negotiation, where he developed a determination that Canada must be allowed to deal with fellow nations on her own terms of independence. . . .
> In countless ways, recognized or subtle, Mr. King for forty years placed his stamp on Canadian political life, Parliament and the Public Service. His tenure as Prime Minister was longer than any other Prime Minister before him in the English-speaking world.
> Today I want to pay tribute to the Canadian statesman and politician who carries so many conflicting descriptions. It is almost impossible to sort out the real Mackenzie King, which was perhaps the key to his great success. . . . Now we can see that he was our greatest revolutionary.

William Lyon Mackenzie King was born December 17, 1874, in Berlin (now Kitchener), Ontario. He was the son of a cultured, inconspicuous father and a dominating, bitter mother. She was the daughter of a famous political rebel of the preconfederation days in Canada, William Lyon Mackenzie. The latter, political crank nationalist and revolutionary, had been expelled from his seat in the legislature of United Canada at least five times for his newspaper writings. As well, he had sought to mount an armed insurrection in 1837 against the government of the day. This was unsuccessful. Mackenzie was forced into political exile and lived for a time in New York State. It was in that bitter exile atmosphere that Mackenzie King's mother grew up. That experience was to be passed on to her son in its full fury along with her rebel father's name. This single inheritance probably influenced King more than any other factor in his youth. For that inheritance apparently directed his political destiny and gave him a deep-seated determination to be a good, if not great, leader of his people.

After an academic career at the Universities of Toronto and Chicago and at Harvard University, King performed social settlement work in Chicago and England. In 1900 he became deputy minister of labour in the Canadian federal government. Eight years later, he was elected to Parliament. In 1918 he published *Industry and Humanity*, a study of industrial relations in the United States. The following year, he became leader of the Liberal party and in 1921 prime minister. He served three times in that capacity, in 1921–26, 1926–30, and 1935–48. He died July 22, 1950, in Kingsmere, Quebec.

Mackenzie King was an exceedingly complex and contradictory personality. It was said by his closest colleagues that no one ever got to know him well. He has been characterized as reserved, colorless, petty, ambitious, sanctimonious. One historian places him among the least attractive of Canada's political figures. Despite criticism, however, he is considered by many to have been the most successful of all Canadian politicians. For he was a pragmatic and consummate compromiser. He equated his Liberal party's good with the good of Canada.

In King's official residence in Ottawa (Laurier House), he kept his mother's picture at one end of his study—with a votive light before it. At the other end of the room, there was a proclamation offering a reward for the arrest of his grandfather in 1837. King was a lifelong bachelor, apparently too devoted to the memory of his mother to give his love to another woman, though he had some ladies as friends. He was not quite a misogynist. Though he has been accused of sexual aberration, there is no clear indication that he was a homosexual. His diaries are only now being published in truncated form. Some scholars say complete publication will be necessary to provide a full understanding of this complex man.

King made his first political contribution and reputation in the field of labor relations. He held the thesis that a realistic program of industrial relations was essential to a strong national economy. He developed this conviction in studies relating to both Canada and the United States, performing some of this study under auspices of the Rockefeller Foundation of New York.

As minister of labour in Laurier's cabinet, he further refined his social-economic ideas. He was wedded to the belief that strikes can be avoided through conciliation and mediation. He disliked theories of governmental intervention, coercion, and forced arbitration. His ideas became ingrained in subsequent Canadian labor legislation. Thereby he made a major contribution to his country's workers.

Prime Minister Sir Robert Borden had headed the Canadian government with combined Nationalist and Conservative support during the years from 1911 to 1920. The Conservatives had proved increasingly unpopular in Quebec during and after World War I. It was clear that federal and provincial leaders must do much to heal the rift now appearing between Quebec and the rest of Canada. Borden felt he should be relieved of the burdens of office. Accordingly, he resigned on July 10, 1920. Arthur Meighen replaced Borden as head of this "Union" government. Meighen's own ultraconservatism, plus the fact that he

appointed only one French-Canadian to his cabinet, made
Meighen, too, highly unpopular in Quebec. Furthermore, as
only four of Meighen's coalitionist cabinet were Liberals,
the so-called political coalition soon began to come unstuck.

The new leader of the Liberal party, Mackenzie King, at
once began wooing Quebec. He himself had been a disciple,
and claimed to be the crown prince, of the highly-respected
Laurier. The resulting election in late 1921 proved a
crushing defeat for the Meighen government. Quebec,
Prince Edward Island, and Nova Scotia went solidly
Liberal, while the Prairie Provinces voted heavily in favour
of a new farmer's party, the National Progressives. Former
Laurier lieutenants all won large majorities. Meighen
resigned on December 29, and Mackenzie King was sworn
in as the country's new prime minister. Since the Liberals
lacked clear majority, they were dependent on support of
the prairie Progressives. Quebec was given five out of nineteen cabinet positions. Its influence, however, was probably even greater than that ratio attested.

When King came to power in 1921, he found major
problems in federal-provincial relations. He believed that
the regimes of Borden and Laurier had been too deferential
to provincial interests, especially those of Quebec. King
believed that priority of such provincial interests would
need to be down-graded in favor of the interests of the entire
nation. Thus he reinvigorated the ever-present but sometimes forgotten concept of Canadian national unity. At the
same time, King had to undertake to lead his country
through a major recession in the twenties and to bring
Canada forward from an agricultural to an industrial base.

In these activities, his background as sociologist and
labor relations expert was tested. But in the process, he
became a seasoned political leader. Strangely enough, he
had to undertake a kind of "negative action" politics in
order to achieve his aims—especially in keeping his country
together through the separatist and conscription issues.
Nonetheless, he succeeded.

As early as 1923, King indicated he would not allow

Canada to become a mere "errand boy" for the British government. In that year, Britain had used an imperial
conference in London to try to enlarge and solidify her
control in certain areas of government within the British
Empire. King refused to permit this, insisting instead that
such conferences should be forums for airing the views of
equal members, not for merely endorsing British views.
Thereby he exhibited his determination to make Canada
sovereign in her own right. As a result, he gained a
reputation for being more "nationalist" than he really was.
This reputation later proved an effective base for further
dealings with the French-Canadians.

Insistence on Canada's independent action and autonomy
in foreign affairs was also demonstrated by King in his
early associations with the United States. During his first
term, a number of treaty questions came up with Washington. Those treaties, King insisted, had to be approved by
the Canadian Parliament before being sent on to London for
the British monarch's signature.

In the elections of 1925 and 1926, King showed particular
political tenacity and acumen. In 1925, the Conservatives
won by a narrow margin, taking 117 of the 245 seats in the
Parliament while King's Liberals won only 101. The growth
of populism on the prairies of central Canada helped the
Progressive party win 25 seats. King lost his own seat in
that election. However, through a working arrangement
between Liberals and Progressives, he was again able to
form a government. This political miracle was achieved
despite the fact that not only King, but several of his cabinet
ministers, were defeated. King was personally returned to
the House of Commons in a by-election called to fill a
vacancy in the constituency of Prince Albert, Saskatchewan. Thus, he was able to continue in his post as Liberal
leader and prime minister.

Immediately after this political success came new
troubles. Revelations of corruption in the Canadian
customs bureau brought demands for King's resignation.
To defend his government before the people, he asked the

governor-general, Lord Byng, to dissolve Parliament and call new elections. Byng refused King's request. However, he permitted the Conservatives, led by Arthur Meighen, to form a government without the formality of elections. King contended that the Conservative-led "rump parliament" and the governor-general's insistence on King's resignation under such circumstances had been unconstitutional. King maintained it was the duty of the governor-general to accept the advice of the prime minister in office. King used this "constitutional crisis" as a contrivance to force new elections. Meighen's government was defeated in the House of Commons. This time Byng granted dissolution to Meighen. In the election of 1926, both the populists of the western prairies and the French-Canadians of Quebec again supported King and his Liberals, who won 129 seats and returned to power. Their principal opponents, the Conservatives, won only 91 seats. Thus, by imagination, constitutional awareness, and political courage, King restored his party and his own prestige.

By this election, King had also managed to take a new measurement of his country's tendency toward fragmentation. He realized that the emphasis of his policy needed to be on national unity and a two-party system. The government of Canada under Laurier, King's mentor, had included, not only its vaunted "sunny days," but, as well, a certain courtliness, courtesy, and charm. All this was gone under King. His rule was matter-of-fact, down-to-earth, sometimes even arrogant, negative, and indecisive. His opponents often contended that King's regime was simply "busy doing nothing—and stayed busy doing it." Throughout the country, people may have found King pedestrian. But they thought him stable and safe, and this suited the mood of the times.

After the depression of 1929 began, the criticisms seemed more valid than ever. King and his government seemed determined merely to stay afloat and to keep in check the discontents of the farmers and the prairie populists. The administration disregarded the growing influences of Quebec nationalism, and they were wholly unprepared for the economic collapse of the early 1930s. A spirit of lassitude, even hopelessness, had settled over the land; King seemed unable or unwilling to meet his political and economic challenges. There was definite, even sharp, reaction against the kinds of economic programs being initiated in the United States. King was characterized as a Canadian Herbert Hoover or a Dickensian Micawber—trusting that something would turn up.

This political inactivity and lack of imaginative leadership brought on increasing criticism. For the country was faced with rising unemployment, increasing farm surpluses, and loss of agricultural markets. There were slowdowns in industry and commerce as well. It was clear that King was sadly underestimating the effects of these conditions. Yet he was said to be so sure of his own political position that, allegedly, after consulting with the spirit world (see below), he decided to call a new general election in August, 1930. But some said that King foresaw bad times ahead and preferred not to be in office to face them.

The Conservatives, now led by a rich Calgary, Alberta, businessman, Richard B. Bennett, won an easy victory, taking 137 seats against the Liberals' 88. King may or may not have misjudged the temper of his country as well as his own political strength. Bennett, strong-minded and conservative in outlook, served as prime minister of Canada during the ensuing five years. He was, in fact, a man of great capability. King and his Liberal colleagues learned a great lesson from their defeat. They realized that Canadians would no longer be satisfied with a status quo of political inactivity and ineptitude.

After his defeat, King at once began an attack upon Bennett's seemingly dictatorial moves. King also challenged the constitutionality of Bennett's later economic programs, which were patterned after some of Franklin D. Roosevelt's New Deal programs. As a result of countrywide pressures, Bennett's leadership, and King's constructive approaches in Parliament, various social reforms were forced through. Among these were unemployment insurance, new credit programs, and work projects designed to overcome unemployment. These reforms so infuriated Bennett's right-wing backers that his Conservative government began to break up. An election was called; King and his Liberals were carried back into office in 1935. Now he had considerable business, as well as farm, support. He and his colleagues agreed to continue pressing for major social reforms, but only after constitutional problems were resolved and provincial responsibilities in the social welfare field clarified.

Oddly, King's emphasis on constitutional underpinnings for these social reforms now made him the darling of the Conservatives and big business. The slogan went up, "It's King or Chaos." His tactics had succeeded in restoring him to power. Yet he knew that he had to continue to institute a modicum of reform.

In 1936, the Canadian courts ruled most of Bennett's social programs unconstitutional. This left King's government temporarily powerless in overcoming social problems created by the depression. Obviously the constitution required amendment. This process King undertook by establishing a royal commission on federal-provincial relations, including the fiscal aspects of the subject.

The commission reported that two major developments in Canadian life had seriously affected the constitution since confederation. One of these had been the undermining of the powers of the federal government as the result of a number of judicial decisions handed down by the Privy Council over a long period of years. (Until 1949, the Imperial Privy Council was the court of last resort for Canada.) The second factor was that the powers of the provinces had been extended far beyond the original concepts of the British North America Act and the Fathers of Confederation. For example, prime responsibilities affecting social services had been taken over by the provinces. Yet the major taxing power remained with the

federal government. Thus the provinces had wide responsibilities but lacked powers to finance them. The problems
presented by federal versus provincial relationships remain unsolved to this day in Canada.

By the Statute of Westminster (1931), all essential
autonomy had been given Canada by Britain. Only the
power to amend the British North America Act was
reserved to the British crown. That reservation remained
only because Canada had not yet decided how she wished to
revise her own constitution, especially as regarded federal-
provincial relations.

During the isolationist and domestically difficult days of
the 1930s, Canada had paid little attention to foreign
affairs. King even sought to limit debate in Parliament on
international issues. It appeared as though he and his
ministers deliberately sought to protect parliamentary
debate and Canadian thought from the world outside. Despite King's evasions, the shadows of World War II were
coming into view. The League of Nations had died un-
mourned. This and other European situations, including
Hitler's rise and his moves into the Rhineland and Austria,
seemed to leave King outwardly unmoved.

But it is now clear from King's diaries that he was deeply
concerned that Canada's certain involvement in the upcoming war on the side of Britain would again bring his
country into trauma. King was especially mindful of the
conscription issue of World War I, which had created such
deep distrust and disunity between Anglo-Canadian and
French-Canadian. He was sure this issue would be
resurrected in these new historical circumstances. King
sensed that the French-Canadians would surely resuscitate their demands for separatism. He knew that, on this
issue, he simply had to bide his time—to drag his feet.
Meanwhile, most Canadians devoutly hoped—even
believed—they would be able to remain out of any new European war.

Thus King, like President Roosevelt, was placed in a
political dilemma. On the one hand, he was forced to hoist a

flag of danger regarding the aims of Hitler and the Axis powers. On the other hand, by reason of his domestic power position, King could not overstress these dangers or fully declare his alliance with Britain for fear of antagonizing the French separatists. Thus, until the last moments before warfare broke out in 1939, King kept most of his feelings to himself. As early as 1937, however, he began quietly to increase and strengthen Canadian defenses. At the same time, he helped furnish Britain with much-needed arms and supplies. When Britain declared war upon Germany, King caused the Parliament of Canada to assemble. Within a week, a resolution of belligerency against the Reich was approved. The British monarch, George VI, signed Canada's declaration of war on the sole advice of Canada's government.

As Canada entered that war, its population was barely 11 million. Despite the fact that the depression had presumably ended, there were still some six hundred thousand unemployed in the country. Faced then with both economic and ethnic problems, King pushed the thesis of full cooperation with Britain in the war effort. However, he insisted there would be no conscription of his countrymen for military activity outside Canadian borders. From the outset, and until the military situation required conscription in 1944, these principles were accepted by the Canadian Parliament and people.

It thus became the task of King to lead his countrymen through six long years of war. This in itself was ironic, since King was one of the least militant of men in habit and thought. In fact, according to several of his biographers, he was reputed to be highly distrustful of the military. So it was that, until very nearly the end of the conflict, King avoided the conscription issue, though at high political—and perhaps military—risk.

It was true that vexation over this problem was deep. Indeed, certain French-Canadian leaders, such as the obstreperous Maurice Duplessis, premier of Quebec, made the most of it in their separatism threats. King's own able

French-Canadian lieutenants, including Ernest Lapointe and P. J. A. Cardin, actually threatened to resign from the cabinet and from government if Duplessis was supported by the voters of Quebec. Duplessis was, in fact, rejected by his electorate and did not reappear in politics for some time thereafter.

At the same time, King had trouble on his Anglo flank. The premier of Ontario, Mitchell Hepburn, contended that King was too weak and too favorably disposed to the French-Canadian cause. As a result of this combination of pressures, King called a new election in March, 1940. He and his Liberal party swept that election, taking every seat in Quebec and most of those in Ontario. King had sagely measured his support and stayed safely in power for the remainder of the war.

Attacks now began on King not from without, but from within his own party. The vexations of the conscription issue remained burning. King had come to believe that Canada could best help Britain and the Allied cause through providing reasonable land, air, and sea forces. But when supply problems became acute in the United Kingdom, the development of a Canadian source of supply became imperative. This was the genesis of the industrialization of the Canadian economy. It also called for training in skills and crafts, and of course it strained the Canadian manpower pool. Certainly, King would have realized that this would happen. He might even have believed that the need for supplies would reduce the clamor for conscription to the army. The conscription issue, however, would not die. There were efforts in the House of Commons to revolt against King's leadership, but even here he was able to hold the line. It was not until 1944 that King was forced to invoke conscription—and then only after a successful referendum on that issue. Meanwhile, of course, many Canadian volunteers had already fought and died overseas. The conscription issue had been propelled by the necessity of reinforcing Canadian troops already in Europe. Once again, King was able to ride through a change of policy—overcoming even a parliamentary revolt on that issue.

One of the most beneficial influences of the war on King's administration was that it helped him gather around him a cabinet of high quality. Prominent among the cabinet members was the former American C. D. Howe, minister of war production and supply. Other men of high caliber were J. L. Ilsley, minister of finance; Angus MacDonald, former premier of Nova Scotia, who became King's navy minister; J. L. Ralston, minister of national defense; and C. T. Power, minister for air. Among the outstanding French-Canadians in the cabinet was the minister of justice, Louis St. Laurent, who was later himself to become prime minister. In short, King's wartime cabinet earned a reputation well deserved— that it was the most capable that had ever ruled Canada. It also gained the undeserved reputation of being somewhat colorless. (It turned out, therefore, that the one real wartime personality, albeit controversial, of Canada was not King, or even one of his ministers, but rather a soldier, Gen. A. G. L. MacNaughton.)

This, plus the fact that the great wartime leaders in other Western democracies—Roosevelt, Churchill, Smuts, de Gaulle—outshone King in personality, popularity, and press relations, caused King to become somewhat incensed. One result of this set of comparisons that particularly troubled King was the fact that he proved to be unpopular with his own armed forces. The unpopularity may have been unjustified, since it was based, in large part, on the comparison of the grandiose charisma of the other great leaders with the unobstrusive leadership of King. His unpopularity, of course, also stemmed from the fact that he had shown a lack of zeal in meeting the conscription issue head-on. The armed forces gave little heed to the fact that this very lack of zeal was contributing to the continuing unity of their country.

It was not until 1945, in fact, that King suffered any real political humiliation over his wartime policies. It was then, at the end of the war, that, in a new general election, King was defeated in his own constituency of Prince Albert. His defeat had actually been caused by the armed service vote in that area. As a measure of his leadership, however, his Liberal party again won the election. This election was held in June, 1945, just after the defeat of Germany and before the downfall of Japan.

King had led his country through war and still kept its unity, yet one other major activity remained to be accomplished by King before his departure from government in 1948. This involved creating a new set of relationships with Britain. The 1931 Statute of Westminster had eliminated Canada's so-called dominion status. It gave Canada virtual autonomy over every field save the right to appeal from Canadian courts to the Privy Council in England and, of course, the right to amend the British North America Act. A Citizenship Act (1947) was adopted, establishing for the first time a Canadian citizenship entirely apart from British nationality. In 1949, the British Privy Council ceased to have final authority in legal cases, and the Supreme Court of Canada at long last came into its own as the final arbiter. Now the British North America Act was amended to permit legal changes to be made in Canada in matters of federal concern—but not of federal-provincial relationships. Thus, the umbilical cord with Britain was virtually severed, leaving only the figurative leadership of the British crown.

At the same time, however, new ties began to develop with Canada's southern neighbor, the United States. These ties were destined to become more and more complex, until, by the early 1970s, they were abrasive and vexing to both sides. First of these important new ties with the United States had been the so-called Ogdensburg Declaration of 1940, by which King and President Roosevelt contrived to establish a Joint United States–Canadian Defense Board. The new relationship between the North American neighbors was said by some biographers to have resulted as much from King's own clear-cut pro-Americanism as from the gradual withdrawal from Britain's arms. The swing toward the United States may, as well, have resulted from the attitude of many of King's personal and cabinet advisors, especially his minister of industry, C. D. Howe, and the highly pro-American O. D. Skelton. The latter, who held the post of under-secretary of external affairs until his death in 1941, was King's closest personal confidant.

King also played an important part in directing Canada into her new and still expanding international role. The formation of the United Nations in 1945 was a move that King enthusiastically supported. However, King and other leaders of middle-level powers were not anxious to have this organization completely dominated by the superpowers. They were determined that their own voices be heard; thus, they pushed for the building up of importance of the General Assembly, with its "one nation, one vote" mandate. Canada also became an early member of the Security Council, and ever since King's day, his country has held a special place of power within the United Nations. King and his cabinet likewise pushed for closer post-war ties with the United States. The Canadians also decided it was essential that they become charter members of the North Atlantic Treaty Organization (NATO). King had turned away from isolation by 180 degrees.

Until 1946, King had personally held the portfolio of minister of external affairs. Late in 1946, however, recognizing the immense growth of this activity and realizing the need for younger men with new ideas, King gave over that portfolio to his minister of justice, Louis St. Laurent. This was to be a stepping-stone for St. Laurent into leadership of the Liberal party and the prime ministry itself.

In November, 1948, St. Laurent became leader of the Liberal party and succeeded King as prime minister. Early in 1949, following upon the spadework of King and other Western leaders, the NATO pact was signed by twelve Western European and Atlantic heads of government. Thenceforth, Canada was formally committed to its new and growing international role.

Yet one more triumph remained for King. This was the Act of Confederation with Newfoundland, which, at long last, filled out Canada's continental profile. Though the formal entry of Newfoundland into the confederation actually took place after King's departure from office, the formal negotiations had all been accomplished during his regime. This was a fit postscript to King's long, constructive career and his constant efforts to secure and strengthen national unity.

When King came into power just after the end of World War I, he found Canada a nation full of anomalies and divisions. There were divisions of class, of cultures, of religions, of economic and social disparities, of political persuasions. There were major chasms between provincial and national interests. There was only a facade of truly national interests—of Canadianism. To build this facade into real national unity, King had to resort to considerable political expediency and opportunism. He faced five great issues during his career as prime minister: (1) restoring a semblance of national unity; (2) bringing his country forward from depression into affluence; (3) leading his country successfully through World War II, even in the face of the conscription issue; (4) helping expand and diversify Canada's international role; (5) restoring power of the central government as opposed to provincial fiefdoms. King achieved goals 2, 3, and 4 without question. Goals 1 and 5 continue as problems for his successors.

In political terms, King can be characterized as a sagacious loner—a shrewd boss—one who possibly has had no equal throughout Canadian history. His legacies to his country are clear. He gave his nation continuing unity through great stress. He gave the Liberal party (which still rules Canada today) the great national foundation that it has exerted in its leadership of Canada during forty of the past forty-five years. Perhaps most important of all, King was the first to sense the reality of a new—international— role for Canada. He left his country independent and internationalist in a world beset by tyrannies and by nationalisms.

A special word now needs to be added concerning King's personality and idiosyncracies. He was a complex man though ordinarily a self-effacing one. Very few people seemed to like or love him—many of his opponents obviously hated him with venom. However, the majority of Canadians continued to vote for him and his party on the theory that his was the best leadership available for Canada at the time.

It now appears that King's belief in the spirit world and in the role of the occult was far deeper than was apparent while he lived. Especially in his later years, King reputedly kept a constant dependence on psychic beliefs and mediums. Through these he sought to keep in running dialogue with dead friends and family members, particularly his mother. It was never clear how much these beliefs intruded into his official life and governmental decisions. They must surely have had some influence. His diaries now reveal that, when faced with hard decisions, he fell back upon his visions of the spiritual for guidance. This philosophy was kept a tight secret by King until after his death, and only thereafter was it revealed by access to his writings and the testimony of his closest acquaintances, including several mediums with whom he associated. Mr. Bruce Huchison's solid biography of King, titled *The Incredible Canadian*, is especially adept at setting forth these peculiar matters.

One interesting incident in King's last term as prime minister illustrates the situation. In 1948, Canada was suffering stringent economic difficulties. In order to alleviate her situation, she sought a large loan from the United States. At the same time, under King's direction, Canada sought to establish a free trade zone with the United States—a prototype of a "common market." Negotiations seemed to be going well, but all of a sudden they collapsed. King had gotten "cold feet." There now appears to be evidence from King's records and from those of his nearest advisors that he allegedly received advice from the spirit world that he should not go through with the program. In retrospect, such a program might have proved highly beneficial to both Canada and the United States in today's world.

Even King's prized pet terrier, Pat, seems to have been involved in King's spirit world. The story was told by King that his dog took seriously ill one night and he feared for the animal's life. At 4:25 the next morning, King's watch dropped from a bedside table while he was sleeping, and stopped. King feared this omen and prophesied the dog's death. Sure enough, a day later, the beloved dog crawled to his master's bedside and collapsed in death throes. King looked at his watch. It was precisely 4:25 A.M.

King took seriously ill in London while attending a commonwealth conference just before his retirement. There he received a last visit from His Majesty George VI, who himself, like Mackenzie King, had only a short while to live. While ill in London, King also received visits from his two British spiritualist friends, Geraldine Cummins and Beatrice Gibbs. (It is even said that these mediums did not know King's identity for a very long time, but actually believed him to be a New York clergyman.) With these housewife mediums, King is reported to have held final seances preparatory to his own arrival in the Great Beyond. It now seems clear that King's lieutenants sought to guard all these activities closely in the conviction that, if they became known, they would prove highly detrimental to King's political role, and he would be laughed out of office. While rumors about King's spiritualism were apparently widely prevalent in Ottawa throughout King's later years, few realized either the depth or the extent of King's spiritual practices and beliefs until after his death.

King was reputed to be both petty and generous and to rely alternately on intuition and on deep rationality and common sense. He was both decisive and indecisive. He believed in signs on occasion but mixed intuitive judgment with some Presbyterian predestinarianism. He seemed to depend more on the "other world" for advice and compliments than he did on the creatures of the world around him.

King was intense in his patriotism but inconsistent in its application. He was forced to employ negative action and political expediency particularly against the baronies and petty "lordism" of provincial chieftains. His policy of allowing provincial interests to dominate over national interests proved unpopular—but successful. It helped King to keep the Canadian national structure together, in a sense, in spite of his policies rather than because of them.

King had aimed at breaking the records of Sir John Macdonald and Sir Robert Walpole as the longest-serving prime ministers in the British Commonwealth. This goal King achieved in twenty-one years of service as prime minister. He retired from office in 1948 and died July 22, 1950, in Kingsmere, Quebec.

Louis St. Laurent

The French-Canadian who followed Mackenzie King as Canada's prime minister was a statesman and jurist of considerable repute when he took office. Louis S. St. Laurent served as head of government from 1948 to 1957, having earlier won his spurs as both foreign minister and minister of justice under King. St. Laurent will be remembered in Canadian history for his efforts to strengthen the country's unity, to increase its economic power, and to develop its special international role. In particular he was the guiding force for bringing Canada into NATO and the collective security of the Atlantic Community.

St. Laurent was born in Compton, Quebec, in 1882 of French-Canadian and Irish-Canadian parentage. Early in life, he associated himself with the Liberal party. He was called to the bar in 1905 and in private practice thereafter specialized in constitutional law. In 1914 he became professor of law at Laval University in Quebec City. He did not enter politics formally until 1941, when he became both minister of justice and attorney general in Mackenzie King's wartime cabinet. Despite his French-Canadian connections, St. Laurent supported the idea of limited conscription during World War II.

After his reelection to Parliament in 1945, St. Laurent led the Canadian delegation to the UN Charter Conference in San Francisco, there playing a leading part in his country's original support of the new international body. He rendered outstanding service as secretary of state for external affairs and was also made a member of the Imperial Privy Council.

In 1948 he took over leadership of the Liberal party from the retiring King and was duly appointed prime minister. Now he became intensely active in domestic as well as foreign affairs. One of his first acts was to conclude (1949) King's basic work of bringing Newfoundland into Canada as the country's tenth province. This completed the nation's geographic and political confederation.

On other domestic issues, St. Laurent's record was also impressive. He encouraged foreign capital investment as the only quick means of developing his country's superb natural resources. He sought to further unify Canada by equalizing revenues—allocating from national taxes to the poorer provinces in proportion to their needs rather than their resources. He pushed through important legislation, as well, in the field of social security, in education, and in support of Canadian arts and letters. Pragmatically, he sought to create a new national unity by bringing his fellow French-Canadians out of their spiritual and economic isolation.

Seeking to achieve a new international role for Canada, St. Laurent's government gave help in the United Nations intervention in Korea. It filled an extremely important role in the peacemaking activities that followed that fracas. Under St. Laurent's direction, and with Foreign Minister (later Prime Minister) Lester Pearson in a special role as mediator, Canada gave similar international leadership in the Suez crisis of 1956. Canadian military men and technicians filled important roles in the "Thin Blue Line" of

UN peacekeeping forces not only at Suez, but also in the Congo, Cyprus, and Kashmir. (Even today, St. Laurent's precedent continues for Canada in the Middle East and Cyprus.)

By this time, the British Commonwealth was beginning to take on a new complexion, both literally and figuratively. The end of the colonial empire was in sight, and the British-inspired commonwealth would soon have a majority of nations whose people were not of European extraction. Among the first of such colonies to gain nationhood were India and Pakistan. In the decolonization process, too, St. Laurent was a preeminent peacemaker, throwing his personal and international prestige into keeping these nations members of the commonwealth after their independence from Britain. At the same time, St. Laurent sought to make Canada more than a junior partner in the commonwealth. Cutting away at Canada's dependence on Britain, St. Laurent arranged the appointment of his nation's first Canadian-born governor-general (Vincent Massey) and sought to draw away from British parliamentary interpretations of Canada's constitutional questions.

Despite this superb background of achievement—and after sweeping victories at the polls in 1949 and 1953—St. Laurent and his Liberals were narrowly defeated in 1957. The loss was less a condemnation of St. Laurent's leadership than it was a judgment that the Liberal party—which had been in office for the greater part of thirty years—had become flabby and arrogant. The country demanded a change. Canadians got that change undoubtedly when John Diefenbaker and his brand of prairie populism gained control in Ottawa. Following the Diefenbaker victories—narrow in 1957, sweeping in 1958—St. Laurent gave up leadership of the Liberal party. He was succeeded by his former foreign minister, Lester Pearson. In 1960 St. Laurent retired from the House of Commons, resuming his long-dormant law practice. He died in 1973 at the age of 91, venerated as much after death as he had been in office. One writer, William Kilbourn, aptly eulogized St.

Laurent thus: "His courtly presence and firm but subtle grip on power lent the office of prime minister a dignity and respect and nationwide acceptance of a sort it had never had before."

JOHN DIEFENBAKER

John George Diefenbaker was born September 18, 1895, in Grey County, Ontario. He served as prime minister of Canada from 1957 to 1963. His regime was particularly important because it interrupted twenty-two years of Liberal rule and represented the high-water mark of economic nationalism and anti-Americanism in a populist-conservative guise. It is for this reason that Diefenbaker is so important in any study of Canada. (After Diefenbaker's defeat in 1963, the national Liberal rule was renewed and continues to this day.)

Diefenbaker was a phenomenon on the Canadian political scene, a genuine folk hero. It was said of him that, early one morning while working as a newsboy on the streets of Saskatoon, he engaged in conversation with the then prime minister, Sir Wilfrid Laurier. As a result of his conversation, Diefenbaker vowed he, too, would be a prime minister of Canada one day.

As a real political outsider—one who found his base among the prairie farmers rather than among the corporate executives or party bosses—Diefenbaker had a long road to tread to attain that goal. In fact, he was to suffer some nine political defeats before success finally shone upon him. Yet when success did come to him, it was constant. For before and after his service as prime minister, he held his seat in the House of Commons in twelve successive parliaments. The seat he holds today, at the age of eighty-three, is from the constituency of Prince Albert, Saskatchewan. This is the same "riding" that was long held by Mackenzie King.

After serving in the Canadian armed forces during World War I, Diefenbaker went into practice of law in Saskatchewan. Entering politics, he first failed in a run for the mayoralty of Prince Albert. He failed four times in races for provincial assembly and House of Commons seats before he finally attained to a parliamentary seat in 1940. Thereafter he was twice defeated for national leadership of his Progressive Conservative party before he reached that post in 1956. Replacing the highly popular Ontario premier, George Drew, as leader of the Progressive Conservatives, Diefenbaker at once sought to remould the party in his own way. His program was against big business, against the status quo, against the American defense establishment, against ethnic minorities—and for the "common man" of Canada. Diefenbaker, being neither true British nor true French, was determined upon a "people's" government.

From 1956 onward, he epitomized an angry Canada. It was a land angered and awed and overburdened by its heavy international tasks. It was angered as well by the condescension and economic domination of its more powerful American neighbor.

Perhaps more important than any of his political issues was the personal impact of Diefenbaker himself. Capable of down-to-earth realism, political courage, and exceptional candor along with a spot of evangelical oratory and apt phrase making, Diefenbaker can be characterized as a Canadian William Jennings Bryan. He was a man who had risen, virtually unnoticed, out of populist pressures of the prairies. He embodied the resentments of the Canadian West against the economic and political domination of Ontario and Quebec.

In personality he was earnest and bluff, suspicious of sophistry, trying to represent the basic human verities. As he himself contended, his greatest sins were those of the heart. In this lay his real political problem—he obviously had great affection for the Canada of simpler and easier days—but these were gone, and his political actions were not necessarily in tune with the times. His egocentric nature and his jealousy of political rivals, even some of his own minions, harmed his courses of action. Yet in certain matters, Diefenbaker was surprisingly innovative. He was the first prime minister to bring women and Indians into senior positions in government. Though he was a non–French-Canadian, Quebec enthusiastically entrusted to him its political fate.

Perhaps the central political issue of the late 1950s in Canadian politics, apart from this Western backlash against the domination of the East, was the tangled skein of relationships with the United States. These ranged the gamut from trade and investment to culture and defense. The attack that the Conservatives, led by Diefenbaker, leveled against the Liberal government of St. Laurent was that Canada was too much under domination of the Americans. Fat and flabby after two decades of leading the country, the Liberals were also showing a surprising lack of concern over public opinion on important domestic issues. The issue of the trans-Canada pipeline, which would give special advantages to American users and financial interests, was the straw that broke the camel's back. The Conservatives' attack on that arrangement was tellingly successful. By that issue, Diefenbaker was able to gain a narrow Conservative victory at the polls in 1957 and to cement himself and his party into power by a wide margin in 1958. In the latter election, Diefenbaker carried his party to an unprecedented victory, winning 208 of the 265 House of Commons seats. This was the largest parliamentary majority enjoyed by any party in Canadian history. It represented the apogee of prairie populism and of economic nationalist sentiment in Canada.

As a result of that overriding victory by the Diefenbaker forces, a whole new era opened in Canadian politics. The country had again turned inward. The Liberals were forced to reexamine their policies, and in so doing they, too, found a new leader in Lester Pearson, the popular former minister of external affairs. The 1958 election had also brought demands for reorientation of national minor parties. These had been very nearly eradicated by the Diefenbaker victory, since he himself had gained such a following on the prairies, ordinarily the seat of strength of these minor parties. The Cooperative Commonwealth Federation (CCF), for example, which won only eight seats in the 1958 election, sought a new alliance with the Canadian Labour Congress. When accomplished, that alliance immersed the CCF into the so-called New Democratic Party (NDP). The Social Credit party, though still strong in some Western provinces, was actually left without a single representative in Ottawa.

During the first years of Diefenbaker's rule, both Canada and the United States suffered severe economic recession with accompanying slowdown of production and serious unemployment. Unemployment figures in Canada reached a high not seen since the worst of the depression years. One of the prime reasons for the economic decline in Canada was the skittishness of American investors. Flow of capital from America not only slowed down—in some fields it actually reversed. This backwash came largely as a result of fears over the Diefenbaker-Conservative attitudes toward American financial domination of Canada.

In addition, Canada's markets overseas, especially in Europe, were shrinking. This resulted from the resuscitation of Europe's own economy as a result of postwar rebuilding efforts including the Marshall Plan. In spite of the industrial slowdown, the agricultural sector was soon revived by Diefenbaker's determination to do all he could for his farmer friends. In addition to providing crop subsidies and technical aid, the Conservative regime was successful in finding new markets for Canadian grains in Eastern Europe and in Communist China. This new agricultural prosperity reinforced Diefenbaker's position on the prairies. Once bastions of protest, these prairies now became Conservative political strongholds.

Diefenbaker's government also made important domestic innovations. To combat slack trade and umemployment, his government established a National Productivity Council. In the realm of social welfare, the administration increased pensions for the elderly and disabled. Diefenbaker also took personal responsibility in Parliament for passage of a national Bill of Rights in 1960. This act guaranteed rights of Canadians to enjoy such personal liberties as freedom of speech and religion, right to fair trial, and habeas corpus. However, it applied only to federal legislation and was to be inoperative in wartime. Unlike the American Bill of Rights, the Canadian protection of personal liberties was not intrenched in the constitution but was simply a parliamentary enactment.

No international question received more serious attention from the Diefenbaker regime than did the question of disarmament. The Canadian minister of external affairs, Howard Green, made serious and continuing attempts at both the United Nations and the Geneva Disarmament Conference to break the stalemate between the superpowers over arms reduction. Canada also pushed hard to institute a ban on nuclear testing. By 1963, these efforts had proven unsuccessful. However, by that time, they had created new difficulties in the field of Canadian-American relations.

Immediately after coming into office in 1957, the Conservatives had signed an agreement with the United States to set up the North American Defense Command (NORAD). This provided for integration of Canadian and American air forces, with defense weapons (including nuclear warheads) under joint defense commands. Despite this agreement, the Diefenbaker government refused to accept nuclear weapons for either Bomarc missiles or fighter aircraft based in Canada or for Canadian forces under NATO command in Europe. The Canadian government argued that if Canada accepted these weapons, that action would jeopardize global disarmament negotiations then taking place. By 1963, Diefenbaker's personal indecision on these questions of nuclear weapons brought rising criticism against his government.

The Diefenbaker cabinet was sharply split on this issue. One side, led by External Affairs Minister Green and his supporters, wanted to repudiate nuclear weapons and pursue goals of disarmament. On the opposite side, the defence minister, Douglas Harkness, considered Canada bound by commitments to NATO, NORAD, and her individual allies. He considered it essential to keep nuclear warheads that were already in place in both Canada and Europe. The row came to a head in January, 1963, when the government had to declare its policy. General Louis Norstad, retiring United States supreme commander of NATO forces in Europe, came to Ottawa and held a press conference. In response to a specific question, he answered that Canada would indeed be reneging on its commitments if it failed to acquire nuclear warheads. His statements created a sensation and contributed to the political storm. Immediately thereafter, Minister of Defence Harkness resigned over this issue. This in turn brought Diefenbaker's government down in defeat in the House of Commons in February, 1963. On the issue, Donald Creighton, one of Canada's most distinguished historians, reported, "The Kennedy Administration regarded Canada with a cold fury of impatience. If the Canadians could not make up their minds on this vital subject—nuclear policy—they must be taught to do so."

In the subsequent April, 1963, election, the central issue was the question of Diefenbaker's leadership. He had been unable to husband and to utilize the great political strength he had amassed.

It is difficult to find a single basic reason for the fact that Diefenbaker disappeared from the scene almost as swiftly as he had emerged. Many attribute his political demise to the fact of his chronic indecisiveness. Others believe that he sought to keep a personal role of leadership, using the party as his private property. There was also a tendency to backtrack on established policies, as was true in Canadian defense relationships with the United States in the nuclear field. As a result of this temporizing, Diefenbaker forced his cabinet ministers into controversy with one another and then into open revolt. In contrast to Diefenbaker, most of his ministers had believed it essential that the Canadian defense arm be in possession of nuclear warheads as soon as possible. The United States government under Kennedy openly sided with the defence minister. Side issues also muddied the waters of understanding between the principals, Diefenbaker and Kennedy. In one particular meeting between Kennedy and Diefenbaker on the defense issue, a now-famous security slip occurred on the American side. Somehow Kennedy had left on the conference table in Ottawa one of his briefing memos on which he had scribbled a note to one of his aides: "How can we deal with this s.o.b.?"

On this issue, as in their rural populist roots, there was a kind of parallel between Diefenbaker and Harry Truman. Truman, a few years earlier, had been challenged by his generals on other grounds, and the revolt among those generals had had a marked debilitating influence on Truman's political power. This was just as true with Diefenbaker.

Diefenbaker loves to reminisce: "I have lived history—I have made history—and I know my place in history." He is a man who takes no one else's assessment than his own. He has said, "President Kennedy sent $1 million and 400 CIA operatives to defeat me in 1963."

Diefenbaker used a helicopter to tour his electoral district. Most top Canadian politicians of the East have assumed that the political reaction of the prairie farmers depends only on wheat sales and price. Diefenbaker, unlike them, has realized that wheat sales mark only one of the prairie farmers' concerns. There are many more problems, not the least of which is the belief that Ottawa is never fair to them—whether that be reflected in transport, tariffs, social welfare, or other policies.

Diefenbaker must be considered as one of the most spectacular as well as the most tragic of all Canada's prime ministers. He had greatness, courage, golden rhetoric—but he was self-destructive. He was a man so full of ego that he was blind to his opportunities. He knew the mood of his rural backers—the mood of his people. Yet his sense of outrage grew so great that it became a personal persecution complex—and his political judgment failed. He has been considered by some to represent the last gasp of the prairie politician, the populist, the perennial protester gone national. He is a man of myth as well as reality, so much so that the two cannot yet be disentangled. Perhaps, however, this politician's greatness must be judged as much by his impact on the public consciousness as by what he did or left undone. Diefenbaker will be remembered in Canada and the United States long after he is gone. To this writer, he was a combination of William Jennings Bryan, Everett Dirksen, and Harry Truman.

In the election contest of 1963, Liberal leader Lester Pearson insisted that Canada's national policies on defense and on nuclear development should be defined, rather than vacillate as they had under Diefenbaker. Pearson contended that Diefenbaker's delays and indecision on these matters were unjustified. Pearson promised that, if elected, he would undertake sixty days of real decision making. The challenge paid off. Pearson's liberals won 129 seats; Conservatives held only 95, and the NDP won 17. Pearson became prime minister. (Diefenbaker held the leadership of his Conservative party until 1967, when he was replaced by Robert Stanfield. Diefenbaker was reelected to his House seat in 1968 and has held it ever since.)

LESTER PEARSON

Lester Bowles Pearson was born April 23, 1897, in Toronto. He died December 27, 1972, in Ottawa. He was politician, diplomat, statesman, and prime minister of Canada. He gained world status as arbiter-mediator of major international disputes.

Pearson served in World War I and afterwards completed his university education at Toronto and Oxford. He joined the Canadian Foreign Service in 1928. He became counselor of the Canadian High Commission Office in London in 1935 and served as ambassador to the United States from 1945 to 1946, when he became ambassador to the United Nations. While there, he helped draft the 1947 Palestine partition resolution. In 1948 he entered Parliament for Algoma East, Ontario, and became minister of external affairs in the St. Laurent government. In 1951 he served as chairman of NATO, and in 1957 he received the Nobel Peace Prize for his efforts to overcome the Suez crisis of 1956. Pearson succeeded to leadership of the Liberal party in 1958 and, in 1963, became prime minister. He resigned that office and retired from politics in 1968.

First under St. Laurent's tutelage, and later on his own as foreign minister and prime minister, Pearson went a long way to promote Canada's place in world affairs. He was an ardent advocate of collective security, of Canada's place in NATO, and of mutual security relationships with the United States. In the last-named effort, Pearson had to bind the wounds left by Diefenbaker in Canadian–United States relations.

When Pearson took office, Diefenbaker and his party had contributed to the decline of Canada's international prestige. However, it was not yet certain that Pearson and his Liberals would be accepted as the vehicles for resuscitating the country's fortunes. The great spread in the vote of 1963 and particularly the growth of the minority parties (especially Social Credit and New Democratic) gave clear evidence of the voters' uncertainty. Nor were voter fears allayed at once after Pearson's takeover as prime minister. It took some time for Pearson and the Liberals to reinstate their reputations.

The promised sixty days of decision seemed to remain days of further indecision, even of fumbling. The first budget presented by the new minister of finance, Walter Gordon, was only the beginning of Pearson's difficulties. In the 1950s, Gordon had presided over a Royal Commission on Economic Prospects for Canada, which had been highly critical of outside (especially United States) investment in Canada. Gordon, following the idea of "Canada for the Canadians," withdraw many special tax privileges for industry and sought to prevent further takeovers of Canadian industry by foreigners. These policies at once brought on contraction of the economy, and the businessmen wailed. Gordon was nearly forced out of office in the resulting furor. Though Pearson defended him, the controversial budget was withdrawn, and a new, far less controversial budget was presented. Gordon and Pearson had suffered a real defeat.

During the next two years, Pearson's government ran into further difficulties. Some of his ministers were accused of personal corruption, and one of them was forced to resign after being accused of bribery. Other questions of bribery and financial mismanagement arose with respect to lower-ranking officials. The minister of justice was charged with failing to carry out his duties with respect to these officials. The Pearson government was finally forced into naming a Royal Commission of Inquiry. This commission, reporting in 1965, indicated that the accusations against the minister of justice had indeed been justified.

It had been recognized by both the Diefenbaker and Pearson regimes that the high dependence of Canadian economic development on outside capital brought on both desirable and undesirable effects. There was agreement between the two leaders, as well as most of their followers, that they did not like to have their major industries owned and controlled outside Canada. Pearson's regime insisted that these corporations, although currently essential to Canada's development, must carry on under the same rules as did Canadian businesses and should share their equity and profits with Canadians. They should have, as well, Canadian directors and managers; should disclose their operations and financial conditions; should purchase their supplies in Canada and share their research with Canada.

During the mid-1960s, Pearson and his external affairs minister, Paul Martin, worked hard to prevent the French, under de Gaulle, from having any excuse for pulling out of NATO and possibly out of the United Nations. Canada remained fairly sympathetic to France as de Gaulle attempted to return to his country some of its international luster. It was only when de Gaulle himself intruded into Canada's own internal affairs—with his famous speech in

Montreal apparently supporting Quebec's independence—
that Pearson's view of France hardened.

The surprising defeat of the Lesage government of Quebec in the provincial elections of June, 1966, had done little
to reduce dangerous frictions between Ottawa and Quebec. Nationalist voices were still vociferous, and sentiment for independence of Quebec was growing. Nearly 10
percent of the electorate had voted for the separatist parties
in that 1966 election. Furthermore, Quebec's new premier,
Daniel Johnson, had committed his party (Union Nationale)
and his leadership to goals of "equality or independence."
He called for revision of the Canadian constitution so as to
give recognition to Quebec as a "nation" within the
confederation. Johnson pressed for a larger role for his
province even in international affairs. He moved to
establish direct relations with France in both cultural and
economic areas, these without reference to Ottawa. He did
so, justifying his actions by contending that, in areas of
provincial jurisdiction, the provinces must be allowed to
deal directly with foreign governments. This view the
federal authorities understandably rejected outright.

The conflict was heightened and dramatized by the visit,
in August, 1967, of President de Gaulle to Quebec, ostensi-
bly to attend the Montreal Expo. The Quebec government
had invited him to inspect that site; then he was to proceed
onward to Ottawa for a state visit. Quebec and Ottawa
bickered over details of the visit, but de Gaulle proceeded
through Quebec ceremoniously, received as though he were
royalty. At a civic welcome given him at the Montreal City
Hall, de Gaulle roared out "Vive la France—vive le Quebec
libre!" Many observers believed that de Gaulle was thus
throwing his support behind the movement for an independent Quebec. Ottawa at once objected, calling the
incident interference in Canada's internal affairs. Thereupon de Gaulle cancelled his projected trip to Ottawa and
returned to France. Now Ottawa took the separatist movement more seriously—even more so when René Lévesque, a
popular Liberal politician (now Quebec's premier), left his

party to form a separatist party in Quebec, Parti Quebecois. At long last, Pearson began talks with Quebec's political leaders on the issues dividing them.

It will be recalled that Pearson, as foreign minister, had successfully led the United Nations arbitration proceedings in the 1956 Suez crisis. He had been accused of being anti-British, which aroused antagonism among the more conservative Canadian Anglophiles; nonetheless, he had the world's grudging admiration. Award of the 1957 Nobel Peace Prize to Pearson had attested to that. In this and subsequent international actions—including his work on the Congo, Cyprus, and Rhodesia—Canada, under Pearson, attained unusual international stature.

For Pearson, as for Diefenbaker, relations between Canada and the United States—entirely apart from the problem of capital intrusion—continued to be complex and full of friction. One problem was the difference of view between the two nations—and leaders—on Vietnam. There were also considerable differences of opinion between Pearson and President Johnson on NATO, on France, and even on Cuba.

Canada was becoming more and more disenchanted with United States participation in the war in Vietnam. There were protest marches; the nation's role as a haven for American defectors and protestors contributed to this Canadian disaffection. Pearson eventually risked good relations with President Johnson by advocating that the United States seek a quick, peaceful settlement in Vietnam. He also suggested revisions of United States policy toward China. These recommendations were made by Pearson on American soil and without President Johnson's foreknowledge.

In April, 1965, Pearson visited Temple University in Philadelphia to receive that school's World Peace Award. In a speech on that occasion, he advocated a pause in the United States bombing of North Vietnam. It was polite but unmistakable criticism of United States policy in Southeast Asia. At once President Johnson summoned Pearson to the presidential retreat, Camp David, Maryland, for a private chat. Canadian press officers tended to downplay the event, but several days later the truth of the affair came out in a Washington news column. More recently, Charles Ritchie, who was Canada's ambassador to the United States at the time of the incident, gave a full story of the event in a Canadian magazine. Therein, Ritchie made it plain that Johnson had been downright offensive to Pearson. Did Pearson give instructions to his press people to soft-pedal this story in order to preserve his own political image? Some defenders of Pearson believe that the prime minister, a very unpretentious man, did not really take Johnson's scolding and blunt language to heart. Pearson did not seem offended, though perhaps he should have been if only in defense of the prestige of his office.

Both Diefenbaker and Pearson had tried, during their terms of office, to prevent division and fragmentation of the commonwealth over racial policies. Diefenbaker had taken a hard stand against South African apartheid as early as 1959. Pearson held the same view and went on to try to mediate between Britains and the black Africans on the subject of Rhodesia as well. The Rhodesian unilateral declaration of independence late in 1965 marked the momentary failure of those policies, but it was not for lack of Canadian effort and mediational leadership. In these efforts, Pearson developed a well-deserved reputation for good faith among the newly independent African nations.

Meanwhile, however, Canada took a more and more independent tack in its foreign policy, diverging from both Britain and America. Canada began trade talks, wheat sales, and diplomatic contacts with Red China far in advance of the United States. Canada pulled some of its troops out of NATO despite the protest of European partners. She continued relations and trade with Cuba over American protests.

By 1967, the end of their first century of nationhood, the Canadians had gradually accepted Pearson as one of their great leaders. They fully approved of his efforts to develop

Canada into a model member—indeed, a leader—of the international community. They proudly accepted this new international role and appreciated the skillful diplomacy that Pearson exerted and that he succeeded in extracting from his cabinet and bureaucracy. The Canadians had foregone the airy idealism and ultranationalism of the Diefenbaker times, and they accepted the pragmatic, compromising, but productive policies of Pearson. In their peacekeeping role for the United Nations and their new and broader trade policies vis-a-vis China, the Soviet Union, and Cuba, the Canadians began to comprehend both the responsibilities and the wisdom of Pearson's realistic yet high-minded foreign policy. This was not only a benevolent role of mediator—it was intelligent self-interest.

Even while the centenary of Canadian confederation was being celebrated in 1967, people were asking themselves whether the country could survive another century. In 1965, one George Grant had published a kind of funeral oration for Canada entitled *Lament for a Nation*. The issues of direct foreign investment in Canada—and the matter of economic independence—as well as of separatism versus confederation continued to be the major topics of national concern. Walter Gordon, former minister of finance, was active in challenging thinking on both fronts. In 1967, he won approval for a commission to study the implications of foreign ownership. His committee report, issued in 1968, called for new policies designed to regulate closely the operations of foreign-owned firms in Canada. The report also encouraged Canadian investment in her own resources. From those ideas rose the Canadian Development Corporation, specifically designed to channel Canadian funds into local development. The report concluded that foreign investment had served Canada as a means of nation building, but this day was gone. New policies required protection of national sovereignty and economic independence. A diversified economy had now emerged, and its growth must be enhanced by internal means.

The direction of Canada's new economic nationalism was

now becoming clear. It marked a path of definite diver-
gence from domination by the United States—a course that
would become even more clear under the subsequent
Trudeau administration. Yet the twin problems of French-
Canadian separatism and of federal-provincial relationships remained unsolved at the end of Pearson's administration. Even intense efforts at bicultural and constitutional changes had brought about only half-hearted
results.

Pearson, nicknamed Mike by his pals, lived all his life
among the "old boys" network of Ontario and assumed that
the whole world was run like this network. It is claimed
that his arrogance was sometimes as sublime as was Lord
Mountbatten's. At the least, he was egocentric, determined,
with his fellows, to "get ahead in the civil service" and then
to "divide the swag." The group that brought Pearson to the
apex of power was a distinctive and close-knit WASP elite.
Most of these were either senior civil servants or fellow diplomats. So close-knit was this group that Pearson even
asked in his last will and testament to be buried in the same
country cemetery plot that was to contain the graves of two
of his closest cronies who had held high positions in
external affairs—Norman Robertson and Hume Wrong. It is
interesting that his own memoirs, entitled *Mike*, thoroughly describe Pearson's group—but do not present much
about Pearson's own dealings with the mighty of the international community. On these people and the events that
concerned them there is actually a dearth of information. In
a sense, Pearson performs diplomatic sleight of hand—
telling innocuous stories on himself in order to evade the
greater truths. One reviewer of Pearson (Heather Robertson in the September, 1973, *Maclean's*) said that thereby
"he appears to bare his soul while saying nothing of
significance." Unfortunately, this probably is the hallmark
of a true diplomat. Yet it was his imagination combined
with his sunniness of nature—his innate optimism—that
enabled him to work hard for great concepts like the United
Nations and world order. As well, by imaginative leader-

ship on the domestic front, he sponsored progress of biculturalism, creation of the country's new flag, and a national pension plan.

Though Pearson was not the most popular of all Canada's prime ministers, he was surely one of the most respected. That respect has increased even after his death, becoming something akin to national affection for him. A recent television documentary covering his life, titled "First Pearson Singular," ably portrayed his superb capacities as diplomat and statesman. In this portrayal, he is shown accurately to have had an elephantine memory, a raconteur's wit and capacity for entertainment; to have been a thoughtful man and a man of simple candor. The author, who was privileged to meet Pearson at the United Nations in 1956, judged him to be incisive but not snobbishly intellectual; down-to-earth but not earthy; shrewd but not nettlesome. Both his autobiography and the television documentary portrayed him truthfully, also, as a man of some smugness and insularity—which might be construed as traits of many Canadians.

In 1968—the 101st year of Canada's confederation—the need of vital new leadership became more and more apparent. Pearson was on the edge of retirement as prime minister and Liberal leader. Diefenbaker, after his 1963 defeat, had not been able to regroup his Conservative forces. Dalton Camp, leader of the Ontario wing of the Conservatives, plumped for a new Conservative party chieftain, and Robert Stanfield, former premier of Nova Scotia, took over the controls. Stanfield, a thoughtful, somewhat colorless man of high integrity and political acumen, was chosen to heal the opposition party's many wounds.

Pearson left the Liberal leadership voluntarily. At once, virtually all the members of the Pearson cabinet announced for that leadership post. Pierre Elliott Trudeau, a French-Canadian who was serving as minister of justice, came to the forefront. He had made an important contribution to recent Canadian political life in a number of ways, not the least of which was to challenge French-Canadian separa-

tism among his own people. He had, as well, a unique personality—a kind of charismatic glamour. He had, an unusual power to communicate and to establish rapport with
younger voters. Thus it was that what came to be called
"Trudeaumania" emerged—and a man who had been only
three years a member of the Liberal party was chosen its
leader.

When Pearson retired, Trudeau at once took the reins.
His first major action as prime minister was to call an
election to capitalize on the interest that his emergence as
Liberal leader had aroused. Trudeau made the matter of
national unity his central campaign theme, and he assured the voters that he would make such constitutional
changes as were needed to cement the country together. In
this connection, he promised to expand bilingualism but
to treat all provinces equally. He assured the voters that he
would seek to eliminate regional economic disparities and
to recapture Canada's ownership of her economy. He also
promised a reassessment of the country's foreign policy,
including that concerning trade and diplomatic ties with
mainland China.

In the 1968 campaign it appeared that Trudeau's viva-
cious personality was even more an issue than were substantive matters. Trudeaumania was sweeping the
electorate. The opposition, led by the colorless personality
and poor speaker Robert Stanfield, was plagued as well by
ambiguities on major issues such as Quebec and foreign
investment. The small parties—the NDP, the Social Credit
Party, and the Railliement des Creditistes—strove to hold
back the tide but were not successful. The election gave
the Liberals the first solid majority government in Canada
since 1958.

PIERRE TRUDEAU

Pierre Elliot Trudeau was born on October 18, 1919, in
Montreal to a French-Canadian father and an Anglo-
Canadian mother. He is the descendent of a French peasant

who emigrated to Quebec in 1659. His family's multimillion dollar fortune was made in oil and real estate. Trudeau graduated from the University of Montreal Law School and did postgraduate study at Harvard, the Sorbonne, and the London School of Economics.

As a youth, Trudeau travelled widely through Europe and Asia. In those travels, he is alleged to have had many special adventures—such as throwing snowballs at Lenin's tomb, being detained in a European jail, swimming the Hellespont, escaping from Arab bandits in the Middle East. He visited Vietnam while the French were still there. He is reputed to have met Mao Tse-Tung and Chou Enlai before they came to power. He was even reported to have been barred from the United States temporarily because of his earlier visit to Moscow.

Trudeau served as desk officer in St. Laurent's Privy Council (1948–51). He founded *Cité Libre*, a monthly review critical of both Liberal and Conservative regimes. In 1951 he practiced law in Quebec province and lectured as professor at the University of Montreal. He was elected to the House of Commons in 1965. In 1966, he became parliamentary secretary in the Pearson government, and in 1967, he became attorney general and minister of justice. In the last-named capacity, he received considerable publicity for pushing for stricter gun control and softer laws on abortion and homosexuality. He became prime minister and Liberal leader in 1968 and retains both positions to this day.

Trudeau first made a national name for himself in a most unusual way. Prime Minister Pearson's final effort to achieve good relations between French and English had been to arrange a provincial-federal conference in Ottawa in February, 1968. This meeting was a kind of constitutional review—even on "reconfederation." Pearson had emphasized its importance when he said, "What is at stake, in my opinion, is no less than Canada's survival." Resulting hot discussion centered about the problem of Quebec. Quebec's premier, Daniel Johnson, demanded greater power for his province in the international sphere as well as in social welfare and broadcasting. Before a nationwide television audience, these demands were brilliantly opposed by Pearson's minister of justice, Pierre Trudeau. Most provincial premiers joined with Trudeau in criticizing and opposing Quebec's demands.

Trudeau's selection as Liberal leader was based in part on his charisma with young voters but partly also on widespread belief in the party that Trudeau, a French-Canadian himself, would not sell the party down the river on the issue of Quebec nationalism. By his opposition to claims of special status in the confederation for Quebec, Trudeau had gained great prestige among Anglo-Canadians. He was firmly opposed to the two-nation thesis for Canada's future. Thus it was that in April, 1968, he assumed Liberal leadership with very strong backing.

When Pearson resigned the prime ministership in June, 1968, Trudeau took over the reins. He grasped power first by helping to install a number of cabinet ministers of French-Canadian background. In fact, never before his coming on the scene had French-Canadians held so many important cabinet posts and high civil service positions in Ottawa. In the same context, he established a real federal presence within the province of Quebec. Thus he sought to guide French nationalism into channels that could be better controlled by Ottawa and to give Quebec some autonomy—but not too much. Thereby, he sought both to redirect and eventually to dominate Quebec's "quiet revolution." He sought to overcome Quebec's parochialism and at the same time to accept national bilingualism as one means of breaching Quebec's walls.

Some of Trudeau's early writings on this matter have applicability even today: "Most English Canadians fail to realize that it is their attitude which exactly determines the extent and force of Quebec nationalism. . . . Central government encroachments which are accepted in other provinces as a matter of expediency, cannot be so viewed in Quebec." That is considered the Trudeau of yesterday.

What about today and tomorrow? Now he says: "I think the linguistic problem is a very important one. . . . [but] there are other problems of national unity. The problem of regional disparity, of national identity. I see nothing retrograde in unilingualism. . . . What is important is that all Canadians be able to communicate with their various arms of government in the official language— whether that be French or English. In that sense Canada is becoming bilingual. . . . " The future Quebec will belong to that party that realizes that Quebec's future is in Canada. The Biculturalism and Bilingualism Commission of 1969 provided a blueprint for carrying out Trudeau's theories, but he has emphasized that these were, in most respects, mere "tokenism." He has insisted that official equality of languages has little significance if not accompanied by equality of economic opportunity.

In Trudeau's first nationwide election, in June, 1968, his Liberals secured a clear majority, winning 155 seats to the Conservatives' 72. The NDP took 22 seats. The French-speaking Creditistes, under their boisterous leader, Real Caouette (now deceased), gained in strength from 8 to 14 seats. The Liberals had done well nationwide, arousing the hope that at least some of the divisive forces of Canada might be controlled.

In recognition of its national base, the new Trudeau regime entered a kind of political honeymoon period. At the outset, it sought to establish what Trudeau called a "just society," the tenets of which were somewhat unclear, but which presumably sought to control French-Canadian separatism and, as well, to eliminate some of the regional and provincial disparities. The administration also sought to reorganize the federal bureaucracy, to complete some of the social measures begun under Pearson, and to institute new social reforms.

Yet by 1970 the political honeymoon was at an end and divisive sociopolitical forces had reasserted themselves. Like his predecessors, Trudeau faced the nagging questions of unemployment and underemployment, of disparities between the poverty of the Atlantic Provinces and the wealth of Ontario, Alberta, and British Columbia. He faced the problem of new markets for Canada's agriculture and industry, the question of foreign investments and United States financial domination. Trudeau also faced the challenge of redefining Canada's international role and especially her complex of relationships—defense, commercial, and cultural—in the Western Hemisphere. Most of all, he faced the pervasive problems of separatism and federal-provincial relationships—the Kingdom versus the Dukedoms and Baronies. The question was, how much leeway could Trudeau allow the renegade dukes and barons in terms of independent provincial authority (especially financial authority) while protecting the confederation itself?

Trudeau's first administration, though preoccupied with domestic issues, made some major changes in Canada's foreign policy. Canada had already established its role of mediator in the United Nations and its prestige in NATO— giving admirable help on the issues of the Congo, Cyprus, and Suez. Trudeau now began to reduce his country's troop strength in NATO and, as well, to move toward fresh new relationships with both the Soviet Union and mainland China. He thus preceded President Nixon in this direction. He also insisted that Canada should attempt to reduce its defense costs, spending that money instead in greater foreign aid for the underdeveloped world.

One of the most important activities of the Trudeau regime has been the calculated effort to move away from domination by the United States. (This matter will be discussed in detail in a later chapter of this book.) This reorientation program has involved two different goals. The first has been to impose new restrictions on foreign (especially American) investment in Canada. The second has been to diversify Canadian trading patterns to find other trading partners. Japan, mainland China, the Soviet Union, Latin America, and Common Market countries have been prime targets of Trudeau's personal salesmanship. In his own words, the aim is to supplement, rather than to supplant, existing Canadian–United States trade patterns. Trudeau characterized these actions in an interview with *U.S. News & World Report*, December 8, 1974: "It's a matter of kicking both ourselves and others in the pants to make sure we don't have all our eggs in one basket, as they are now. . . . We are believers in multinational trading patterns. We are only telling businessmen from Canada and other lands, 'If you want to make trade multinational, then it shouldn't only be United States/Canada.'"

Underlying the direction of relations between Canada and the United States, in Trudeau's view and in the view of his cabinet ministers, are the propositions that Canada must redefine her own national interests, protect her national unity from intrusions by the giant neighbor to the south, and reassert her own national identity. In realigning associations with her southern neighbor, Canada has been faced with only three options: (1) maintaining the status quo with continued domination by the United States; (2) allowing closer integration with the United States, with threat of total submergence by that country; and (3) taking steps designed to reassert Canada's own independence and freedom of action in all fields. To help decide on a course of action, Trudeau, in 1972, set up a foreign policy study commission that decided upon the third alternative—reassertion of Canada's "own thing."

In his personal relationships with American officials, especially Presidents Nixon and Ford, Trudeau may be portraying the basic difficulties between these two neighbors—Canada and the United States—as much as showing his private vexations with America's leaders. What gripes most Canadians is not that the United States is really antagonistic to Canada, which it is not, but that it tends to be condescending toward Canada, to ignore her, which it does.

It has already been noted that Diefenbaker and Pearson, Trudeau's immediate predecessors, had their own kinds of troubles with American Presidents Kennedy and Johnson.

During the Nixon and Ford administrations, relations between Canadian and American leaders continued their slippage. In President Nixon's unilateral announcement (August, 1971) of the surtax on imports, he created a gaucherie—calling Japan rather than Canada America's best customer. It took a subsequent visit to Ottawa by Nixon and a Nixon address to the Canadian Parliament to cool off Canadian feeling over this gaffe. Even after that, Nixon once more muddied the waters of United States–Canadian relationships. Having promised Trudeau that the United States would join Canada in cleaning up the highly polluted Lake Erie, Nixon thereupon impounded funds appropriated by Congress for the American side of that venture. The psychological shocks of the 1971 Nixon surtax; the controversies over the Vietnam issue; and especially the Watergate revelations of Nixon's taped derogation of Trudeau as "an asshole" have all helped to hasten the downhill slide. These traumas have been given further impetus by the more recent substantive conflicts between the two nations over the energy crisis, meat quotas, and pollution problems. (In his farewell appearance before Canadian officials and fellow diplomats in Ottawa in December, 1975, outgoing United States Ambassador William Porter used the occasion to warn both Americans and Canadians that relations between these two nations were indeed deteriorating and requiring prompt lubrication.)

Even Prime Minister Trudeau's meeting (December 4, 1974) with President Ford illustrated the difficulties between the two nations and their leaders. For the Canadian prime minister was not the most important foreign visitor in Washington on that day. Instead, for official Washington, it was the West German chancellor. Once again, it appeared that Washington officialdom, including President Ford and Secretary of State Kissinger, was taking Canada—America's best customer—too much for granted.

Trudeau appears to have got off on better footing with

the Carter administration. He was the first Canadian prime minister invited to address a joint session of the American Congress. This session, broadcast throughout Canada, took place February 22, 1977. Trudeau used the platform to bluntly warn his fellow Canadians and all North Americans of the dangers of Canadian separatism. He contended that Canada would not break up, but he admitted the need of constitutional changes to hold Canada together. This Washington visit gave clear indication that the Carter administration was using this occasion to make Americans more Canada-conscious.

The October, 1972, election, in which a far less popular Trudeau faced the voters, had reduced the Liberal's absolute majority to a minority position. Despite the shrinkage of seats from 155 to 109 (against the Conservatives' 101 and the NDP's 31), Trudeau managed to stay in power with a minority government. He maintained that situation only with the sometimes tacit, sometimes open, support of the socialistically inclined NDP. It was surprising to most observers that he was able to stay in power, given that weak position, for some eighteen months. In return for that NDP backing, the Liberals were forced to send through the Parliament a series of NDP bills. These included higher welfare and food benefits for the elderly and other social welfare proposals.

In May, 1974, the quasi alliance between Liberals and the NDP was torn asunder. The NDP leadership was tiring of Trudeau's conservative approach and began to go after the big corporations with demands for a new "soak the rich" tax structure. Trudeau's budget became the major issue. A "no confidence" motion on that proposed budget was sustained on grounds that the administration's financial plans failed to deal effectively with Canada's growing inflation. Success of the "no confidence" vote brought the Trudeau government down.

The resulting election on July 8, 1974, was characterized as a "great Liberal comeback" by the London *Economist* and the Canadian press. Once again, the Liberals had a clear majority. They won 141 of the 264 seats in the House of Commons. The Progressive Conservatives won 95 seats; the NDP won 16; the Creditistes 11; Independents 1. It was a striking personal victory for Trudeau. Yet, in addition to all his prior problems, Trudeau and his reorganized government faced several new ones. Not the least of these was how to deal with inflation, rising unemployment, and a broad array of strikes. Trudeau and his Liberal colleagues instituted an Anti-Inflation Board (AIB) presumably designed to control both prices and wages. This body instituted harsh measures to achieve its goals, even insisting on rolling back wage increases already won—thus voiding many bargaining agreements. Less spectacular have been its battles against price rises. Inflationary pressures have continued strong. As a result the AIB has become a whipping boy for parliamentarians, labor groups, and the public. (It is now being phased out.) To avoid running his ship of state onto these political shoals, Trudeau, in September, 1976, completely overhauled his cabinet. He brought in seven newcomers, made nine reassignments, and added two new portfolios, enlarging the cabinet to thirty-one ministers.

The realities of power—ever complex and kaleidoscopic in movement—are always difficult to measure. As regards Prime Minister Trudeau's most influential advisers, his "inner cabinet" or "super group," there is some myth and some truth. Members of his personal staff and of the Privy Council do have extra access—therefore extra power. Trudeau has special long-time friends on whom he depends particularly. A few senior civil servants sometimes labeled "mandarins" also have special position.

Of Trudeau's main advisers, the six who seem to have special influence are these: Marc LaLonde, minister of health and welfare; Ivan Head, speechwriter and specialist on foreign affairs, who was also influential with Lester Pearson; Jim Coutts, Trudeau's chief of staff; Peter Roberts, Trudeau's press secretary; Senator Keith Davey; and Gerard Pelletier, Canada's present ambassador to

France. A second coterie of power is, by some, considered to include Donald Macdonald, former Minister of Finance; Al Johnson, secretary of the Treasury Board; Allan MacEachen, president of the Privy Council and House leader; Jean Chretien, Minister of Finance, and External Affairs Minister, Don Jamieson.

Until recently, the presumed heir apparent to Prime Minister Trudeau's mantle of Liberal leadership was John W. Turner, the country's exceptionally capable former minister of finance. However, Trudeau and Turner publicly differed on the issue of inflationary controls. Turner favored installation of some form of price and wage ceilings; at the time, Trudeau would not buy this concept. On that difference, Turner departed the cabinet, though he did retain his parliamentary seat. The successor to Turner's portfolio of finance was Donald Macdonald, formerly minister of energy and resources and as noted above a Trudeau intimate. (Macdonald did persuade Trudeau to accept price and wage controls, but these are now being discontinued. This was the very issue on which Trudeau had won the 1974 election. At that time, his Conservative opponent, Robert Stanfield, had advocated such controls while Trudeau had condemned them.)

At this writing, John Turner cannot be ruled out as a future leader of the Liberal party and eventual prime minister. His successor, Donald Macdonald, as well as Canada's former minister of external affairs and present House leader, Allan MacEachen, also appear—at least today—to be among possibilities for the role of Trudeau's crown prince.

Pierre Trudeau came upon the country "like a stone through a stained glass window." This was the estimate of one astute Canadian newsman, Gordon Donaldson, in his book *Fifteen Men*. Trudeau was novel, exciting, a kind of political "flower child." He had—and has—imagination, intelligence, decisiveness. Some even say that he had—and has—compassion. His language is both colorful and ribald. He is, for example, credited with an ironic reversal of Lord

Acton's famous phrase that "power corrupts. . . . " Trudeau's version is that "lack of power corrupts and absolute lack of power corrupts absolutely!" In House of Commons debate as well as in press conferences, Trudeau's choice of words sometimes requires censorship and sometimes is unprintable.

To many Canadians—both his champions and his critics—Trudeau has turned out to be a paradox. For example, following his first election in 1968, he ended up not quite as advertised. He had earlier been seen as a champion of the "just society." Instead, for a time after his first election he was remarkably conservative on most social issues. His attitudes on abortion and homosexuality were exceptions. In his election campaign, he claimed to be a champion of major political and parliamentary reform. Thus far he has turned out no major reforms of this variety. His critics have contended that he is more occupied with managerial flow charts than with humanitarian solutions. He claims, however, to be willing to bring public opinion to bear on major decisions so as to attain a participatory democracy in his Canada. Yet today, he seems to be swinging between free enterprise and a managerial state—closer to Keynes than to Friedman.

On civil liberties, his reputation preceded him into office. He helped to settle a famous miners' strike in Quebec before he became prime minister. Yet, when confronted by postal strikers on the streets of Ottawa, he is reported to have issued the sobering, dirty expletive "Mange la merdre." Sometimes arrogant, occasionally humble, he is often perplexing. Touted as a champion of civil rights, he is at times autocratic. He has sought to curb the separatists via a War Measures Act and proudly presents a computerized processing of government rather than a humane, people's government.

When he came to power, he was an arch-exponent of free trade. Instead, in the face of the energy crisis, commercial rivalry with the United States, and determination to come out from under the American umbrella, Trudeau and his cohorts are beginning to look "crusty"—like economic nationalists.

Prime Minister Trudeau's most valuable political characteristic appears to be the capacity to hold and exercise power and to shift with political wind currents. His greatest personal characteristic is that of adaptability and resilience, the ability to roll with the punches. When his country thought it needed a "swinger," he gave them one. When he thought they needed a highly domesticated married man, well, he gave them that, too.

Trudeau's young, now estranged wife, Margaret, has herself been described as a "perfectly preserved flower child." She produced for her husband three sons in a period of seven years. Though Margaret Trudeau openly objects to violation of her privacy by her heavy public duties as a prime minister's wife, she did much to assist her husband in the 1974 campaign. In that effort, she delivered some highly quotable and popular campaign speeches. In one now famous speech, she innocently spoke of her husband as "quite a beautiful guy"—who taught her about love. This was a naive, but highly successful, comment in an otherwise ribald and harsh political campaign. Following up allegations of some journalists that the Trudeaus were the only prime ministerial couple to have had a real sex life, *Macleans*'s newsmagazine on June 13, 1977, carried a background article on the subject. This article reported a question asked of Margaret Trudeau in the tense days prior to the Trudeaus' marital break. Margaret was asked what she and her husband had ever had in common. "We f—— a lot," she explained suavely.

Self-indulgent and erratic, Margaret Trudeau recently kicked up an international scandal by chasing around with the rock group Rolling Stones and by a New York visit in which she contended she was "abdicating." Clearly she had become a political question for her husband, already besieged by massive problems of separatism, inflation, and unemployment. At this juncture, the question asked by inquisitive Canadian, British, and American news hawks is, Will the Trudeau marriage break up or survive, and what will be its effects on the future of Canada's ruling Liberal party?

So, despite all the artful advertising—the concern with the public image—Trudeau appears to be turning out to be both an ordinary and an extraordinary politician. Petty yet generous, clever yet obtuse, Trudeau is a man of great personal foibles and vanities, political strengths and frailties. The well-known Canadian pundit Marshall McLuhan has called Prime Minister Trudeau "a man in a mask," his image shaped by the Canadian culture gap—an eighteenth-century Frenchman who has outstripped his nineteenth-century country to become a twentieth-century leader.

Trudeau's popularity reached an all-time low during 1976. With the election of the Parti Quebecois in Quebec late that year, a new period of risk was ushered in, and there was a period of recovery for him.

After a thumping in the by-election of October 16, 1978, Trudeau was called upon by many major newspapers and members of his party to step down to allow new blood to lead his Liberals. The vote was not necessarily for the opposition but a vote against his government. The ten Premiers have unanimously expressed their dissatisfaction with his constitutional proposals and the economy. For the past year Trudeau, behaving out of character, has isolated himself from his Cabinet and most of his coterie of advisers. Lately, he has been profoundly impressed with the writings of the American social critic Robert Heilbroner on "civilization malaise."

The federal election will be held before July, 1979, when Trudeau's five-year mandate expires. The question now is Will he bounce back and lead his Liberals to victory, to Loyal Opposition, or will he "abdicate"? The stage is set with other Liberals such as John Turner and Tory leader Joe Clark in the wings. The country desperately needs a healer who can speak for all parts of Canada in this critical phase of its history.

7

Dukedoms and Baronies: The Provinces

W ith the provincial premiers, the "dukes" and "barons" of this princely realm, Prime Minister Trudeau, like his predecessors, carries on constant political "warfare." This continuous duel between the central government at Ottawa and the various provinces is a tug-of-war for power, tax receipts, and control of resources. It involves such diverse questions as autonomy in Quebec; business privileges in Ontario; the control of taxation of natural resources in British Columbia, Alberta and Saskatchewan; solution of transport and agricultural problems in Saskatchewan and Manitoba; the elimination of economic disparities between the Atlantic Provinces and other parts of the country. This competition between Ottawa and the provinces, between leaders and regions, works as a deterrent to Canadian unity and to strengthening of the federal system. There have even been moments in Canadian history when provincial premiers have held sway over an entire region. Thus far, however, no provincial premier has been able to exercise his will over the entire nation.

Of overriding concern between the two major ethnic groups—French and English—and between federal government and provincial capitals is the polarizing question of bilingualism. This matter provokes bitter controversy. In their efforts to foster study, understanding, and application of both languages in government, business, and academe, virtually all Canadian rulers from Lord Durham to Pierre Trudeau have run into trouble. Today, by law, Ottawa dictates official use of both languages throughout the nation despite provincial counterattacks. In particular, in their own bailiwick, Quebec's leaders seek to restore French as the single legal and preeminent language. Some Anglo-oriented constituencies either neglect or openly combat bilingualism. The program costs approximately $500 million yearly, and political controversy on this issue is ubiquitous and never ending.

All this is, in part, a reflection of the phraseology of the British North America Act of Confederation. It stems also, in part, from the differences between the geography, economics, and cultures of the various constituencies. It is likely that solving these problems will eventually require amendment of that act. Such amendment is bound to take many years. The eventual solution could even prove to be the determinant as to whether Canada remains one confederacy or fragments into several autonomous nations. In order to better understand these tensions, one must have some perspective of each of the constituent parts—each of the provinces—each of the dukedoms and baronies.

Canada is divided into ten provinces and two territories. The provinces have specified authorities as provided in the British North America (BNA) Act of 1867. These authorities have been expanded, especially in the field of social welfare, by judicial acts and subsequent constitutional changes. As a result, each province and provincial administration has considerably more authority than is given to an American state government.

The four original provinces—Quebec, Ontario, Nova Scotia, and New Brunswick—were formed into the confederation by the act of 1867. The provinces added since that date include Manitoba in 1870, British Columbia in 1871, Prince Edward Island in 1873, Saskatchewan and Alberta in 1905, and Newfoundland in 1949. (The Yukon Territory was created in 1898, and the Northwest Territories in 1905. These territories, administered directly by the federal government under the Department of Indian

Affairs and Northern Development, are described in Chapter 11.)

In each of the provinces, there is a legislative assembly to which members are elected from constituencies termed ridings. Each legislature must meet once a year. Elections are held every five years, or sooner if the current majority party rule is overridden in the assembly or if the provincial government so chooses. These are the same parliamentary arrangements as exist in the federal parliament. The administrative and legislative head of each province is the premier. That official is also normally the head of the political party that has a majority in the legislature. If no single party holds a clear majority, then it is possible for the leader of the largest political party to assume office as premier through a coalition of several minority parties. Through that coalition, he must maintain a voting majority on all major issues. Failing this, the province must face a new election.

The premier appoints members of his own or of the coalition parties as heads of the various departments of the provincial government. These are known as ministers. The permanent head of each department, however, is usually a senior civil servant of long standing. This official is usually given the title of deputy minister. In each of the provinces, there is a lieutenant-governor whose role is very similar to that of the governor-general of Canada. The lieutenant-governors are appointed by the governor-general of Canada on the recommendation of the prime minister.

The BNA Act sets forth seventeen fields of provincial jurisdiction. These have been enumerated in Chapter 5. Most provinces are big territorially, rich in resources; they have more or less viable economies. They may not be individually self-sufficient, but they come closer than most states of the United States do. Hence, they have more clout as they confront the federal authorities.

Canada has an unusual, even exemplary, system of taxation and fiscal sharing between the national government and the various provinces. Ottawa pays each province 28 percent of the federal income tax collections with added income from sixteen other taxes shared on an equalizing process. This scheme is based on a national average in which the richer provinces, notably Ontario, British Columbia, and Alberta, share their largesse with the poorer provinces. Recent political pressures—resulting from inflation, urbanization, the energy crisis, social welfare, demands for separatism and regional parity—all produce continuing insistence on additional federal allocations. Federal increases, in turn, bring forth provincial demands for constitutional changes in taxing powers so as to guarantee provincial incomes. This question still remains moot.

As in the United States, the provinces can, to a degree, be classed in regional groupings. The Maritime Provinces are similar to our own New England states. Quebec and Ontario might be categorized as the industrial heartland, comparable in some respects to the highly industrialized American mid-Atlantic and northern Appalachian regions. The so-called Prairie Provinces of Manitoba, Saskatchewan, and Alberta are comparable to America's plains states. The large and mountainous Province of British Columbia has similarities to our own Pacific Northwest. Thus, the Canadian provinces are grouped regionally by geography, climate, mutual economic interests, and resources.

History, religion, cultural and ethnic attitudes also contribute to regionalism. Most of the residents of the Maritimes are of English, Irish, or Scottish descent, as is the majority of the populace of Ontario. In fact, a preponderance of the people in all provinces except Quebec are essentially British in ethnic origin. In Quebec however, 80 percent of the people are of French origin. The percentage of the population originating in the British Isles varies from 93 percent in Newfoundland to 12 percent in Quebec, averaging 40 percent throughout the nation. However, those figures are now being diluted by immigration from Central Europe, from Asia, and from the United States.

As to provincial politics, the three Atlantic Provinces excluding Newfoundland traditionally hold Conservative party views. So, too, does Ontario. Newfoundland has long held Liberal views but is led by the Tories. Prince Edward Island is the lone Liberal province. Quebec has been either Liberal or tending to separatist with its Parti du Quebecois and similar organizations. The three Prairie Provinces have experimented with populist ideologies from Social Credit (SOCRED) to Co-operative Commonwealth Federation (CCF) and the more recent New Democratic Party (NDP). Today, however, Alberta has swung Conservative, largely because of its oil riches. British Columbia has tended to experiment with SOCRED and NDP rule. The two principal national parties—Liberal and Conservative—have had little influence in that province's politics during the last quarter century.

Representation in the central Parliament at Ottawa is made up according to population by constituencies from the provinces and territories. There will be 282 seats with the 1979 election, divided as follows: Ontario, 95; Quebec, 75; Newfoundland, 7; New Brunswick, 10; Nova Scotia, 11; Prince Edward Island, 4; Manitoba, 14; Saskatchewan, 14; Alberta, 21; British Columbia, 28; Northwest Territories, 2; Yukon, 1. The disparity of representation in the federal Parliament results in the objection from Western provinces and the Maritimes that there is too much centralization of legislative and administrative authority in Ontario and Quebec. This complaint has validity with regard to the Parliament, the cabinet, and the federal bureaucracy. Thus the claims of the outlying provinces that they have long suffered regional discrimination have some justification. This situation in turn creates sectional problems in Canadian politics. As a result, provincial political leaders arise who, on their own, become highly important, controversial figures in regional, national, even international affairs. These are the men whom we must call "dukes" and "barons" and whom Canadians themselves describe as "the First Ministers."

It is almost axiomatic in Canadian political life that leaders and political parties both in Ottawa and in provincial capitals enjoy extraordinarily long periods of power. It is as though the Canadian voter, accustomed to the comfort and fit of these politicians—like old shoes or favorite sweaters—simply refuses to discard these leaders until they wear out or disappear. This kind of situation has been evident in the stories of major national leaders—Macdonald, Laurier, and King—set forth in pages just past. The same phenomenon appears in the record of provincial leadership. For example, W. A. C. Bennett, with his Social Credit Party, led British Columbia for twenty years, and Joey Smallwood of Newfoundland led his party into confederation and sat thereafter in the premier's chair for some eighteen years. Angus MacDonald (Liberal) served as premier of Nova Scotia twenty-three years, and E. C. Manning (Social Credit) was leader of the Alberta government for about the same length of time. Furthermore, there appears to be a kind of longevity built into Canadian politics, national and provincial. Canadians are singularly loyal to their proven leaders, and that loyalty in turn seems to beget long life, both politically and chronologically.

In Canada (as in the United States), there is sometimes the view that all power resides in Ottawa (as in Washington). This view assumes that little or no real power rests with the provincial premiers (in Canada) or with the state governors (in the United States). During recent years there has been a new shift in this opinion. In Canada today, the men of Ottawa do not run the country—they have only the image of power. Ottawa runs itself; the provincial premiers really run the country. These are the decision-makers—the men who matter to the ordinary citizen. Their actions are in the areas that really touch people's lives—transport, utilities, housing, land use, social welfare, and environment. These premiers of the Canadian provinces are not necessarily widely known. Yet within their provinces, they are the real rulers—some acting like feudal dukes or barons—most of them colorful and young. In a country where national leaders tend to be younger than in the United States, the prime minister is now only in his late fifties, but he is older than any of the provincial premiers. Their average age today is about forty-nine. A decade ago, none of them was in power. The rises of all have been meteoric. These men and their fiefdoms are deserving of special attention. Chapters 8, 9, and 10 describe each province—west to east—its geography, economy, politics, and leadership.

The Western Provinces

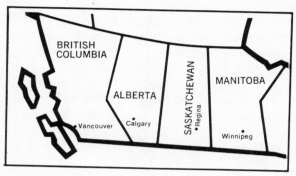

BRITISH COLUMBIA

British Columbia is considered Canada's spiritual as well as geographical frontier. Canadians who have not moved there are jealous of those who have done so. B.C. is a kind of California—a rainbow's end of the Canadian mind as well as of Canadian geography. This province has its own allegiances, its own "manifest destiny." Its people are for British Columbia first and for Canada second. They are alternately isolationist and internationalist. Most of all, they are self-contained. As some have aptly put it, B.C. is a piece of land completely surrounded by envy.

The provincial populace is vital and versatile in its life, its work, its play. It has dynamism and a creativity that is lacking in much of the rest of Canada. Strange it is that the bureaucrats in Ottawa have not yet been able to rein in and utilize the dynamism of this province. For those bureaucrats still appear to believe that Canada is Atlantic oriented and Ontario centered, rather than a two-ocean country.

In British Columbia, nothing is done by halves. Seven years ago, the highly conservative Social Credit party (SOCRED) of Premier W.A.C. Bennett was thrown out of office after twenty years in power. It was replaced by the leftist-oriented, welfare-oriented (NDP) directed by Dave

Barrett. The latter proved to be (along with Richard Nixon) the most controversial leader of government on the North American continent. He was replaced in 1975 by the conservative SOCREDs and premier Bill Bennett, Jr.

Thus, British Columbia continues to fascinate and exasperate the rest of Canada. This province is highly inconsistent. It is alleged to have the best prison system in the country; yet it has the highest crime rate. It has the largest percentage of unionized workers and the most repressive labor legislation in the commonwealth. It has the highest marriage and divorce rates in the country. It has the best social services and the highest number of drug addicts. It has one of the fastest growing populations and yet the lowest population per square mile in all Canada.

British Columbia, third largest province in Canada, entered the confederation in 1871. Today it has an area of 366,255 square miles (equal to Washington, Oregon, and California combined) and a population of 2.5 million. Some three-quarters of the population occupies only 5 percent of the total land area. Most of the people are concentrated in the southwestern sector of the province, known as the Lower Mainland. While only 2 percent of the province is considered fit for cultivation, that area is intensively utilized.

The geography of the province embodies parallel ranges of mountains cutting southeast and northwest, leaving broad fertile valleys and a coastline cut by magnificent tree-lined fjords. With its contrasts of rugged mountians towering ten thousand feet or more, its green valleys, and its island-specked seacoast, the province is among the most scenically striking areas in the world. The rugged coastline is reminiscent of Norway's. The sagebrush plateau land of the northeast looks like parts of Texas. The green and fertile central valleys resemble western Oregon.

Coastal regions of the province have mild winters and cool summers because of the Japanese current and Pacific winds. Inland areas have greater temperature extremes and much less rainfall than the seacoast. All in all, the province's spectacular scenery is varied. Given the greatest economic potential and best climate in all Canada, the province is the Shangri-la of tourists, immigrants, and retired prairie farmers.

Though European explorers and fur traders visited British Columbia briefly in the seventeenth and eighteenth centuries, no permanent settlement was accomplished until the 1840s. Both Spain and England were early claimants to what is today the coastal area of the province; the famous British explorer Captain James Cook laid firm claim to the region in 1778 when he explored the coastline seeking the elusive Northwest Passage to Asia.

In the years 1792–1794, British sea captain George Vancouver charted the region for the British monarchy. About the same time, Alexander Mackenzie reached these Pacific shores in the first European crossing of the northern part of the continent. Conflicting claims of British and Americans to this region were not settled until the controversial "Oregon question" was laid to rest by adoption of the present Canadian-American boundary at the 49th parallel in 1846. The main settlements of the province—Victoria, Vancouver, and New Westminster—all owe their beginnings in part to the fur trade, in part to the California and Alaska gold rushes, and in part to completion of the transcontinental Canadian Pacific and Canadian National railways. For detailed treatment of these matters, see Chapters 4 and 6 of this book.

The provincial capital, Victoria, was first established as a fortress headquarters for the Hudson's Bay Company in 1843. Located on the southern tip of Vancouver Island and named in honor of Queen Victoria, the site was chosen in part to strengthen British claims to the region prior to settlement of the "Oregon" boundary question. The fort and adjacent settlement subsequently became the supply base for the 1859 Fraser Valley gold rush. Today the city has 187,000 people and serves as both provincial capital and west coast naval base. Noted for its gardens and its dry, mild climate, Victoria has a distinctly British air and a heavy tourist trade.

Vancouver, the metropolis of the province, has a populace exceeding 1.2 million. Established in the 1840s and incorporated as a city in 1886, it has a spectacular mountain-and-sea backdrop. It is important in manufacturing, in shipping, in educational activities, and in tourism and ranks as a financial, industrial, and cultural center of the Canadian West. Vancouver today has the largest seaport of Canada and one of the busiest in North America. With its frost-free natural harbor and the western terminus of the transcontinental rail systems, it is the funnel of Canadian trade with Pacific Rim countries.

The province is a mixture of cultures, British, Continental European, and American, with an overlay of Chinese and South Asian. Ethnic origins of the province include British, 67 percent; Scandinavian, 6 percent; German, 5 percent; French, 4 percent; Netherlands, 3 percent; Amerindians, 3 percent; Chinese and East Indians, each 2 percent. Vancouver now has the second largest Chinatown in North America. Only San Francisco's is larger. There are about sixty thousand French-Canadians now resident in B.C. They are dispersed widely throughout the province and are occupied chiefly in forestry and mining. The Amerindian community is concentrated on the Queen Charlotte Islands, in the Vancouver metropolitan area, and in the eastern part of the province. In religious terms, the province is divided as follows: United Church, 29 percent; Anglican, 27 percent; Roman Catholic, 15 percent; Presbyterian, 8 percent; Lutheran, 5 percent; Baptist, 4 percent. There are also thousands of adherents to Hebrew, Muslim, and Oriental faiths.

British Columbia's economy is both varied and abundant. It is primarily dependent on extractive industries—forests, mining, waterpower, and fisheries. There is also considerable wealth from agriculture on large and small farms. Timber production and mining copper, coal, and petroleum represent growth industries. Consumer and secondary industries are all dependent on these primary products. Tourism, too, is moving up fast.

British Columbia has surprising importance to the United States in terms of natural resources, secondary products, and various forms of power. The province furnishes about 60 percent of the newsprint for West Coast American newspapers and about 60 percent of all natural gas for the Pacific Northwest. B.C.'s hydroelectric-power exports to the United States make it a key factor in the Western states power grid. In addition, its fisheries, minerals, petroleum products, and timber are of great importance to the American economy. The total value of B.C. exports to the United States is in excess of $2 billion annually. After Ontario and Quebec, B.C. is the most important Canadian province exporting to the American market.

Representative of the broad range of conflicts that have arisen between Ottawa and Washington are the several major issues between British Columbia and the United States government. These problems range from energy and water to hydroelectric power and natural gas sales. The question of oil tanker pollution along the western Canadian coast as a result of Alaskan oil developments is also a major new problem, and even more recently, there is the two-hundred-mile fishing agreement (see Chapter 16).

Illustrative is the so-called Great Columbia Giveaway. The pertinent Columbia River Treaty of 1964 is considered "a bone in the throat" of many Canadian politicians, especially ex-Premier Barrett. This treaty was ratified at the Peace Arch in Blaine, Washington, by President Johnson and Prime Minister Lester Pearson. On that occasion, a check for $290 million was presented to then Premier W. A. C. Bennett for British Columbia. This check represented a major portion of payment for water rights and flood control in the Columbia basin. In return, the B.C. government agreed to build three dams—at Duncan, High Arrow, and Mica. An associated dam was to be built by the Americans at Libby, Montana. These enormous concessions, involving flooding of vast areas of Canadian valleys behind the dams, were presumably to attain short-term benefits of flood control and cheaper hydro power. B.C. critics now contend that they not only gave the Columbia River away but also subsidized the Americans in the process. Bennett had promised the people of B.C. that the sale of the downstream benefits would pay for the three treaty-promised dams and also meet part of the cost of generators at the Mica Dam. It now appears that the Americans will have met only half of those costs promised by the treaty. British Columbia taxpayers are now forced to pay an additional $300 million because of inflated costs of the projects. These figures do not include the costs of the environmental destruction that has resulted. This controversy became a major issue in the 1972 provincial election which W. A. C. Bennett's party lost to the NDP. Then Barrett, the new NDP premier, asked Prime Minister Trudeau to have the treaty reopened with the United States. Trudeau dismissed the request, saying only it was tough luck for the province and Ottawa was not going to Washington for more money now. In its new opposition role, the NDP (led by Barrett) will continue pressuring Ottawa and Washington on this and related matters. They have a strong case, since the Columbia River Treaty was never ratified by the British Columbia legislature.

Especially during the past several years, British Columbia has been a battlefield for competing ideologies. This conflict has involved the electorate in massive social turmoil—creating a tug-of-war between socialist and free-enterprise forces, between capital and labor. Given the rich resources of British Columbia, that conflict is probably destined to continue for some time.

Labor organizations in British Columbia are extremely powerful, both politically and economically. Many of the working groups are now associated with the NDP. In contrast, the agrarian community and business and commercial interests have sought political haven in the two older federal parties—Liberal and Progressive Conservative—as well as in the present ruling group, the Social Credit party. Regional and agricultural diversity have been so great in this province as not to permit populist amalgam of political pressures from the agricultural sector, as has been true with the prairie wheat farmers. Thus it appears that, in general, the rural and agricultural peoples of the province are essentially conservative, while the industrial sector ranges from conservative to liberal, and the labor grouping liberal to radical. In some ways, then, British Columbia's polity is a fractured community, with political and economic divisions stemming from both class and community roots. The religious and racial cleavages notable in other provinces of Canada do not seem to be of such consequence here. The provincial community is too polyglot and of too materialistic bent to make religious-racial matters of much importance. Instead there is an unusual spirit of acquisitiveness which is measured in the commercial-financial demands of the tycoon and in the wage and social welfare demands of the working class. Provincial premiers and political parties, whether led by Bennetts or Barretts, are determined to try to keep the riches of this province for their own people—not to have them commandeered by the federal government. Thus, the federal government remains the whipping boy of provincial politicians, no matter who is in power in Victoria.

The twenty years of Social Credit leadership (1952-1972) primarily represented conservative, free-enterprise rule. The subsequent NDP regime was primarily socialist and welfare-oriented. The SOCRED are orthodox; the NDPs are definitely unorthodox—innovators and conscious do-gooders. The earlier SOCRED rule covered a boom period in commerce, industry, transport, and physical development. The NDP rule was oriented toward the working class, with the initiation of massive nationalization schemes. In sum, the SOCRED generally have represented the economic elites of the province. The NDP claims to represent the blue-collar workers.

The NDP rule in 1972–75 placed Barrett and his party among the most controversial governments on the North American continent, surpassed in this respect only by the Castro and Nixon regimes. In that four years, the NDP government expanded the various social welfare or "mincome" programs; brought into being various crown corporations including a nationalized auto insurance scheme; and imposed heavy burdens on natural resources ranging from mining to timber. The economic and political results were dramatic. The provincial treasury went from a modest surplus to a deficit of some $400 million during Barrett's short regime.

British Columbia's legislature has fifty-five seats. As a result of the December, 1975, elections, the Social Credit party holds thirty-six seats, the New Democrats hold seventeen, and the Liberal and Progressive Conservative parties each have one seat. This election reversed the results of 1972, when the NDP came into power with thirty-eight seats amassed from only thirty-nine percent of the popular vote.

Premier William Richards Bennett, aged forty-five, is a newcomer to politics. A prosperous businessman in association with his father and brother, Bennett was kept from early entry into politics by the very fact of his father's long-time service as premier. It now seems certain that the father wished the son to enter politics—even to assume the former's mantle as SOCRED party leader. However, it took the fortunes of politics and the choice of the electorate to accomplish that. Bennett is a middle-of-the-roader, a champion of free enterprise, not a fiery orator but a down-to-earth and commanding speaker. Bennett first entered formally into politics by winning his retiring father's legislative seat in the South Okanagan riding. This by-election took place in September, 1973. Two months later, young Bennett was selected as his party's leader, winning that post on the first ballot. At that convention, Bennett adopted as his political theme the Rooseveltian song "Happy Days Are Here Again." Relatively shy and mild-mannered, hard-working and a loner, Bennett is determined to get his bureaucratic machine working properly. He has an uphill fight to swing his province around from NDP days.

A tough election campaign and postelection proceedings (including the massive inherited financial mess) have not only given Bennett a baptism of fire but have shown his mettle. Shortly after he took office, a cabinet meeting was rudely broken up by the intrusion of some seventy-five unemployed men and women. The demonstrators threatened the cabinet members with picks and shovels. Bennett, displaying courage and tact, took the riotous leadership to his office to pacify. He pushes for five regions within "one" Canada—nationally, "We want a say."

Given the vagaries and tensions of the British Columbian political scene, it is essential to say something of ex-Premier Dave Barrett. For he remains very much on that scene and is still titular head of his controversial and highly vocal opposition NDP. He was born in Vancouver in 1930, the son of Russian Jewish immigrants. He was educated at Seattle University (B.A. 1953) and at St. Louis University (M.S.W. 1956). He served as a social worker and probation officer in Missouri for some time before returning to his native Vancouver. He was first elected to the B.C. legislature in 1960 and reelected in all subsequent elections from his constituency of Port Coquitlam. He became premier and minister of finance of the province on September 15, 1972.

Maclean's magazine (June, 1973) has characterized Barrett as "a Socialist in the land of plenty." Despite his Jewish upbringing, he is now said to be an agnostic, though influenced by social justice writings of recent popes as well as St. Thomas Aquinas and Bertrand Russell. He has respect for American people but dislikes the American political system, which he considers "government by establishment." It is said the only Canadian leader he respects is former Prime Minister Diefenbaker.

As a result of Barrett's movement toward his kind of "social democracy," American investors have become hesitant. During Barrett's rule, *Barrons* magazine recommended caution, calling B.C. the "Chile of the North." Surprisingly, however, B.C. bonds still rate double A in the New York money market, and Arab investors have made substantial loans to the provincial government. Nonetheless, the Barrett government looked with avaricious eyes on American petroleum profits in the province and was determined to have a major voice in control and transmission of B.C.'s natural gas to American consumers. Barrett tripled the export price of natural gas during 1975. As a result, American customers characterized Barrett as the "Arab of the North."

Given its immense economic riches, there still remains a serious question as to how the Province of British Columbia will develop. Will it yet blow its chances in a massive class struggle, or will it prosper through enlightened self-interest and free-enterprise? Will it be able to spread its bounty directly to its own people and indirectly to all of Canada? Will the polity of this rich dukedom choose the course of capitalism, take a path back to Fabian socialism, or venture something even more radical? Given the conservatism and puritanical work ethic of the Canadian character and the proximity of the capitalist American leviathan, the chances seem heavily weighted against the long-term development of a socialist island of British Columbia.

ALBERTA

Alberta, first of the Prairie Provinces (which term includes also Saskatchewan and Manitoba), is one of the fastest growing, most prosperous, and most conservative of all Canadian provinces. Producing most of Canada's petroleum and natural gas as well as a great deal of her wheat, Alberta has often been characterized as Canada's Texas. Led by her dynamic, young, and arch-conservative premier, Peter Lougheed, the Albertans and their prairie partners have long contended they have been too dependent "on God, the federal government, and head offices of the Ontario-Quebec financial establishment." Finding these "managers" insufficiently trusting and benevolent, the prairie politicians and businessmen have determined to take some of that control into their own capable hands. Alberta, in particular, in the wake of the international energy crisis has been able to do just that. For here the branding iron of years past is replaced by the oil-drilling rig.

The prairie provinces were first bound together by agrarianism—the combination of indigent farmers organized to oppose the presumably despotic rule of Ottawa and the Eastern financial interests. Though the wealth of oil and mineral finds as well as increases in grain prices brought these people new-found political power, some even riches, there are still heavy marks of agrarianism on their political life.

Alberta was a part of the original Hudson's Bay Company grant known as Prince Rupert's Land. It was first explored by European trappers and later became the scene of squabbles between indigenous Indian tribes and intruding white settlers. The building of the transcontinental Canadian Pacific Railroad, which reached Calgary in 1883, opened up the territory first to cowmen and sheepmen, next to the wheat-farming homesteaders, and finally to the oilman. With the newly built railway, the northern portion of the province, centering in the capital of Edmonton, developed rapidly. Late in the last century, that sector became important as a provisioning point for the Klondike gold rush. The name of the province was chosen in 1883, honoring Queen Victoria's daughter the Princess Marie Louise Alberta, the wife of the then–governor-general of Canada. The province was admitted to full membership in the Canadian confederation in 1905.

Alberta has a considerable range of topography. The western edge of the province embraces the eastern wing of the spectacular Canadian Rockies (which includes the famous parks of Banff and Jasper). From those western mountain ramparts of the province, the land slopes downward through foothills of the Rockies to the highly arable plains. Central Alberta has belts of good timber. The southern area is mainly treeless with irrigated farmlands.

One of the most arable localities is the far northern Peace River valley. The entire province has a considerable range of climate, intensely hot in summer and extremely cold in winter. However, these temperatures are subject to swift variations under the impact of the so-called Chinook winds, which can change temperatures as much as sixty degrees within a few hours. These are warm, humid winds that blow out of the southwestern mountains; they are named for the Chinook tribe of Indians that once inhabited that mountain region. Rainfall is sparse, snowfall heavy, and there is considerable sunshine.

The Province of Alberta has 255,285 square miles (the size of Texas) and a population of nearly 2 million. By ethnic origin, the population is British, 49 percent; German, 12 percent; Ukrainian, 9 percent; Scandinavian, 8 percent; French, 6 percent; Polish and Netherlands, each 3 percent; Amerindian, 2 percent. In religious terms, the province is divided as follows: United Church, 29 percent; Roman Catholic, 20 percent; Anglican, 13 percent; Lutheran, 9 percent; Presbyterian, 6 percent; Baptist, 4 percent; Greek Orthodox, 4 percent; Ukrainian Catholic, 4 percent; and unaffiliated, 11 percent.

Edmonton, the provincial capital, has a population exceeding 380,000. It was incorporated in 1904, but the site has had white inhabitants since a Hudson's Bay Company fort was established there in 1794. The fort's builder, George Sutherland, named the settlement after the Edmonton River in England. This post was the locale for both missionary and fur-trade activities for more than a century. When the Canadian National Railway reached the city in 1891, Edmonton's civic life was given new impetus. It remains an important marketing area for livestock and grain as well as an important tourist center for Jasper National Park and other scenic regions. Recent nearby oil and gas discoveries have also made of the city an important pipeline and refining center.

Calgary, the fastest growing metropolis in Canada today, has now passed 400,000 in population. Many of the newcomers are Americans, and most of these are indeed Texans. This city is the home of the far-famed Calgary Stampede, a colorful rodeo held each July. Calgary was founded in 1875 by North West Mounted Police who used the site as a headquarters and stockade. The name Calgary (a Gaelic word meaning clear running water) was given the settlement, located at the junction of the Bow and Elbow Rivers, by a well-known Canadian Mountie, Colonel McLeod. He had taken the name from his earlier home in Scotland. Calgary is considered the petroleum capital of the country. It is also an important center for distribution and marketing of agricultural commodities.

Until after World War II, the economy of Alberta was almost totally dependent on agriculture. As in the other Prairie Provinces, that sector had suffered greatly during the depression of the thirties. A major change in Alberta's economic and political life came about in 1947, when great oil discoveries were made. The largest of American oil companies were involved in these finds, and they have since spawned subsidiary industries. Though agricultural and livestock production still rank high, the principal economic developments continue to be associated with oil, gas, petro-chemicals, and related industries. As a result of the impetus given by oil and other mineral discoveries (principally coal), the province's industrial activity is said to have increased by six times in less than two decades. Agricultural output, though increasing too, now accounts for only 20 percent of provincial production. Construction and manufacturing have doubled in recent years and continue their upward swing.

Alberta is, by all odds, the prime producer of oil and natural gas among all the Canadian provinces. That production accounts for 80 percent of Canada's total output and now amounts to 2.2 million barrels daily. In the face of the recent energy crisis, there have been efforts to expand this production. In turn, there has developed bitter controversy over provincial versus federal distribution of royalties and taxes. Two of the longest crude-oil pipelines in the world move oil from Edmonton to Port Credit, Ontario, and Edmonton to Vancouver, B.C. The world's longest natural gas lines also extend from Alberta eastward into Ontario and southward into the United States as far as California. A large number of American companies are engaged in production, refining, transmission, and in new exploration. In 1978, there was another great natural-gas find, called Deep Basin, straddling the northern Alberta-B.C. border.

Associated with Alberta's new economic dependence on petroleum developments has been the new and fascinating Syncrude project. This is a massive $2-billion effort to produce oil and gas from the so-called Athabascan tar sands of northern Alberta. It is expected to bring on stream a total of some 125,000 barrels of crude daily from reserves estimated at 300 billion barrels (equivalent to Middle East reserves). Syncrude is financed by joint private and governmental means. Associated with the project are Imperial Oil of Canada (a subsidiary of Exxon), Canada–Cities Service, and Gulf Oil. The Canadian Government, along with the provincial governments of Alberta and Ontario, is also helping to finance the venture.

Like those other Prairie Provinces, the provincial government of Alberta has developed unusual antagonism toward the central government in Ottawa. This antagonism has expanded over the past five decades, fed by troubles of depression, war, and inflation. As the farmers suffered the special privations of the depression years, believing they were neglected by Ottawa and by national political parties, they developed their own local brands of politics. Some of these were based on farmers' cooperative groups, some on trade union associations, some on Fabian socialism or "funny money" theories designed to gain more support.

Alberta has had only four changes of government in seventy years. The Liberal party ruled the province from 1905 to 1921. The United Farmers Association controlled the legislature from 1921 to 1935. The Social Credit party was in the driver's seat from 1935 to 1971. The Progressive Conservatives have ruled since 1971.

In 1935, after United Farmers groups had ruled Alberta for fourteen years, there came into power a crusading radio preacher, William Aberhart. Under the Social Credit banner, he propounded a variety of economic and social panaceas, including a guaranteed handout of twenty-five dollars monthly to every adult in the province. Aberhart was succeeded by a fellow Social Credit leader of more orthodox economic views, Ernest Manning, who remained in office until 1968. His successor was Premier Harry Strom, who was finally replaced by the Progressive Conservatives in 1971.

When Prime Minister Diefenbaker, the Conservative darling of the prairie populists, swept into power in 1958, the prairie groups, now tending toward conservatism, found themselves in the driver's seats in Ottawa for the first time. However, the prairies, including Alberta, followed Diefenbaker into a minority government in 1962 and into defeat in 1963. Since then, Ottawa has continued in Liberal hands, but the prairies have been in opposition, with Alberta turning heavily Conservative. In 1971 the Progressive Conservatives turned the Social Credit Government out after that party had been thirty-six years in office. In the 1975 provincial elections, the Conservatives cemented their huge mandate into place. They now control sixty-nine of the seventy-five seats in their Legislative Assembly, with Social Credit holding four seats, the NDP, one seat, and one Independant assemblyman.

Because the province has been so long on the Loyal Opposition side, Alberta's demands on Ottawa have generally been ignored. There has been running controversy between the young and able Conservative premier, Peter Lougheed, and the national Liberal government of Prime Minister Trudeau. As was the case in British Columbia, much of this controversy has centered upon distribution of tax revenues and royalties from the production of minerals, especially petroleum.

For the first time, in 1969, Alberta joined in medicare and social insurance programs. It also changed tack by accepting the official language bill (bilingualism) after many years of opposition. Alberta sought some benefits from Ottawa in return. The provincial government threatened separatist pressures if Ottawa were not forthcoming, especially on problems of transport and tariff. Premier Lougheed has contended that Western provinces (excepting only Manitoba) are in a better position to separate or secede than any other part of Canada. Westerners like Lougheed believe that no province of Canada should have special status, particularly Quebec. Westerners also believe that special deference to Quebec's demands is only postponing the resolution of Canada's problems of national unity. Given the new-found power in the field of energy, the Westerners, especially the Albertans, should be able to enforce their demands against Ottawa.

Peter Edgar Lougheed was elected premier of Alberta in 1971 and reelected in 1975. He was born in Calgary in 1928. A graduate of the University of Alberta and Harvard School of Business, he practiced law in Alberta until entering politics. In 1965 he was elected to the Alberta Legislative Assembly representing Calgary West and also became provincial leader of the Conservative Party. Proposed for national leadership of the Progressive Conservative party, Lougheed was an unwilling candidate and rejected formal nomination. It is said that Lougheed's idol, Winston Churchill, helped the Canadian form the conviction that politics is the center of one's life. Lougheed believes the greatest problems facing Canada today are (1) creation of jobs for all, (2) maintenance and expansion of international markets, and (3) attainment of national unity. He believes it essential that both province and nation shift from overdependence on other nations to self-sufficiency and control of the country's own natural resources. Premier Lougheed is definitely a "Canada Firster."

One most unusual factor of Alberta's political life is the influence of a single family—the Horners. At the crest of Diefenbaker's political power in 1958, there were four Horners representing Alberta in Ottawa: Senator Ralph Horner, and his two sons and a nephew in the House of Commons. One of the latter is Jack Horner, who until recently has been a power among Progressive Conservatives. However, in April, 1977, Jack Horner crossed the "aisle" and joined Trudeau's Liberals—receiving a cabinet ministry as a reward. Ralph Horner's daughter Jean Horner Rowan has been secretary of the Progressive Conservative party. There is even a branch of this feudalistic family operating on the political scene in Saskatchewan. With the present premier, Peter Lougheed, a firm ally of the Horners, and with yet another family member, Hugh Horner, Lougheed's deputy premier, the family's political control in the province is enormous. Given this "family committee" operation, politics in Alberta is said to "be measured in terms of the Horners."

One other political Albertan is worthy of special note; this is Joe Clark, thirty-eight-year-old centrist member of the Canadian Parliament. Early in 1976, after a hectic intraparty battle, Clark won the leadership of the Federal Progressive Conservative party, replacing Robert Stanfield. As leader of this main opposition party, Clark could eventually become prime minister of Canada if Trudeau's Liberals are defeated. In six federal by-elections held in May, 1977, Clark received a political "baptism of fire." The Conservatives lost all contests. The Liberals won five seats, and the Social Credit party took one seat. The Conservatives, however, rallied their strength in the October, 1978, by-election when they won 10 seats (a gain of 4); the Liberals, 2 seats (a loss of 5); NDP, 2 (1); SOCREDS, 1.

SASKATCHEWAN

Saskatchewan has been called the grain-rich and cash-poor province of Canada. This was true until very recently, when potash and oil made it a "have" rather than a "have not" territory. Saskatchewan has also found a basis for new wealth in its uranium mines, and for the first time in many years the province's population has actually increased. Saskatchewan has a population of 925,000 and an area of 237,975 square miles.

Like Alberta, this province was a part of the Hudson's

Company fiefdom until purchase by the federal government in 1869. During its first two centuries of European
association (1690–1870), Saskatchewan was mainly
involved in fur trade. There were few permanent settlements until Hudson's Bay Company gave up its territorial
rights. In the mid-1880s, however, the province became the
scene of the final acts of the Louis Riel rebellion, in which
Indians and Metis made their dramatic last stand against
the European intrusions. (See Manitoba section following.) This settled for all time the conflict over land rights
that had arisen between Indians and immigrants. The
region finally became a province in 1905. The name of the
province derives from the Saskatchewan River (originally
Kisiskatchewan), an Indian word meaning "swiftly flowing water." This river is the longest in the Prairie
Provinces.

The southern two-thirds of the province comprises a
great plain sloping gently to the east and north. It is extremely fertile, representing one of the great grain-growing
areas of the world. The northern and southwestern sections are more hilly and rugged. Most of the river systems
of the province empty into Hudson Bay and the Arctic
Ocean. Central Saskatchewan has an important belt of
timber. The northern third of the province lies within the
Canadian shield. The province has a dry climate with
much summer sunshine. There is little precipitation, and
the frost-free period ranges from June through mid-
summer.

Ethnic backgrounds in the province form a real mosaic:
British, 42 percent; German, 16 percent; Ukrainian, 9
percent; Scandinavian, 7 percent; French, 6 percent;
Netherlands, 4 percent; Polish, 3 percent; and Amerindian,
3 percent. By religion, the province is divided among
United Church, 30 percent; Roman Catholic, 24 percent;
Anglican, 12 percent; Ukrainian Catholic, 5 percent;
Greek-Russian Orthodox, 4 percent; Presbyterian, 4 per-
cent; Baptist, 2 percent; and unknown 19 percent.

The capital city, Regina, incorporated in 1903, now has a

population of 150,000. In the 1880s it became an important midway point along the prairie route of the transcontinental Canadian Pacific Railway. At the same time, it became the headquarters for the North West Mounted Police and the administrative capital of what was then the Northwest Territories. The name Regina (Latin for "queen") was selected for the city by Princess Louise, wife of the governor-general, in honor of her mother, Queen Victoria. Today, the city is an important distribution center for wheat-growing farmers of the region.

Saskatoon, second-largest city in the province, has a population of 125,000. Lying northwest of Regina, it is an important distribution and educational center.

The horrors of the depression era of the 1930s have always weighed heavily on the prairie agricultural industry. In the decades following—even until today—farmers there have been determined to achieve stable prices and assured markets for their produce. Saskatchewan has a third of the agricultural land of the entire country and fully half of the nation's wheat acreage. Livestock production, dairying, and mixed farming are also of considerable consequence to the provincial economy. Furthermore, within the past quarter century, the province has become an important producer of petroleum, and with oil has come industrial development. Saskatchewan now produces 10 percent of all petroleum pumped from the ground in Canada. There are also important sources of uranium, of potash, and of paper products. Agricultural and mineral production are now essentially in balance.

In a deliberate program to help retain its population and to help keep its young people "down on the farm," the Saskatchewan · government has recently initiated a land-purchase and leasing program. This has been essential, since the province lost half its farm population during the past decade, many of the farmers emigrating to other provinces or to urban areas. The program is a means of special benefit for individual and family farmers, rather than corporate agribusiness interests. Though the program has been controversial and avowedly a centerpiece of the socialist-oriented NDP, it still may provide helpful patterns for other agricultural centers in North America, especially in view of world food shortages. The *Wall Street Journal* of February 5, 1975, reported on the program with enthusiasm, noting that in its two years of existence, the plan has helped to resettle more than fourteen hundred families in Saskatchewan.

Like all the Prairie Provinces, Saskatchewan has usually been on the political "outs" with Ottawa. In the eyes of the prairie farmers, Western needs have frequently been ignored by the central government. Prime Minister Trudeau has given tacit or verbal support to a kind of "new deal" for the prairies, which has been slow in coming. Major differences have centered upon transport costs; assured prices and markets for agricultural commodities, and improved tariff rates allowing farmers to buy imported machinery and supplies at cheaper prices. Federal-provincial conferences have been helpful for discussion if not for solution.

The difficult economic times of the depression-ridden 1930s produced on the prairies a number of splinter-type political parties of socialist cast. As noted earlier, the Social Credit party had its origins in Alberta but eventually developed strong branches in Saskatchewan, British Columbia, and even Quebec. The Co-operative Commonwealth Federation (CCF), with roots in Manitoba, also had adherents in Saskatchewan, Alberta, and Ontario. The CCF was later merged with a trade union group to become the NDP. This in turn gained a balance of power situation in the national Parliament of the early seventies. The political popularity of these parties rose and fell with the economic tides. However, in the mid-1950s, they merged in support of the Progressive Conservative leader, John Diefenbaker, from Prince Albert, Saskatchewan.

It was his support of a south Saskatchewan irrigation project that gave Diefenbaker his early political footing in this region. It was, as well, his vocal determination to make Ottawa shift its priorities and give attention to the needs of the prairies that brought him to national attention. As Diefenbaker and his constituents saw it, this was the time for Ottawa to stop favoring Ontario and Quebec, to give greater balance to the needs of the Western provinces. Thus, when the darling of the prairies, John Diefenbaker, swept into the prime ministership in 1958 with his massive parliamentary majority, the prairies found themselves politically in the driver's seat for the first time. At that moment, forty-six of forty-seven ridings in the prairies were controlled by Diefenbaker.

In 1962, the prairie voters followed "populist" Diefenbaker into a minority government. Since then, Ottawa has been in Liberal hands. The political opposition from the prairies remained of conservative bent but tended once more into splinter party groupings.

One of the founders of the CCF and later of the NDP was T. C. Douglas, who served as premier of Saskatchewan from 1944 to 1961. Today Douglas is an MP, holding an NDP seat in Ottawa for Nanaimo, B.C. Douglas was followed as premier by Woodrow Lloyd. The CCF and Lloyd were defeated in 1964 by Ross Thatcher, a Liberal and former member of the CCF. In the early 1970s, when low wheat prices and the shrunken potash market depressed the economic situation in Saskatchewan, the Thatcher Liberal government found itself in trouble. In 1974, Allan Blakeney, leader of the NDP, pushed Ross Thatcher and his Liberals out of office. Today, Blakeney and his party control forty-four seats in a legislature composed of sixty-one members. The Progressive Conservatives received 17 seats and the Liberals none in the October 18, 1978, provincial election.

During the prior decade, Blakeney had sought to recreate the NDP in the image of the old CCF that had ruled Saskatchewan from 1944 to 1964. Thatcher's Liberal administration had reversed many of the nationalization schemes that had been initiated under the previous CCF regimes. Blakeney, though agreeing that the province needs to diversify and industralize, is swiftly reversing Thatcher's policies.

Premier Blakeney has recently become the center of an active international controversy involving provincial takeover of the highly profitable potash industry. These deposits have been developed by twelve foreign concerns, and they are now valued in excess of $1 billion. Seven of these concerns are American owned, while others are French, British, German, or South African. Provincial legislation covering the takeover insisted on expropriation if price of properties could not be agreed upon. Forty percent of output is provincial-controlled.

Blakeney seeks to avoid the label of outright socialist. He continues, however, to have as his prime interests the condition of the wheat farmer and the repopulation of his province which has lost some seventy-five thousand people in the past five years.

Premier Blakeney was born in 1925 in Bridgewater, Nova Scotia. He calls himself a "composite Canadian" and an intense nationalist. His father's ancestry includes a two-hundred-year Canadian lineage; his mother came from Europe. He attended Dalhousie University in Nova Scotia and Oxford University (where he picked up his political ideals). He pursued his legal career in Ontario and Saskatchewan. As Saskatchewan's minister of health, he brought in Canada's first medicare plan. He is a fighter as well as an intellectual. He admits to a fear of absorption by the United States—cultural, economic, political. He also fears inter-provincial conflict, especially the disaffection of Quebec. He insists on the need of full employment and equal opportunity for all Canadians. While working to reduce his province's dependence on agriculture, he still believes the family farmer has an important place in Saskatchewan life. He insists on the need for Canada to build a society neither better nor worse than America, Britain or France—but different.

MANITOBA

Manitoba has long been considered the poorest of the prairie provinces—in fact, one of the poorest in Canada. In the mid-nineteenth century, it appeared to have a very bright future. It had been assumed that the province and its capital Winnipeg would become gateways to new growth by virtue of their mid-point position on the continent. However, following the opening of the Panama Canal in 1915, Manitoba's importance, in terms of all Canada, materially diminished. Since that day of dimunition of their dreams, Manitobans have tended to look northward for realization of their economic potential. Thus far, that potential has not been fully realized.

The province is dotted with an immense number of lakes, large and small. One of the largest is Lake Manitoba. This name is derived from an Indian word, *manito*, which means "strait of the spirit," referring to a narrow channel between an island and the shore of Lake Manitoba where the waves constantly dash against the rocky shoreline. Other great lakes include Lake Winnipeg (larger than Lake Ontario) and the famous Lake of the Woods.

A great coastal plain stretches west and south from Hudson Bay in the far north and reaches a maximum elevation of 2,700 feet. In the southern part of the province, the soils are rich and varied. Winters are long and extremely cold, summers warm. Only three months of the year are generally frost free. Manitoba has the heaviest rainfall of the Prairie Provinces, but its snowfall is comparatively light for Canada.

The territory was first explored by the fur traders. Later there ensued bitter struggles between these and the permanent farmer-settlers as well as struggles between Indians and whites. Like Alberta and Saskatchewan, the territory was a part of the original Hudson's Bay Company grant from King Charles II. That territory of Prince Rupert's Land was sold to the government of Canada in 1869, and a year later, Manitoba became the first portion thereof to be made a province. (Present boundaries of the province were not fixed, however, until 1912.) The years immediately following 1869 were notorious for the fact that a Metis named Louis Riel led an uprising at Red River against the Ottawa government. He set up a provisional regime and attempted to dictate terms whereby the new province would enter the dominion. However, Prime Minister John Macdonald succeeded in quashing the uprising and bringing Manitoba into the confederation.

The site of the city of Winnipeg—Fort Garry on the Red River—was also the place of birth in 1873 of the famous North West Mounted Police. This group, originally numbering 150 men, was established to maintain law and order on the Western plains. It had the specific task of protecting the Indians and Metis against the depredations of the fur traders and whiskey traders. Highly romanticized in film, song, and story—with the motto "They always get their man"—the organization had an important function, then as now, in protecting the good guys from the bad guys. In 1920, this original territorial North West Mounted Police amalgamated with the Old Dominion Police Force and became the Royal Canadian Mounted Police, an organization with nationwide paramilitary as well as ordinary police functions. Composed of ten thousand men watching over the largest police jurisdiction in the world, the Mounties are famous for their scarlet-jacketed dress uniform and their horsemanship. They also pilot their own planes, sail their own ships, drive their own sleds and snowmobiles. Today, the RCMP retains its high standards and reputation of yesteryear. Although publicity swirls about "CIA tactics" and allegations about and the source of responsibility are still in controversy, the RCMP has the hearts of the Canadians.

Manitoba has an area of 251,000 square miles and a population just in excess of 1 million. More than any other province, Manitoba represents a true ethnic, linguistic, and religious mosaic. The ethnic composition is British, 50 percent; Ukrainian, 13 percent; French, 9 percent; German, 7 percent; Netherlands, 5 percent; Polish, 5 percent; Scandinavian, 5 percent; Eskimo and Amerindian, 3 percent; Metis, 2 percent; Icelandic and Hungarian, each 1 percent. Religious affiliations have the population divided as follows: United Church, 29 percent; Roman Catholic, 20 percent; Anglican, 16 percent; Greek Orthodox, 9 percent; Lutheran, 6 percent; Presbyterian, 5 percent; Ukrainian Catholic, 3 percent; and unaffiliated, 12 percent.

Over half the population of the province resides within the environs of the capital city of Winnipeg. The British poet Rupert Brooke characterized Winnipeg as "just a little more American than other Canadian cities, but not unpleasantly so." Today the city of Calgary might compete with Winnipeg for that characterization.

Incorporated in 1873, Winnipeg lies at the junction of the Assiniboine and Red rivers. The city's name is derived from the local Cree Indian word for this place: *Wi-nipiy* meaning "murky waters." Originally a fur-trading settlement named Fort Rouge (established 1738), the community was renamed Fort Garry when it became Hudson's Bay Company headquarters.

Winnipeg really came into its own with the completion of the transcontinental railway in 1885. A junction and transit point, it developed an important grain commodity market with associated transport and a financial center. It has since become, as well, an important literary, educational, and performing-arts center, being, among other things, the home of the famous Winnipeg Ballet.

More than half the province lies within the Canadian Shield, and it is in this area that Manitoba's mineral wealth is stored. However, despite the fact that Manitoba is the most industrially diversified of the three Prairie Provinces, its greatest wealth still lies in its agriculture, chiefly wheat farming in the southern third of the territory. Canada's great wheat-growing capacity saw its birth in Manitoba. In fact, the quality of all bread wheat is still measured against the paramount grain—Manitoba hard spring wheat. Today the province produces a variety of

agricultural crops, including other grains, livestock, poultry, and dairy products. Forestry is proving to be a new
and growing industry. While commercial fishing is still
comparatively small, sports fishing and tourism are
important. Fur production, historically valuable, remains
an essential business of the province, with five hundred li-
censed fur farms in operation. In the minerals field, the
largest nickel mine in the world is located at Thompson in
central Manitoba. This mining complex produces nearly 20
percent of free world nickel. There are, as well, important
deposits of copper, zinc, and tantalum.

Until the twentieth century, class voting has been less of
a fact in Canada than in many European countries. Yet
social stratification and class vote have probably been
more noticeable on the prairies, particularly in Manitoba,
than in most of the other provinces. Party politics in
Manitoba has generally been the result of the action and
interaction of two groups. The first of these is the Anglo-
Canadian community, consisting mainly of British immigrants and settlers from Ontario. This group, primarily
landowners and industrialists, held power for nearly a
century (1840– 1930). The second, a heterogenous working-
class group, comprises various European ethnic strains
(Ukrainian, French, Icelandic, Hungarian) along with
Metis and Indians. This class came into power before the
depression.

From the outset, the Conservatives were associated with
the first group, the Liberals with the second. In recent
years, however, both the national parties saw their political bases in Manitoba, as elsewhere on the prairies, frag-
mented into right- and left-wing populist farmers' and
workers' parties. Out of these amalgams came first the
prairie progressives; next the Cooperative Commonwealth
Federation (CCF), and now the NDP. In fact, the prototype
of the prairie splinter parties emanated from a strike-torn
Manitoba and was formed in the 1920s. This was the CCF
founded by James S. Woodsworth. From 1921 until his
death in 1942, Woodsworth represented a Winnipeg con-

stituency in the Canadian Parliament. In his CCF, Woodsworth had sought to align Western progressives, farm and labor, with Eastern trade unions and intellectuals.

Woodsworth was followed as leader of the CCF by M. J. Coldwell, another Manitoban. In 1961, Coldwell, with Saskatchewan's Premier T. C. Douglas, helped to combine the CCF and the Canadian Labour Congress to form the NDP. Both nationally and provincially, the early CCF and the later NDP have supported policies of full employment, subsidized job training, broad social insurance schemes, and public ownership of utilities. The NDP, in general, has been only slightly less socialistically inclined than was its predecessor CCF. The two world wars softened the effect of such groups, but economic disparities combined with employment and inflationary strains had resuscitated their political effectiveness. For example, Manitoba's NDP, inheritor of the CCF mantle, was back in the saddle in the provincial capital of Winnipeg under a "political comer," Edward Schreyer, from 1970–1977 for two four-year terms.

Born in Manitoba in 1935, ex-Premier Edward Schreyer was a graduate of the University of Manitoba. He was the youngest member ever elected to the provincial legislature. He served in the Canadian House of Commons from 1965 to 1969. He returned to Manitoba to become leader of the NDP and provincial premier, defeating Walter Weir, Conservative. Schreyer considered himself a "social democrat" in the European tradition rather than an "old-line socialist." Thereby he sought to reassure those businessmen who he knew were essential to Manitoba's economic progress. He inaugurated social legislation a small step at a time. A Catholic and bilingual, he feared neither Protestant Ottawa nor French Catholic bilingualism. In his election campaigns he became known as "a man for all reason." He is clearly a charismatic politician. (See page 65.)

An election was called for October 1977, and the NDP lost to the Torys. The surprise wasn't the victory but the size of it. Manitoba voters had decided to retrench, to terminate their eight-year experiment with democratic socialism. The Conservatives were given a clear majority in the legislature with an unprecedented 49 percent of the popular vote. The Progressive Conservatives won thirty-three seats in the fifty-seven-seat House, with NDP winning twenty-three seats, and Liberals, one seat.

Premier Sterling R. Lyon was born in 1927 in Windsor, Ontario. He studied law at the University of Manitoba, receiving his LLB in 1953. He was a Legislative Member for Fort Garry, 1958–1969, while serving as Attorney General, 1958–1963 and 1966–1969, and has held many provincial ministerial posts. Lyon was defeated by James Richardson in 1974 but was returned to provincial parliament in 1976.

During the campaign of 1977, Lyon offered little in the way of traditional goodies. Instead he said the provincial and municipal governments would have to do "a better job with existing financial resources." *Maclean's* describes Premier Lyon's aims thus: "He set himself the tightrope task of maintaining the NDP's social programs, while cutting income taxes and doing away with succession duties, gift taxes and the acreage taxes levied on mining companies. Many government-owned businesses would be sold off, and the bulk of the $50-million development project in Winnipeg would be scrapped."

9

Ontario and Quebec

ONTARIO

The highly industrialized province of Ontario, half again the size of Texas, has 412,000 square miles and a population of more than 8 million. Though it is an inland province, Ontario has a massive shoreline of 2,300 miles on the Great Lakes and a salt-water shoreline of 680 miles bounding Hudson and James bays. Most of the northern portion of the province lies within the rocky Canadian Shield, but the southern lands of clay and loam are highly satisfactory for farming. Thus Ontario's northlands are forested or sparse, the southern part pastoral.

Ontario is intensely cold in winter and extremely hot in summer. Throughout the province, there is a wide variance of daily temperatures, and some precipitation occurs in nearly half the days of the year.

Even before Europeans settled the area, this part of Canada was reputed to be its most densely settled region. Here the Huron Indians were dominant. The French explorers and fur traders came into close commercial association with the Hurons and used them as prime sources and middlemen for development of the rich fur trade of the territory. Ontario was the site of the first European settlement in the interior of North America, this being Sainte-Marie, founded in 1639 near Georgian Bay, some 90 miles north of Toronto and 800 miles inland from Quebec City. Originally, Ontario was a part of New France and the province of Quebec. As a result of the American Revolution, however, the province received a large influx of Loyalist refugees from the American colonies. These so-called United Empire Loyalists had implanted in them the seeds of the American revolution despite their fidelity to Britain. Almost at once, the new settlers pushed for introduction of British civil law, personal rights, and representative government. Thus in 1791, the British Parliament was forced to divide Upper Canada now Ontario from Lower Canada now Quebec under terms of the Canada Act. Upwards of ten thousand Loyalists settled within the new province at that time. Several Indian tribes from the New York region, still faithful to the British side in the Revolution, also moved north into Ontario.

Success in repelling the American invaders during the War of 1812 only served to strengthen the determination of these peoples to remain independent of the United States and to form their own government. Following the end of that war, as happened following the American Revolution, this territory of Upper Canada received a great influx of both American settlers and European immigrants. By 1815, three-fifths of Upper Canada's population of eighty thousand had originated from the United States. The rebellion of 1837 (already described in the background of Mackenzie King's ancestral heritage—see Chapter 6) brought on renewed pressures for independence and culminated in the confederation of 1867, with Ontario's major politicians leading the way to Canadian independence. As a result of Ontario's Loyalist origins, patriotism there has always been extremely high. The provincial motto illustrates this fervor: "As loyal she began, so shall she ever remain." So, too, does the provincial flag. For in 1965, when the Red ensign was removed as Canada's national flag, it was adopted as the provincial flag of Ontario.

The word *ontario* is of Indian derivation and means "rocks standing in the river," apparently referring to Niagara Falls and its nearby rocky escarpments. The principal city, Toronto, located near the western end of the Lake Ontario, was originally settled in 1720 and quickly became an important fur-trading center. Toronto was chosen in 1793 as the capital of the new province of Upper Canada, and it has continued both as metropolis and provincial capital of Ontario to this day. The name Toronto is also of Indian origin: the word *Tarantou* meaning "place of meeting" and referred to the merger of fur traders' trails from west, north, and south. Today Toronto is the country's financial capital as well as the base of Canadian industrial control. With a metropolitan population of 2.7 million, it is also an important cultural center.

Canada's capital, Ottawa, is also located within the province of Ontario. This city was founded as a trading center called Bytown in 1827 and was renamed Ottawa in 1855. At the time of confederation in 1867, it was chosen capital of the new Dominion of Canada. Ottawa is located on the provincial border between Ontario and Quebec, and some of its suburbs lie across the dividing line formed by the Ottawa River. Ottawa and adjacent cities in Ontario are now combined into a regional municipal government called Ottawa-Carleton, aggregating some six hundred thousand people.

Ethnically, more than two-thirds of Ontario's population—or nearly 5 million persons—have their origin from the British Isles. Some 10 percent of the populace is of French extraction. Germans number 5 percent; Italians, 4 percent; Netherlands, 2 percent; Ukrainians, 2 percent; Polish, 2 percent; other Europeans, about 5 percent. Some sixty thousand Ontarians are Amerindians. The preponderance of Ontario's population is also urban. Today, seven of Canada's fifteen largest communities are located within the Province of Ontario. Religious roots of the Ontarians show that 30 percent are members of the United Church; 25 percent are Roman Catholic; 21 percent are Anglican; 10 percent are Presbyterian; 5 percent are Baptists; 3 percent are Lutherans, and 2 percent are Jewish. Others, including agnostics, total 5 percent.

Ontario appears to be the greatest wealth-producing province of Canada in nearly every field except petroleum, timber, and fishing. It is the most highly industrialized and urbanized of all the provinces, but it still contains the largest number of farms of any of the provinces. Yet, there remains much virgin agricultural and timber land in the province's northern regions. It has been contended that northern Ontario still holds the greatest single area of undeveloped agricultural lands in the world—perhaps some 20 million acres. Canadian statistical services report that the Province of Ontario produces manufactures equal to those of all the rest of Canada combined. There is a diversity of available raw materials in the province ranging from iron ore to uranium. As well, there is an abundance of hydroelectric power. This factor is aided by southern Ontario's strategic proximity to the Great Lakes and the associated ease of transport to the great American markets of the Midwest. Perhaps more than for any other province of Canada, Ontario's economy and prosperity are directly tied to and affected by that of the United States.

It has been a commonplace in the Canadian political scene that the major parties' operations at the national level, and even some of the parties' operations at the provincial level, have had extraordinarily long terms of life. These extremely long periods of control have been singularly exemplified by Conservative control in Ontario. In fact the Conservatives have governed this province almost without interruption since the beginning of the century. This is in sharp contrast to the fact that, during the same period, the Liberals have most often been in control in Ottawa. Thus the local-level control seems to bear no relationship whatsoever to the control at the national level— at least in Ontario.

Why then do Ontarians ambivalently vote for Liberals federally and for Conservatives provincially? This probably has had to do with the strikingly effective organization of the Ontario Conservatives—a kind of Tammany-type political grouping called the "Big Blue Machine." In the June, 1977, provincial election, that machine delivered 58 of the 125 legislative seats to the ruling Conservative party led by Premier William Davis. The Liberal party won 34 seats; the NDP won 33.

In recent years, however, there has been a considerable growth of the splinter parties within the province, this surely as a result of heavy industrialization. Like the Democrats in the United States, the Liberals and NDP leaders in this province have directed their appeals to a heterogeneous grouping of farmers, workers, and professional people. The recent proselytization by the splinter parties has come from the Liberal ranks. The Conservatives, on the other hand, continue to hold on to their industrial-financial-commercial polity. All this has tended to make for a continuing three-cornered political fight in Ontario, with the Conservatives holding the edge.

In highly urbanized, no longer agricultural Ontario, class warfare is entering into the political system in a degree as marked as anywhere in Canada. The movement is similar in some respects to the beginnings of agrarianism on the prairies. The industrial working classes here are steadily increasing their power. Thus, Ontario's politics has a stamp all its own—one that might be said to be in the final stages of full industrialization, with financial and labor interests still competing.

It is especially interesting to note that this province has had three decades of steady Conservative party rule. The last three premiers, Leslie Frost, John Robarts, and William Davis, have all contributed to the stability and economic growth of the province.

Ontario's present premier, William Davis, has proved to be an exceptionally popular, youthful, and attractive figure. He was born in 1929, in Brampton, Ontario. He took his collegiate training at Toronto University, receiving his B.A. from there in 1951. He proceeded through Osgood Hall Law School and began the practice of law in 1955. Davis was first elected to the Ontario legislature in 1959. He served as the province's minister of education and minister of university affairs from 1962 to 1971. (As minister of education, he insisted on Canadianizing text-books and developing Canada's own cultural "stream.") He became provincial premier in March, 1971. Davis attributes to his father his entry into public life. Today, the premier contends that the greatest problems his province faces are unemployment, inflation, taxation, and environmental concerns. He believes in the need of a "real Canadian identity," and he supports a healthy, but not strident, Canadian nationalism. He does not understand why Canadians seem at times to be so lacking in self-confidence as to be continually asking, How is our Canadian identity to be found? He considers that a background as provincial premier is highly useful, if not essential, for any Canadian prime minister. Davis must be considered a possibility for eventual national leadership of the Progressive Conservative party, even a future prime minister.

QUEBEC

The Province of Quebec is the cradle of the first colonization of Canada and the seat of French-Canadian culture. It is the largest of all the provinces (594,860 square miles) and the second in population (6.3 million). It is a region of vivid contrasts and many facets, from history and geography to culture and politics.

More than 80 percent of the province lies within the Canadian Shield—an area dotted with lakes, rolling hills, and plateaus and bearing heavy forests. The southern portion of the province is dominated by the St. Lawrence River, one of the great waterways of the world. This was first a "highway" for explorers and settlers coming into the Canadian hinterland. The adjacent St. Lawrence lowlands are well suited to intensive general farming. The Appalachian Mountains extend along the south side of the St. Lawrence and eastward into the Gaspé Peninsula. This peninsula comprises a succession of plateaus and plains, much of which is wooded.

Summers are hot and humid along the riverway, but areas of Quebec's far north have little or no summer. Both the St. Lawrence valley and the far north are rigorously cold in winter. Frost-free periods run about five months yearly in the south, which has comparable periods of rain or snow. By comparison, the regions around Hudson Bay have frost-free periods of only six weeks, with precipitation—mainly snow—ranging over four months.

The origins of French Canada are set forth in detail in the historical sections of this book. Although Cartier had landed in what is now Quebec in 1534 and proclaimed the region under French sovereignty, it was not until 1608 that Champlain established a permanent settlement at Quebec City. From then onward, there followed intense conflict between the fur traders and those settlers involved in the seigneurial system, who wanted to concentrate on agricultural enterprises. As the trappers and fur traders moved westward, the French manorial settlements remained. The defeat of Montcalm by the English general Wolfe on Quebec City's Plains of Abraham in 1759 brought an inevitable weakening of French backing for colonists in New France. Despite the victory, by the time of the British takeover in 1763, the territory of New France had become a well-established agricultural society of about a hundred communities. The population by then was some sixty-five thousand—a people becoming Canadian as well as French.

The settlement of thousands of American Loyalists along the upper reaches of the St. Lawrence in the days just following the American Revolution brought a complicating element into New France. This group of Tories was Protestant and Anglophile, commercial as well as agricultural. In cultural, ethnic, and religious modes, they were in direct contrast to the long-established habitants of the

French seigneurial system. The Canada Act of 1791 divided the territory of New France into Upper Canada (Ontario) and Lower Canada (Quebec). By this division, making Upper Canada English speaking and Protestant, Lower Canada French speaking and Catholic, the British government hoped to separate the two groups, thus avoiding internal dissension. By the same act, the British also preserved and guaranteed French civil law, the Catholic religion, and French custom for the inhabitants of Lower Canada.

Other steps that the British government took between 1791 and 1867 to cement the various sectors of Canada—French and British—into place as a future nation took only half-hearted note of cultural and religious differences and the means to dispel them. There was never at any time a real effort at integration or development of a single culture and unilingual system. Most of the bicultural differences were further established by the British North America Act of 1867. Thus the chance for developing a nation on the American model was passed up, and the position of the French-Canadian was recognized.

The Province of Quebec entered the new confederation in 1867 on condition that it would be entitled to retain its traditional institutions, including its language, its civil law, and its Catholic religion. For more than eighty years following entry into that confederation, partly because of the strong influence of the Catholic church, Quebec remained what might be termed an agrarian-classical society. There was little industrialization, and the province fell behind other parts of Canada, especially Ontario. As a result, there was considerable emigration of the unemployed of the large French-Canadian families into other regions—including New England, Ontario, and the Canadian West. Whether they moved or stayed behind, the French-Canadians fought to retain their religion, culture, individuality, and language. (That language today, with its atypical colloquialisms, is more akin to seventeenth-century Norman French than to modern Parisian dialect.)

Nationalism and the theory of "separatism" of Quebec—
even of its eventual independence—became continuing
political forces among these people.

Quebec City, the provincial capital and the first permanent settlement in this region, is an important seaport. It
lies upriver some 460 miles from the Gulf of St. Lawrence
and 160 miles downriver from its sister seaport, Montreal. The name Quebec is believed to stem from the Indian
word *kebec*, which, translated, means "the river narrows
here." (Even so, the St. Lawrence at this point is a mile
wide.) This city remains the center of French culture and
political activity in North America. Quebec is the only
fortified city on this continent, part of the upper city being
still encircled by those walls. Highly picturesque—
resembling a medieval European town—Quebec is a mecca
for tourists from all nations. Today, tourism is the city's
most important industry—apart from politics. Quebec is
also the site of Laval University, which was first established as a seminary in 1663 by Bishop Francois de Mont-
morency Laval. With its Citadel (summer home of Canada's governor-general) and its famous Chateau Frontenac
dominating the heights above the great river, the city is
indeed one of the most picturesque in the world.

Downriver some twenty miles from Quebec City is the
famous shrine of Ste. Anne de Beaupre (*Beaupre* meaning
"beautiful meadow"). Tradition has it that, in 1650, a group
of sailors beset by a storm on the river were saved. In grat-
itude to Heaven, they. built a chapel on the shore where
they landed—especially thanking Saint Anne, mother of
Mary, for their deliverance. In 1922, a magnificent basilica
was built on the site near the small chapel. This became
the most popular Catholic shrine in America—the grail of
pilgrims seeking miraculous cures.

The largest city both in the province and in Canada is
Montreal. Its population today is about 2.75 million. This
city, founded in 1642, rests at the confluence of the St.
Lawrence and Ottawa rivers. It became the base of operations for explorers, fur traders and, eventually, merchant

princes. It is one of the most cosmopolitan cities in North America—a multilingual, multicultural center now somewhat uneasy as a result of its separatist political drives. It is also one of the world's greatest seaports. Like Quebec, Montreal is more French than English. The city is famous for its various forms of winter sports, ranging from hockey to tobogganing. Montreal was also the site of the 1976 summer Olympic Games.

The mention of Montreal brings up yet another important matter: the art of gastronomy and gourmet cooking. Along with San Francisco, New York, and New Orleans, the Canadian cities of Montreal, Quebec, and Vancouver must be considered among the gastronomic capitals of North America. Montreal alone has five thousand restaurants. Some three hundred of these are said to deserve top starring in any *Guide Michelin*-type listing for Canada. The city also has at least thirty active gourmet groups—an epicurean elite.

In ethnic terms, the population of Quebec Province is divided as follows: French, 82 percent; British Isles, 12 percent; other European, including many Jews, 6 percent. By religion, the major groups include Roman Catholic, 88 percent; Anglicans, 4 percent; United Church, 3 percent; Jewish, 2 percent; others, 3 percent.

As noted earlier, farming provided the original basis for the economy of the province. This in spite of the fact that only 4 percent of the total land area is classed as arable. Most of the farms are small, concentrated on dairy products, and in the valley of the St. Lawrence. The far larger Canadian Shield area, originally considered a wasteland, is today the center of new activity embracing wood, water, and minerals. In timber production and related activities, Quebec is second only to British Columbia. In pulp and paper activities, Quebec ranks first, specializing in production of newsprint. The textile industry is also important, products ranging from cotton fabric to clothing.

Quebec is also the richest of Canadian provinces in

terms of waterpower resources, generating today about half of all the country's hydroelectric power. Some of this power is exported to New York State. As a result of its cheap hydropower, Quebec is also one of the world's greatest producers of aluminum. The fabulous James Bay development, destined to associate hydroelectric and uranium production, and costing more than $6 billion, is underway.

The St. Lawrence River, together with its important adjunct, the St. Lawrence Seaway (described in the economic chapter of this book), is vital to both Canadian and American marine transport in and out of the Great Lakes. Almost two-thirds of Canada's foreign trade moves through this major waterway system. The Port of Montreal, though more than a thousand miles from the Atlantic, is second only to Vancouver in total tonnage handled. Icebreakers are able to keep this port open through most of each winter.

Quebec is also highly favored with iron ore deposits, the richest of these being the fabulous Ungava Mine. The province is also an important producer of copper, gold, zinc, uranium, asbestos, and waterpower. As a result of all these activities, Quebec is beginning to catch up with Ontario as a major industrial province.

In line with the great economic and social changes that Canada, and especially Quebec, have undergone in the post war period, the French administrators of the province have continually insisted on more autonomy for their area. They have gained greater control over their province's industry and commerce—removing much of that control from Toronto and Ottawa. Many argue that Quebec must eventually become a separate nation-state.

Nationalism and the threat of separatism (secession) have formed a paramount issue in Quebec during the past half-century. In fact, their seeds were planted even earlier: Henry Bourassa, their chief proponent in the province, spoke out on that issue over a period of fifty years (1896–

1945). Bourassa, politically independent publisher of *Le Devoir* and parliamentarian, sat in federal or provincial parliaments for over four decades. For him and other arch-nationalists, French-Canadian conscription became one of the chief issues in Canadian politics during both world wars. The fact that a majority of French-Canadians flatly refused to be conscripted or to accept overseas service in either World War I or II was the principal reason why Canada maintained only a partial or qualified military draft.

In addition to the major social and economic dislocations that took place so swiftly following the end of World War II, the government of Quebec province during the period 1936–59, under Premier Maurice Duplessis (leader of the Union Nationale party), became corrupt and highly repressive. His administration sought to limit change despite the intensity of social unheavals, including the migration of large numbers of the habitants from settled rural environments to unsettled and (usually unemployed) urban existences.

In 1960, trying to make amends, the provincial administration undertook what some called a "quiet revolution." During this time, educational processes were completely taken from the hands of the autocratic and anachronistic Catholic hierarchy of the province. Thus the people of Quebec suffered the shattering of their traditional social codes and of their educational and religious institutions. This upheaval, combined with their intense resentment against political and economic domination of French-speaking by English-speaking Canada, were all root causes of the movements toward revolution. Federal and provincial authorities in fact underestimated or failed to comprehend the real aims of the revolutionaries. The "quiet revolution" also brought about a flowering of new attitudes and pride toward French language and culture—but the revolutionaries sought to protect this culture in the wrong way.

From the late 1950's until the present, French-Canadian

nationalism has assumed new proportions and violent facets. As a result, Quebec's role in the Canadian confederation has undoubtedly been Canada's principal political problem. Though agrarian and religious influences of French Catholicism have declined within the province, trade unionism and separatism have now replaced these earlier pressure points. There have been gradual elimination of the classical education concept and movement away from the discipline of Catholicism. These are being replaced by new kinds of training for French youth in technical and management fields. This new educational motif has also served as a basis for separatist pressures. Extremists in this movement have demonstrated their feelings and their goals through riots, terrorist bombings, kidnappings, even killings.

When Queen Elizabeth (Canada's own reigning monarch) visited Quebec in 1964, the police were forced to hammer the heads of young dissenters who shouted, "Vive Quebec and down with Ottawa!" This was only one incident in Quebec's long drive to self-determination. A high point of this period of bad feeling came in 1967 at the moment when French President Charles de Gaulle stood on the steps of Montreal's city hall and shouted in French, "Vive le Quebec libre" ("Long live a free Quebec"). As a guest in the country, de Gaulle had shattered all illusions—and broken his hosts' best china.

The terrorists' program reached a new apogee in 1970 when Pierre Laporte, provincial minister of labour and immigration, was kidnapped and murdered. Earlier the same month, the British trade commissioner in Montreal, James Cross, had also been kidnapped but later was released. These and other terrorist activities had been the work of the most extreme of the separatist political groups in Quebec, the *Front de Liberation Quebecois* (FLQ). This group, a loose-knit political organization formed in the early 1960s, had been created by immigrant European revolutionists who designed their work on the model of the Algerian freedom movement of the late 1950s. Recognized aims of the FLQ appear to have been (1) separation of Quebec from Canada; and (2) ending of political and economic domination of Quebec by English-speaking Canadians (and Americans).

Four thousand troops were moved into Ottawa in 1970 immediately after the foregoing kidnappings. This action was aimed at restoration of calm as well as protection of federal officials. At the same time, more than five hundred presumed agitators were arrested. A War Measures Act was also invoked to overcome the situation. This act permitted police officials to perform search and detention without formal charge. Meanwhile the FLQ was declared to be an outlaw organization.

In response to the demands of the separatists and the more conservative French cultural defenders, the federal government passed an Official Language Bill (1971). This bill made both French and English official languages of the federal administration and provided bilingual regions in which both federal services and schools would be available to the public in both languages.

It is interesting to note that the last Liberal-led provincial government chose the public education system to help shape the province's future. In an oddly reactionary 1974 legislative enactment, termed Bill 22, they managed to reverse the idea of bilingualism and biculturalism. This bill insists that French must again be the sole official language of Quebec. The proposal brought on explosive debate in both federal and provincial parliaments—and, by its passage, rescinded, for Quebec, the earlier nationwide legislation that made French and English coequal official languages. In mid-1977, the Quebec legislature passed a controversial bill making French the official language of education, business, and government in this huge eastern province.

As this book is being written, the question of bilingualism in Canada has flared up again in most virulent form. The French-speaking air traffic controllers in Quebec Province are insisting that all pilots and control-

lers operating over Quebec use both French and English.
English-speaking pilots object on grounds of safety and on
grounds that English is the established international air
traffic language. One Trudeau cabinet officer, Jean Mar-
chand (minister of environment and a close personal friend
of the prime minister), has resigned over the issue, and
other political fragmentations are likely. The whole issue
further polarized relations between French- and English-
Canadians.

A special word is required on the problem of Quebec's
separatism. This is not the same kind of issue as that
which disturbs other Canadian provinces—say Alberta or
British Columbia. For those entities, the issue is solely
economic control over their own affairs. For Quebec, a
much more deep-rooted issue exists, and that is the matter
of French survival—political, social, economic, cultural.

The most ardent proponents of French-Canadian separatism have insisted that the basic equipment of Quebec's
real independence is control of immigration and of citizenship; control of media and manpower; control over economic and cultural development; and eventually, full
control over external affairs. Quebec already possesses
many of these items. She is, as well, gaining fiscal power
over education, research, and health. (It is important to
note that the federal government gives to the Province of
Quebec more than $450 million annually in equalization
payments. This represents the largest payment to any of
the Canadian provinces. The provinces of Alberta, British
Columbia, and Ontario do not receive any such monies.)

Quebec is a distinctive—and separate—presence both in
Canada and abroad. She is even accepted as a "francophon nation" in some parts of Europe and Africa. Her last
provincial leader, Robert Bourassa, was considered a
prime minister—never a premier as in other provinces.
His was a national, not a provincial, assembly. In a recent
visit to France, Bourassa was accorded the kind of welcome ordinarily given to a chief of state.

The ultranationalism seen in Quebec in recent years has

had a tendency to drive out capital and energies needed to gear up the unused labor force of the province. At the same time, trade union pressures have intensified, and strikes and walkouts have been all too frequent. Corruption in provincial and municipal government as well as in trade unions has also been commonplace. While officials of federal and provincial governments have been aware of these ugly facets of Quebec's social revolution, they have not always been willing or able to control them—or even to comprehend their ramifications. Never was this failure to comprehend provincial problems more clearly demonstrated than in the results of Quebec's provincial election of November 15, 1976. In that election, the separatist-minded Parti Quebecois, led by René Lévesque (pronounced Leveck) swept the sitting provincial (Liberal) leader, Robert Bourassa, and his party out of power. This was a shock, not alone to the Liberals in Quebec and Ottawa, but to a majority of all Canada. No one appeared to be more shocked—disheartened—by those election results than Prime Minister Trudeau himself.

Quebec's provincial legislature—known as the National Assembly—has 110 seats. At the time of the subject election (November, 1976), the Liberal party held 100 of these seats. Robert Bourassa, provincial premier, had been a loyal disciple of Trudeau and the federal Liberal party leadership. Bourassa's group had been in full control of the province since 1973 and had apparently been so confident of its situation that it called the November election two years prior to constitutional requirements.

The Parti Quebecois won a total of sixty-nine seats. The former Liberal majority ended up with only twenty-seven seats. Even Premier Bourassa lost his seat. The remaining fourteen seats in the legislature were won by smaller antiseparatist parties—Social Credit (Creditistes) and Union Nationale.

Quebec's new premier, René Lévesque, is the son of a lawyer. He was born in Bonaventure, Quebec, in 1922. He attended law school at the University of Laval and interrupted his law studies during the Second World War to become a war correspondent. From 1952 to 1956 he was chief of CBC's French network news service and afterwards was a free-lance radio and television commentator. In 1960, Lévesque was elected as a Liberal member of Quebec's provincial government; he resigned in 1967. (During those seven years, he held three provincial ministerial appointments and was instrumental in nationalizing Quebec's hydroelectric power.) In 1967, he became cofounder of Mouvement Souveraineté-Association and the Parti Quebecois, of which he is now president.

Lévesque is the author of a book on separatism—*Option Quebec*—and of a number of magazine articles setting forth his views on independence for Quebec. Perhaps the most important of these is an article that appeared in the prestigious American journal *Foreign Affairs* (July, 1976), entitled "For an Independent Quebec."

In his political campaigning and in his writings, Lévesque constantly emphasizes needed economic and social reforms for his province. He has also promised his people a referendum on full autonomy or independence for Quebec. This referendum he planed to hold within two years. He has promised that, if such a referendum shows a majority of Quebeckers desire independence from the rest of Canada, "There will be no Berlin Wall on the shores of the Ottawa River." Instead he seems to envision a continuation of economic ties through a kind of Canadian "Common Market" and scoffs at Prime Minister Trudeau's new constitution initiative as a "stillborn mouse".

It is important to realize that Levesque's aim has always been to *persuade* his Quebec compatriots into independence—not to *coerce* them into that judgment. He has gradually gained more and more adherents to his views—winning 23 percent of the popular vote for his separatist theories in 1970; 31 percent in 1973; 41 percent in 1976. Given the massive economic stagnation that has upset earlier provincial governments, Lévesque's Parti Quebecois, now in the position of responsibility, could face resistance in enlarging upon its base. Yet, if Lévesque, as an activist leader, does succeed in putting his province on its feet economically, his dreams of independence may indeed gain broader support—even autonomy. However, it is interesting to note that Quebec had a net loss of 23,300 persons from June 1, 1976, to May 31, 1977.

Quebec Province, with its large population and area, has extensive commercial ties with the United States. Furthermore, American multinational concerns have a large investment stake in Quebec. United States–controlled companies are reported to account for about 30 percent of Quebec's manufactures. American investment in the province is conservatively estimated to be in excess of $5 billion (second only to that in Ontario). Almost 25 percent of jobs in the industrial area of the province are on American payrolls.

Financial marts (especially New York) took the results of the November, 1976, election seriously. Canadian stocks tumbled at once on domestic and international exchanges. The Canadian dollar slipped eight cents in value within ten days. This was the most precipitous decline for that currency since May, 1962. (New low October, 1978)

Immediately after the results of the Quebec elections were known, Prime Minister Trudeau took to the airwaves. He insisted that the people in the rest of Canada should not panic over the potentialities of the Quebec election. He insisted, too, that any referendum involving Quebec's people on the issue of independence must be accompanied by a referendum of the Canadian people as a whole on the same issue. This process, he stated, would ensure that Canada would remain one nation. He admitted, however, that, in order to keep Canada as an entity, there might well be some further devolution of power from Ottawa to provincial capitals. This move would make the provincial government of Quebec even stronger.

Leaders of the two major national Opposition parties— Progressive Conservative and New Democratic—immediately followed Trudeau with countrywide broadcasts of their own. Both Joe Clark of the Progressive Conservatives and Edward Broadbent of the NDP sought to calm their followers on the issue of Quebec's independence, saying that such departure was not imminent. However, they laid much of the blame for this matter at Trudeau's feet, contending that he had been too lax in his national leadership on matters of bilingualism/biculturalism and on federal-provincial relations as a whole.

On the separatism issue, Trudeau has several dilemmas. Outside Ontario and Quebec, his Liberal party is largely in the minority. Furthermore, if Lévesque were bullied by Ottawa, that action could well swing more Quebeckers toward separatism. Conversely, if Quebec were given more federal assistance or autonomy, the rest of Canada would berate Trudeau or any successor. Though separatism is not presently in the fiery revolutionary stage that it was in 1970, the economic situation in Quebec keeps it smoldering. Those flames can always flare up.

In the author's view, there is no real hope for continuing Canadian unity unless the English-speaking people of Canada fully understand, accept, and implement the Pearson-Trudeau bicultural-bilingual policies. French-Canadians must be satisfied by Ottawa, first on the issue of political autonomy over their own affairs, and second on the proposition that they are getting an even break in meeting pressing economic and social needs. If there is not wholehearted nationwide acceptance of bicultural, bilingual, political and economic equality, the Canadian confederation could be doomed. Furthermore, if Quebec should depart the existing confederation, it would be highly unlikely that the rest of the Canadian confederacy could hold itself together. Other provinces, too, might decide to go their own way, especially in the West. There might also be a gravitational pull southward toward the United States for the Maritime Provinces. Already, as a result of the Quebec election, French-Canadian nationalists in New Brunswick and Nova Scotia are becoming restless.

As the esteemed London *Economist* (November 20, 1976) put it, this may be "Canada's Last Chance." The magazine went on to say, "Canada has always been a triumph over geography, but not even Canadians could be expected to maintain a unity stretching 4,000 miles from Newfoundland to Vancouver if there were a gaping hole in the middle of it. . . . If Canada breaks up, the United States will have a sort of Caribbean to its north as well as the Caribbean it already has to the south."

Some French-Canadians say the issue is not *whether* Quebec will one day be independent from the rest of Canada. That is settled, they say. The questions are only *When?* and *How?* That is, will the new nation of Quebec be socialist or capitalist, and will it remain a French-speaking nation inside or outside a Canadian—or North American— "Common Market." As this book goes to press, these questions remain unanswered.

10
The Atlantic Provinces

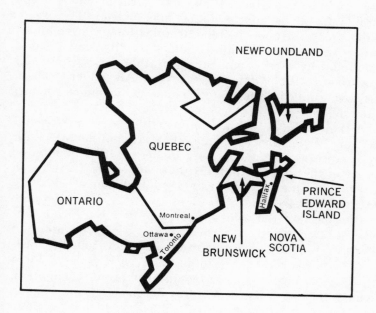

NOVA SCOTIA

The Province of Nova Scotia is a picturesque peninsula—a combination of history, scenery, and fisheries. Considered as the focal center of the Maritimes, it has more than eight hundred thousand people in an area of 21,425 square miles. It is almost completely surrounded by water—the Atlantic Ocean on the east, the Gulf of St. Lawrence on the north, and the Bay of Fundy on the west.

The peninsula is some 390 miles in length, and the land

is mainly rocky. However, in the center of the province there are fertile plains and river valleys. Cape Breton Island, considered part of the province for administrative purposes, lies just to the northeast. This is a rugged upland plateau, cut almost in half by a salt water inlet or lagoon known as Lake Bras d'Or (Arm of Gold). Cape Breton Island is approximately one-quarter the size of Nova Scotia proper, being 110 miles long and about 85 miles wide. This island is joined to the Nova Scotia mainland by a mile-long causeway that carries both rail and road traffic. A famous American, Alexander Graham Bell, who loved Cape Breton Island as his summer home, now lies buried there.

Although Nova Scotia is obviously a Maritime-coastal region, the climate is nonetheless continental, with temperatures somewhat more moderate than in interior areas of the same latitude. Winters are stormy, and fog is prevalent. There is either rain or snow during at least five months of the year.

It is certain that Norsemen and other Europeans, including Portuguese fishermen, came to Nova Scotia and Cape Breton Island even before John Cabot made his "official" discovery of the region in 1497. The first permanent settlement, however, awaited the coming of Champlain, who in 1604 established Port Royal. This is the third oldest settlement in North America (following St. John's, Newfoundland, and St. Augustine, Florida). Today, Port Royal is known as Annapolis-Royal. This original capital is located across the Bay of Fundy from Saint John, New Brunswick. Not long after Port Royal was settled, it was attacked and conquered by English invaders from the American colonies. The French following Champlain gave to the territory the name Acadia from the Indian-named river, *Shubenacadie*. However, in 1621, the first British charter was awarded to Sir William Alexander. To his new possession, Alexander gave the name *Nova Scotia* ("New Scotland"), honoring his own birthplace. During the next 150 years, the territory changed hands from French to

British and back again a total of six times until it finally passed into permanent British control. Sometimes these changes came by treaty, more often by war.

During these troubled decades, the French concentrated their settlements in the southern part of the peninsula, along the Bay of Fundy, and on Cape Breton Island. Britons settled mainly along the Atlantic coast. To protect their interests, the French built a fortress at Louisbourg on the east coast of Cape Breton Island. To counter it, the English built another fortress, the Citadel, which still dominates the city of Halifax, now the provincial capital.

In 1755, some six thousand French settlers (habitants) of the area were sent into exile by the British governor. They were dispersed to other British-American colonies along the Atlantic and Gulf coasts as well as the Caribbean. Many families were broken up in the process. It was this event that Americans will recall as the basis for Henry W. Longfellow's sentimental and sad epic poem *Evangeline* (see Chapter 3). Today the village of Grand Pre near Halifax is filled with mementos of that event and that epic. There are festivals to memorialize the occasion, these taking place near the restored chapel and statue dedicated to Longfellow's "Evangeline." Today in Louisiana, the Cajuns (Acadians) trace their heritage to that French-Canadian settlement in Nova Scotia. With the destruction of the French fortress of Louisbourg by the British in the mid-eighteenth century, French control of the area was eliminated once and for all. Halifax, established in 1749, became the colonial capital and an important venue for British naval operations during both the American Revolution and the subsequent War of 1812. Following the Revolution, Nova Scotia also became the locale for settlement of a large number of United Empire Loyalists fleeing from their earlier homes in the American colonies. It is now estimated that more than thirty thousand of these settled in Nova Scotia alone.

Nova Scotia is also famous as the site of the gathering and eventual departure of yet another large group of refugees. During the decade following the American Revolution, many Negro slaves, the "property" of the Loyalists escaping the American War of Independence, had been settled in the various Maritime Provinces of Canada. Most of these were there given their freedom. From Halifax, in 1792, local authorities, inspired by the abolitionist cause, helped some eleven hundred former Black slaves return to their ancestral homeland in Africa. Most of these were resettled at the port of Freetown on the African west coast. There, inspired by their colonial American and British heritage, these former slaves built the foundations of a new nation—Sierra Leone.

The present provinces of New Brunswick, Prince Edward Island, and Nova Scotia, as well as a slice of the state of Maine, were originally united as the colony of Nova Scotia. New Brunswick and P.E.I. were shed immediately following the American Revolution. That portion now incorporated into Maine was taken away as a result of the boundary settlements following the War of 1812. As late as 1867, however, just at the time of Canadian confederation, consideration was given to reuniting the three Canadian Maritime provinces. This move was unsuccessful, though within a decade all three separately joined that confederation.

Nova Scotia today includes: those of British origin, 75 percent; French, 11 percent; German, 5 percent; Dutch, 3 percent; and other, 6 percent. By religious preference, the Roman Catholics have 34 percent; United Church, 22 percent; Anglicans, 18 percent; Baptists, 14 percent; Presbyterians, 7 percent; and unaffiliated, 5 percent.

Halifax, located on one of the great harbors of the world, was known in Indian times as *Chebucto*—a Micmac Indian term meaning "great, long harbor." Halifax, named for the British Earl of Halifax who had much to do with the city's founding, is today one of the prime seaports of the Atlantic. It proved essential to wartime convoys in World Wars I and II. It is situated some six hundred miles nearer London than is New York and is an ice-free port year around.

Halifax is the province's center of commerce and culture as well as the home of the famed Grand Banks fishing fleets. Its population is about 225,000.

The city of Sidney, second largest in the province, was the capital of the earlier Cape Breton Island colony. Today it is an important industrial center of some hundred thousand people—the site of major coal and steel production.

With its many excellent harbors and lush interior valleys, Nova Scotia is famous for fish and fruit, and for tourism and industry. The present highly mechanized fishing fleets continue to take great catches of lobster, cod, halibut, hake, and mackerel from the Grand Banks and coastal bays just as was done by European fishermen some three hundred years ago. In fisheries production, Nova Scotia is second only to British Columbia. The province is famed for its apples, too, these being exported in great quantity. Though farming is limited, cultivation is intense and diversified. Hay is the largest field crop. Half the province is heavily forested, with pulp and paper production developing. In addition to its coal, Nova Scotia also has some gypsum, salt, and base metals. There have been recent finds of oil and gas offshore, but these are in preliminary stages of development. Tourism is an advancing industry serving some one million visitors annually. Despite the commerce and industry, however, Nova Scotia continues to remain among the poorest of all Canadian provinces.

Charles Dickens, the great English novelist, watched the proceedings of the Nova Scotia legislature in 1841 and characterized the experience as "like looking at Westminster through the wrong end of a telescope." Nova Scotian politics today may not be much changed. From 1974–78, the legislature has had thirty-one Liberals, twelve Progressive Conservatives, and three members of the NDP. Despite the party labels, politics here has been traditionally conservative with a small c. As in Ontario, politics here bears little relationship to the national scene. In Nova Scotia, the so-called Family Compact arrangements have operated: the oldest, most prestigious families of Upper Canada (Ontario) and the Maritimes functioned together in a kind of oligarchy. A so-called Council of 12—comprising a business-oriented "Mafia"—actually operated Nova Scotia as a "fiefdom" during many of the early years. These relationships dominated Nova Scotian politics until the beginnings of World War II, and traces remain even today.

Angus L. Macdonald, perhaps the most popular premier ever to rule Nova Scotia, held office for more than two decades, breaking off only to join the wartime cabinet of Mackenzie King.

One of the more successful and popular premiers was Robert Stanfield, who led the province from 1956 to 1967, when he was drafted away by his party to assume national leadership of the Progressive Conservatives. He has several times since, always unsuccessfully, challenged Pierre Trudeau for the position of prime minister of Canada. Under Stanfield, in the late 1950s, there was set up an "operation bootstrap" for the province: a crown corporation called Industrial Estates, Ltd. This organization persuaded more than sixty foreign companies to locate in Nova Scotia.

Stanfield was followed into office by his former deputy and reputed "hatchet man," George Isaac ("Ike") Smith. Smith was an ardent monarchist, opposing both French-Canadian separatism and too-close association with the United States. He was a "Canada Firster"—but with Nova Scotia a close second.

The previous premier, Gerald ("Gabby") Regan, was formerly a radio sportscaster and news director. He was born in Hants County, Nova Scotia, in 1928, the son of a small shopkeeper. After studying law at Dalhousie University, he entered politics. He was elected in 1963 to the federal House of Commons but remained there only two years. He returned to provincial politics and attained the post of premier in 1970, leading his Liberal ("Grits") party to victory with twenty-three seats in the legislature. In the next election (April, 1974), his Liberals won thirty-one seats, Progressive Conservatives, 12; NDP, 3. Regan had been critical of his predecessors' actions in "bailing out" some of the private companies that had been encouraged to settle in the province.

According to a recent interview, Premier Regan is "a passionate Nova Scotian who opposes Maritime union." He believes that action would "weaken rather than strengthen us." He believes outsiders have too much authority over Nova Scotia business and seeks more local direction thereof. He believes in the need of greater decentralization, saying that the national government must represent all ten provinces—not just one (Ontario). Restless and vital, he is, throughout, a practical politician, with national and global, as well as provincial, views.

Gabby Regan believes the prime provincial problems stem from the lag between public revenues and public needs. He is also much concerned with the continuing problem of unemployment and with the need for national policies beneficial to the economically backward provinces such as Nova Scotia. He contends that the provinces are too "distant" from the central government—this tending to splinter the nation.

The provincial election on September 19, 1978, was an upset. The Conservative Party led by John Buchanan, aged 47, defeated the Liberals. Premier Buchanan had campaigned for a subsidy on power rates until coal-powered generating plants become operation in the 1980s, greater support for small business, restraints on government spending, and a reduction in the 11 percent unemployment rate. His party won 17 seats and the Liberals won 15 seats out of the 32.

NEW BRUNSWICK

New Brunswick has been characterized as complex and subtle, remaining a secret even to itself. It lies northeast of the state of Maine, fronting on the Bay of Fundy and the Gulf of St. Lawrence. Its population is 685,000 and its area 27,985 square miles. This territory was originally a part of the French colony of Acadia, which also included Nova Scotia and Cape Breton Island.

New Brunswick owes it very existence to the fourteen thousand Tories—British sympathizers—who came out of the American colonies to settle there as United Empire Loyalists. Most of these arrived in the years just following the end of the Revolution (1783) and took up their new habitation on the shores of the St. John River and the Bay of Fundy. Developing an intense dislike of the colonial government in Halifax, then capital of New Brunswick as well as Nova Scotia, and inspired by the very revolutionary views they had left behind in the American colonies, these new settlers promptly agitated with London for a colonial government of their own. The British Parliament reacted quickly to these demands, setting up the new colony of New Brunswick in 1784. It was named in honor of the House of Brunswick, the family name of the reigning monarch, George III.

The capital, Fredericton, originally an Acadian settlement, had been expanded by the infiltration of the many Loyalists refugees from the colonies. It was given its name by these new settlers in 1784 in honor of Prince Frederick, the son of George III. Formally made the colonial capital in 1788, it was given "city" status in 1848 by Queen Victoria. This action was taken in order to make Fredericton "a fitting location for Christ Church Cathedral, the first new Cathedral built on British soil abroad since the Norman Conquest." Fredericton is some sixty miles up the St. John River from the Bay of Fundy. Today it has a population of thirty thousand.

While Fredericton is an important commercial center as well as the capital, it also has an interesting literary role. This role stems from the University of New Brunswick, which is located in Fredericton. Here has developed an important literary clique that designates itself as "the poets' corner of the world." Among the more important Canadian poets associated with this venture are Bliss Carman, Charles Roberts, and Alden Nowlan.

The largest city in the province, Saint John, has a metropolitan population exceeding a hundred thousand. It has the distinction of being the first incorporated city in British North America. Located on the Bay of Fundy, Saint John is Canada's only year-round ice-free Atlantic seaport besides Halifax. It has a splendid harbor and one of the largest dry docks in the world. Like Halifax, Saint John proved its worth to the Allies in their wartime Atlantic convoy activities. It is the site of the famous "Reversing Falls," where half the time the St. John River empties into the Bay of Fundy and half the time the Bay of Fundy empties into the St. John River. At the latter time, the tide raises the water level in the harbor about fifteen feet above the level of the river mouth, and so the tidewaters disgorge upstream.

Nearly rectangular in shape, the province has an extensive seacoast. Hilly rather than mountainous, New Brunswick has its highest elevation, 2,690 feet, in the vicinity of Grand Falls on the St. John River. Much of the territory's soil is rocky and unfit for agriculture, but the heavy rainfall produces excellent forests. The principal river, the St. John, is over four hundred miles in length. The Bay of Fundy, which separates New Brunswick from Nova Scotia, has the world's highest tides (reportedly sometimes exceeding fifty feet). There have been recurring proposals, as yet unsuccessful, to harness these tides to produce electric power. The climate, reflecting the moderating effect of the sea breezes, is similar to that of Maine. There is a short growing season, with extreme variations of temperature, and only four months of the year are frost-free.

In New Brunswick, the ethnic ratio is British, 57 percent; French, 38 percent; and all others, 5 percent. Major faiths in New Brunswick include: Roman Catholic, 51 percent; Baptist, 18 percent; United Church, 14 percent; Anglicans, 12 percent; others, 5 percent.

The southern and western parts of the province are populated by those of British heritage, Protestant and politically Conservative. In the north and northeast, the communities are mainly French Catholic and Liberal. Most of the French-Canadians are concentrated in and around the communities of Bathurst and Moncton. Many of these are descendants of the original Acadians.

Though the French-Candian influence is growing, the British tradition in the province—the legacy of the Loyalists—remains pronounced. In New Brunswick, the designation United Empire Loyalist still means a great deal. Even today, descendants of the United Empire Loyalists are permitted to sign U.E. after their names—this being the only hereditary distinction now allowed in Canada. The province has furnished unusual gifts of her subjects to the motherland, Great Britain. Among these were the imperialistic newspaper magnate and friend of Winston Churchill, Lord Beaverbrook (formerly Max Aitken), and the 1922 British prime minister, Andrew Bonar Law. The latter was the only prime minister of the United Kingdom ever to have been born outside the British Isles. The province is also famous for the site of Franklin Roosevelt's summer home, the island of Campobello.

The province is known for its tourism and its salmon fishing. Its important fisheries, ranking just behind those of Newfoundland, British Columbia, and Nova Scotia, produce in quantity lobsters, oysters, clams, and the various deep-sea varieties. New Brunswick's agricultural activity lies mainly in mixed farming to satisfy the local market, with potatoes the main product. Coal mining has been important, but manufacturing is now the leading industry of the province. Among those manufactures are forest products, shoes, confectioneries, shipping materials, and automobiles. One interesting extension of manufacture has been the New Brunswick government's encouragement of and investment in local production of the ill-fated American-designed sports car, the Bricklin.

One of the more surprising of cultural links between Americans and Canadians in present-day New Brunswick has been the support afforded by residents of that province to the Boston Red Sox. Indeed, the people of New Brunswick are as ardent rooters for that baseball team as any to be found in Fenway Park. Their pleasure knew no bounds when their favorites batted their way into the World Series in 1975. Part of this remarkable support stemmed from the fact that a Canadian pitcher, Reggie Cleveland, was on the Boston roster. However, the affection of the people of New Brunswick for what they delight in calling the "Boston States"—meaning especially Maine and Massachusetts—comes from the long-standing economic association of the two areas through a transport linkage, the Boston and Maine Railway.

The provincial legislature has fifty-eight members. The present Conservative premier is Richard Hatfield, elected in 1970, reelected in 1974 and 1978. His party controls thirty seats as opposed to the Liberals' twenty-eight. Some observers here have characterized provincial politics as intensely parochial, sometimes even stagnant and anachronistic, reminiscent of politics in Nineteenth-century prereform Britain, or New York in Tammany days. These two old parties have been successfully kept in place by gerrymandering and by ancient loyalties, by ethnic and cultural antagonisms. There has been little room for "participatory democracy" or populism. As Liberals and Progressive Conservatives have dominated the governmental structure in turn, there has been a lack of development of third parties.

Some academic observers have characterized New Brunswick's legislature as a partisan forum for conflict and development of patronage rather than a deliberative body. The province normally has about eighty-two hundred regular employees and about the same number of casual patronage appointees. The legislative assembly is said, then, to be more concerned with patronage and the parish pump than with major issues. Mass media politics have as yet found little place in this province.

Prior to the accession of the present premier, Hatfield, the man in charge of the province was Louis Robichaud. He served as the first Acadian premier of New Brunswick and was in office for ten years (1959–1970). An ardent exponent of bilingualism, he proved intensely controversial, but he managed to ram through the legislature heavy new taxes designed to expand social welfare benefits for his poor French-Canadian constituents. At the same time, he sought to bring new industrial development to his native Acadian northeast.

One important political battle that occurred in the province during the Robichaud regime is worthy of special note. This is the conflict that arose between Robichaud and the billionaire industrial tycoon Kenneth Colin Irving. Irving is the owner of a chain of service stations located throughout the Atlantic Provinces and Quebec. As well, he owns refineries, shipping businesses, bus lines, hardware and sporting goods chains. He also owns the five major newspapers in the province and the several TV-radio outlets. His holdings are said to be in excess of a billion Canadian dollars, representing perhaps one-third of all New Brunswick's land and economy. Robichaud and Irving, close associates in their early years, are now said to be mortal enemies—the main source of difficulty coming from Robichaud's determined tax policies and the usual French-Canadian versus Anglo-Canadian rivalries. Robichaud is now a senator, and Irving lives in Bermuda.

The present, Progressive Conservative premier, Richard Bennett Hatfield, gained office on grounds that his predecessor's fiscal program was "irresponsible." Hatfield is generally considered to be a level-headed, conscientious, serious minded premier. He was born in 1931 in Hartland, New Brunswick. Educated at Acadia University with a B.A. in 1952, he received an LL.B. from Dalhousie University (Nova Scotia) in 1956. After a varied career in private business, he practiced law for five years, then became a member of Parliament in 1961, elected from Carleton riding. He became leader of the Progressive Conservative party of New Brunswick in 1969. He has served as premier since 1970.

Hatfield contends that the pressure of friends and the recognized needs of his province directed him into political life. He states that Jose Ortega y Gasset's book *Revolt of the Masses* was of profound influence on him, also helping to guide him into public life. As to the problems of his own province, he cites major issues as unemployment, lack of opportunity, and lack of adequate revenues for essential social welfare.

Premier Hatfield believes that, in Canada, there is a definite tendency to oversimplify complex problems and that there is far too much inequality of opportunity in his country. He believes that both these tendencies weaken Canadian federalism and nationhood. As a Canadian, he tries to identify with his country's drive and diversity. He defines a "True Canadian" as one who has compassion for all his fellow citizens and for the aspirations of all people universally. He characterizes most Canadians as a people essentially polite, serious, and, most of all, reasonable. He believes that all Canadian premiers—and prime ministers—should have a consuming ambition for good government.

PRINCE EDWARD ISLAND

Prince Edward Island has been characterized as a tranquil garden. About the size of the state of Delaware, the island lies in the Gulf of St. Lawrence northeast of New Brunswick. With inhabitants numbering some 120,000 and a land area of 2,184 square miles, the province is the smallest in all Canada. Separated from the New Brunswick mainland by the nine-mile-wide Northumberland Strait, this crescent-shaped island is 140 miles long and has an average width of 20 miles. The otherwise rigorous climate is somewhat modified by the sea breezes of the Gulf of St. Lawrence. The frost-free period ranges from May through October.

This island was discovered by Jacques Cartier on his first voyage to New France in 1534. The name originally given by the French was Isle St. Jean. Though settlement by the French was not extensive, the island was used as a fisheries concession by the French crown. With the British takeover of French possessions in 1763, this island was separated from the colonial administration of Nova Scotia and made a separate colony and, later, province. In 1763, the population numbered only 250. Small holdings were then given to English settlers and later to some American Loyalist refugees. In 1799 the name of the territory was changed to Prince Edward Island in honor of Queen Victoria's father, the Duke of Kent, who then commanded British troops in North America.

Population growth and economic development came slowly, mainly because most land on the island was held by landlords resident in Britain. This situation was not changed until Canadian confederation was achieved. Though the island did not actually enter that confederation until 1873, its metropolis, Charlottetown, was the site of the 1864 convention that first framed and promulgated the idea of Canadian independence by confederation.

This provincial capital, Charlottetown, has about twenty thousand inhabitants. Originally named Port La Joie by French explorers, the city was renamed by the British in 1768 in honor of Queen Charlotte, consort of George III. The city is the commercial, cultural, and administrative center of the province.

More than 80 percent of the present population of Prince Edward Island is of British extraction. Those of French origin compose about 16 percent. There are a few Americans, and Europeans of other nationalities, also resident on the island. By religion, the Roman Catholics, with 44 percent, are predominant. United Church adherents form 26 percent; Presbyterians, 12 percent; Anglicans, 6 percent; Baptists, 5 percent. The remainder are unaffiliated.

The irregular coastline of the province provides many bays and inlets for fishing. The soil is rich, and 80 percent of the island is suitable for agriculture. Prince Edward Island is particularly famous for its potatoes and bent grass. Beef, bacon, and dairy products are also produced and exported to New England. Manufacturing is limited to processing of dairy products and fish. Other than quarries there is no mining, and forest land is now nearly nonexistent. Per capita income is small, and the island is heavily dependent on federal support for its people's subsistence.

For some years past, the federal government at Ottawa has promised to construct a causeway across Northumberland Strait to permit easier access to and from the island. This scheme—now estimated to cost more that $300 million—would, of course, transform the entire social and economic structure of Prince Edward Island. Thus far, the project remains only a dream, and the federal government has increased its subventions and economic development funds for the island in lieu of the larger plan.

Prince Edward Island is the least viable of the Maritime Provinces. This island province is equipped with all the political machinery of the much-larger Quebec or Ontario. This cumbersome political/administrative establishment must be heavily supported by federal grants in order to survive. In fact, P.E.I. has even been characterized as simply a "colony" of Ottawa. The island thus depends on politics as a major business along with its farming and fishing and tourism.

In some respects, Prince Edward Island reflects the overweening proportion of government installations in Canada as a whole. For it should be remembered that this nation of 24 million people has eleven different sets of government institutions to handle its affairs. In some parts of the world, governments of similar size would be sufficient for several hundred million people. It is easy to question, then, whether P.E.I. should actually be a separate province. Nonetheless, it is a distinct, and highly politicized, geographical entity with a political tradition of its own.

Prince Edward Island's legislature has thirty-two members—sixteen two-member constituencies. The cabinet has ten members, so one-third of the legislature are also members of the executive. Cabinet thus dominates caucus, legislature, and administrative set-up. Debate is in

Cabinet rather than legislature. Each opposition party has complained bitterly about this political setup. Furthermore, the extraordinarily small size of the constituencies encourage highly localized electoral battles on extremely narrow political issues. This high cost of politics per capita appears to have only one real compensation—that is, an extremely large proportion of islanders participate both in political discussion and in governing. They represent their neighborhoods—and, as a result, develop a high sense of political democracy and political linkage between one another. Thus democracy must be said to be a thriving business on Prince Edward Island. Party organization is highly personalized. No other group in Canada is said to have so many party gatherings and so much political machinery.

As a result of the 1978 election, the Liberal party won seventeen seats, a loss of nine seats; and the Progressive Conservatives won fifteen, a gain of nine seats. This grouping still reflects the general Liberal-leaning orientation of the island in recent decades. The leaders of the island's administration, particularly the former premier, A. B. Campbell, downgrade ethnic differences, religious differences, and provincial-federal disputes in the interests of a stronger Canada. Nonetheless they have been constantly disturbed that recent federal administrations in Ottawa have continually "let them down" on the issue of building the causeway to the Canadian mainland to permit the island to become more prosperous. They believe that the federal government has pawned off this development in favor of less expensive ferry routes and social welfare services.

Ex-Premier Alexander Bradshaw Campbell, the second-youngest first minister in Canada, was born in 1933. He was educated at Dalhousie University, Nova Scotia, later entering law and political life. He is the son of Prince Edward Island's chief justice, himself a former Liberal premier. Campbell had been Liberal premier of the province since 1966, when he took over from his defeated Conservative predecessor, Walter Shaw.

Campbell is hard pressing and hard pressed. He believes that, if Quebec should separate from the confederation, British Columbia would declare independence as well, and there would then be common action for unification by the Atlantic Provinces. These latter, in turn, might seek political association with the United States. However, he presses for "federalism" rather than provincial "separatism" or "balkanization" of Canada into several smaller nations.

He also believes that the British monarch should continue to be sovereign head of Canada. He does not believe Quebec Province should hold a special place in the confederation any more than should his own province. He does not favor the two-language idea, believing that linguistic differences are divisive. He believes, too, that regional disparities must be overcome and that the young must be held at home. He says brains and talents are far more worthwhile than are equalization payments coming out of Ottawa to support dying populations.

Campbell has led his "spud-islanders" in a hard-pushing effort at economic betterment. His province has allocated to this purpose some $700 million to be spent over a period of fifteen years—only one-third of those funds coming from Ottawa. He emphasizes that his people's prime needs continue to be capital investment, employment, and settlement of their transport problems. He continues to hope for his causeway.

Unexpectedly, on September 11, 1978, Campbell resigned, handing the reins to Prince Edward Island's Finance and Education Minister, Bennett Campbell (no relation), aged 35. He was elected leader in a December convention. The 32-member Legislature is divided—Liberals, 17; Tories, 15.

NEWFOUNDLAND

Newfoundlanders, sometimes known as "Newfies," do not like to be considered as a part of the Canadian Maritimes, but rather separate from the other three provinces. This stems in part from their isolation, in part from their history. Newfoundland did not join the Canadian confederation until 1949. Till then, it had been a British colony. In fact, it was the oldest of all British overseas possessions and in the late nineteenth and early twentieth centuries considered the prospect of going independent on its own, rather than joining Canada.

The province includes the island of Newfoundland, some 42,734 square miles, plus the mainland peninsula of Labrador, 112,630 square miles. The two are separated by the Strait of Belle Isle, which is nine miles wide at its narrowest point. The total population of the two sectors is about 560,000. Most of these reside along the coastal region of the island and in its capital, St. John's.

Both sectors of the province are rocky, hilly, and rugged. Much of the area is barren, though there are a few heavily forested areas. The climate of island and mainland is kept cold by the Labrador Current, which flows out of the Arctic Ocean. As a result, there is a very short summer, there being no more than four months of frost-free days. The territory has rain, snow, or heavy fog about two-thirds of the year. The peninsula of Labrador, being further north, has an even more rigorous climate than the island of Newfoundland. It is snow covered nearly half the year. Newfoundland is reported to have no snakes, skunks, poison ivy, or hay fever. There are, however, many moose, caribou, deer, bear, and otter.

Newfoundland derives its name literally from the fact that the English fishermen who first used its welcome harbors called it their "New Found Land." Today the name is accented on the last syllable—NewfoundLAND. Viking explorers visited Labrador about the year 1000 A. D. There are some archeological sites in the area that attest to this. One of these Norse settlements has been found at L'Ansa-aux-Meadows on the northern peninsula of Newfoundland. European fishermen, Portuguese and Spanish, are said to have worked the famous Grand Banks as many as fifty years before Columbus discovered the New World and before John Cabot ventured into that region. The latter either discovered or rediscovered Newfoundland and asserted British sovereignty over it in 1497. A Portuguese navigator, Corte-Real, explored the coast soon after. His action in behalf of Spain brought about Spanish claims to ownership. However, the British explorer Sir Humphrey Gilbert reasserted English ownership finally and firmly in 1583. Until 1700 it was actually illegal to settle in Newfoundland—this because the wealthy English absentee landlords of the fishing fleets wished to protect their monopolies against the intrusions and competition of domestic fishermen. Nor, indeed, did the British sovereign incur political problems with this colony, instead believing the long fishing voyages to Newfoundland represented superb training for her future naval recruits. As noted earlier, however, this was still considered to be Britain's first real colony—the foundation stone of the British Empire. Even today, about 80 percent of the residents of Newfoundland are descendants of the early British fishermen and 98 percent of the populace speaks only English or a special Newfoundland dialect thereof. Many locations bear fascinating names such as Hug My Dug Island, Bake Apple Island, Little Tumbledown Dick Island, Joe Batt's Arm, and Change Islands Tickle.

Newfoundland became a self-governing colony in 1855, continuing this autonomous form of government until 1934. At that time, her financial problems brought on suspension of her "responsible" government. The colony was then placed under a special Commission of Government appointed by the British crown. In 1946 the people were asked to vote on whether they wished to remain under this Commission structure; to return to internal self-government and eventual independence; or to be united with Canada. In 1948, after two votes were held, the choice of union with Canada narrowly won out despite the fears of many Newfies that, as a "have not" province, their homeland would suffer domination and oppression by Ottawa and richer sister provinces. When Newfoundland finally joined the confederation in 1949, it lagged far behind the rest of Canada both economically and politically. It is still in the catching-up process. Almost thirty years after Newfoundland became the tenth province, there is no doubt that starvation and malnutrition there have been heavily curtailed and minimal social welfare needs of the population are being met. While standards of living have risen, however, employment is not yet what it could be. As there is not sufficient work, the prime export of the province is said by some cynics to have shifted from fish and sealskins to its young men and women who seek work elsewhere in Canada.

By ethnic origin those Newfoundlanders from the British Isles comprise 93 percent; French-Canadians approximate 3 percent; the remainder are from other European stock or are aboriginal. By religion, major groups include Roman Catholic, 34 percent; Anglicans, 31 percent; United Church, 24 percent; Salvation Army, 8 percent; unaffiliated 3 percent.

The provincial capital, St. John's, has a population of 120,000. North America's oldest town, it was first settled by Devonshire fishermen about 1527 and was incorporated as a city in 1888. Located on the southeast coast of Newfoundland, the city is some 540 miles by sea from Halifax, its nearest Canadian provincial neighbor. The city's name derives from the traditional view that the discoverer, John Cabot, first visited the city's harbor on Saint John's day— June 24, 1497. The town became a popular rendezvous for the European fishermen working the Grand Banks. Sir Humphrey Gilbert, making his first visit there in 1583, described the town as "populous and much frequented."

St. John's has a fine, landlocked harbor with wharves, dry docks, machine shops, and foundries. It has row on row of flat-roofed houses with big bay windows. Many of these homes were built by wealthy merchants who founded their fortunes on purchase of fish and extension of credits to the outlanders who worked the Grand Banks. It was claimed that this fabulously rich mercantile class made St. John's disproportionately wealthy in per capita terms. As late as 1950, that city was reputed to house more millionaires per capita than any other city in North America.

One looks down the city streets and sees the ships at anchor at the water's edge. Here, too, however, skyscrapers and freeways are beginning to intrude. Belatedly, but determinedly, St. John's is changing its Victorian vistas. The city's quaintness is going—regrettably, progress is equated with modernity.

There are few urban centers in the province, apart from the capital. The second largest municipality is Corner Brook. This city of some thirty thousand is located on the island's west coast. It is the center of a new iron and steel industry. (International air travelers and military veterans will recall the safe haven that two Newfoundland airport communities—Gander and Goose Bay—provided for trans-Atlantic adventurers during the exciting days of World War II and immediately after.)

More than 40 percent of the populace of Newfoundland still lives in villages of less than 1,000. The prime reason for this distribution has been the territory's historical dependence on fisheries. Newfoundlanders became true "people of the sea," dependent on oral tradition alone for maintenance of their history and socializing with one another only by sea. During the last four hundred years, more than thirteen hundred so-called outports, or small fishing communities, grew up, each clustered about its own harbor, bay, or inlet.

In the past twenty years, a controversial resettlement of many of these outport villages has been accomplished. The program has resettled the residents of some three hundred outports into larger communities. This has been done in order to provide better health, educational, and physical amenities and occupational prospects for those people. Among the elderly, these resettlement schemes have not been popular.

Of the ten provinces, Newfoundland is by all odds the poorest. The territory has little land suitable for farming and, as the growing season coincides with the main fishing season, agriculture has never been accented. Of the labor force of some one hundred and fifty thousand, only thirty-five hundred are actually employed in farming. Agricultural out put is essentially for domestic use, only eggs being produced in sufficient quantity for export. Some governmental efforts, federal and provincial, are now being directed at expansion of agriculture, but the results are slow.

Today fishing ranks fourth among Newfoundland's economic activities, producing only 10 percent of the provincial wealth. However, fishing still remains important in the social structure. Most fishermen must now depend on part-time logging and timber work for their livelihood. There is some additional revenue brought into the province, however, by the various services that the port of St. John's furnishes to foreign fishing fleets.

Associated with fisheries has been the Newfies' long-standing interest in hunting baby harp seals in Labrador and on gulf islands. Though this is a million-dollar business (receipts $1.4 million in 1977), the annual spring slaughter of these white-furred "pups" has become a subject of international controversy between environmentalists and hunters.

There are several pulp and paper mills in operation in the province. Exports from these earn more than $100 million annually. The attendant labor income for the province is an important economic factor. There are now considerable efforts underway for improvement and reforestation of timber lands.

Labrador's new hydroelectric plants and its iron ore production are of special importance in the provincial economy. Most of the iron ore is exported to new markets in Japan and continental Europe.

A new oil refinery is now being completed at Come-by-Chance, ninety miles from St. John's, where oil from the Middle East is expected to be processed at the rate of 100,000 barrels daily. Here supertankers too large for other Atlantic ports can be handled. Production from the refinery will be made available to Eastern Canada. It is possible that this plant may be expanded into petrochemical production as well.

As a result of the combination of governmental and private business initiative, it is possible that Newfoundland's economy may be given a real boost. Most economists believe that the province must come to depend on resource industries and on local processing of those resources. At the present time, however, more than 60 percent of the provincial income is drawn down from the federal government through equalization grants. Those equalization funds are running into Newfoundland at the rate of nearly $100 million annually.

Newfoundland's current provincial assembly has fifty-one members, with Progressive Conservatives holding thirty seats; Liberals sixteen; NDP four; Independents, one. The present premier is Frank D. Moores, Progressive Conservative. Politics in Newfoundland and Labrador had been dominated for more than thirty years by the preceding Liberal leader and premier, Joey Smallwood. Confederation in 1949 had been achieved by only the narrowest margins—52 percent of Newfies voting for and 48 voting against. It was Smallwood who turned support of confederation with Canada into backing for his Liberal party. He and his colleagues thus became allied with Canada's most successful federal party. The opponents of confederation, in the main, thus became associated with the Progressive Conservative party.

In the 1930s, when the province was being administered by seven commissioners from Britain, Joey Smallwood first came into public view. At that time he had a nightly radio program titled "The Barrelman" (meaning the lookout on a sailing ship). For more than thirty years thereafter—during twenty-two of which he held the post of premier—Smallwood pressed the cause of his province. After talking Newfoundlanders into confederation with Canada, he sought from the various Canadian prime minis-

ters the finances with which to endow his province industrially and its people with better social services. In later
years he concentrated on encouragement of foreign investment for his province—successfully bringing in an oil
refinery, a shipyard, and a massive hydroelectric scheme.
He finally became too imperious, and his voters apparently tired of his "political chicanery." Yet he refused to
give up his premiership under a contested election
(1971–72) until forced to do so by court order. Smallwood
finally retired from Newfoundland and politics. Born in
1902, he has recently written his autobiography, titled *I
Chose Canada*. Of his book, he says that "Churchill would
be remembered by history because Churchill wrote it
himself; so too, with Smallwood and Newfoundland."

Frank Duff Moores, premier of Newfoundland, was born
in Carbonear, Newfoundland, in 1933. Educated at Saint
Andrews College, Aurora, Ontario, he worked in the
fisheries business for more than fifteen years before start-
ing his political career. During those years, he became an
authority on Canadian fishing and its related economic
problems.

In 1968, he was first elected to the House of Commons as
a Progressive Conservative representing the riding of
Bonavista-Trinity Conception. He won the leadership of
the Progressive Conservative party in Newfoundland in
1970 and was reelected to the House of Commons in 1971.
He became premier in January, 1972.

Frank Moores loves the solitude of his province and tries
to get away from the drives of his office into that solitude
for several weeks each year. He entered politics in the
belief that, given the long dominance of Joey Smallwood
over the political life of Newfoundland, that province
sorely needed new people and new ideas. He considers that
he and his party have a real obligation to improve the lot of
the Newfoundlanders. He is a disciple of the former
Progressive Conservative leader Robert Stanfield. Moores
believes that Newfoundland's problems remain economic
and ecological, some of these the result of Smallwood's

earlier mismanagement. He believes that under Small-wood's leadership, industrialization was overemphasized while the province's natural resources—especially timber and fishing—were neglected. He believes that tourism can be developed and marine resources expanded and that more employment can result from deurbanization.

Premier Moores belives that all the provinces of Canada have drawn too much inward, thus enlarging the problems of regionalism and the forces of separatism. He cites the Province of Quebec, with its separatist drives, as being the most obvious case in point. He considers that the very size of Canada aggravates this problem. He thinks that Canadians have concentrated much too long on being disunited rather than united. He insists that the economic policies of the Trudeau regime have not helped solve this situation. He believes that Canadian "identity" has yet to be crystallized—that Canadians must be more forceful—must be "themselves."

Newfoundland celebrated its twenty-fifth anniversary in the Canadian confederation in 1974 by promoting its tourist and business potential as the "last Canadian frontier." It is interesting to recall that the temporary, and later permanent, settlements along the Grand Banks fishing grounds were being established as much as a century before the other English settlements in Virginia, New England, and along the St. Lawrence.

Like the people of Quebec, the people of Newfoundland have kept a firm hold on their culture through mythology and language. They have clung to their aspirations through thick and thin—even in conflict with their environment and economy. Only with confederation in 1949 were these special situations of human history made partially Canadian and only partially bettered. Even today the atmosphere of Newfoundland remains something quite apart from the rest of Canada. By song and story, there has remained here the inscription of man's triumph over fearful odds. The Newfoundlanders bear their social upheaval and their continual fight against the elements with hurt but with dignity.

As a footnote to foregoing discussions of the Atlantic or Maritime Provinces—Newfoundland, Nova Scotia, New Brunswick, and Prince Edward Island—it should be noted that there has been recurring discussion of union of these into a single province. In 1968–70, an official governmental study was undertaken on this proposition, largely inspired by New Brunswick's then-Premier Robichaud. This study, half financed by three provinces, half by Ottawa, simply awakened distrust and further indecision on the matter. Though it made a half-hearted recommendation for union of three provinces—Nova Scotia, New Brunswick, and Prince Edward Island—that recommendation did not include Newfoundland. In fact, then-Premier Smallwood of Newfoundland wanted no part of any such union.

11

The Colonies of the North

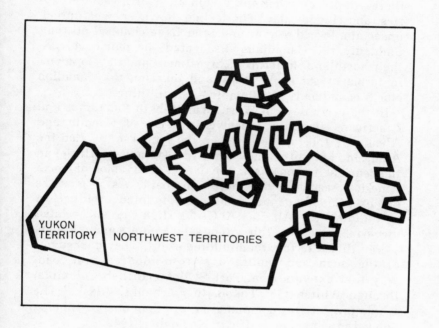

Canada's North has long been romanticized in song and story as well as on the silver and TV screens. Until recently, most Americans, even many Canadians, believed it inhabited only by gallant Canadian Mounties and beautiful Indian maidens; by trappers and Eskimos; by wolves, caribou, and polar bear; by ice and snow. It was, in essence, the epitome of the literary dreams of Robert Service and Jack London, and the screen story of

Nelson Eddy and Jeanette McDonald in Rose Marie.

A vague feeling has existed that the Far North was up there—in places called the Yukon, the Northwest Territories, and Hudson Bay. The feeling, however, was unreal, uncertain. World War II and after have changed all that. Suddenly the Canadians discovered—or rediscovered—their northland. In terms of investment and development, in terms of scholarly study and tourism, the Canadian North is suddenly fashionable—"the in thing."

In the early days of World War II, both Canadians and Americans feared a massive invasion of Canada and Alaska by the Japanese. When the Japanese invaded the Aleutian chain of islands early in 1942 and hostilities in the near Pacific increased, the danger of invasion of North America seemed even more imminent. As a massive defense, Canadians and Americans mounted a joint effort at building the Alaska (ALCAN) Highway and related airports. More than thirty thousand soldiers and civilians were utilized in this roadbuilding effort. They hacked out of the bush and tundra a sixteen-hundred-mile roadway that extends from Fort St. John, British Columbia, through Whitehorse, Yukon, to Fairbanks, Alaska. The whole project was completed in less than one year, being opened to vehicular traffic in November, 1942.

Just as the earlier gold seekers moved on from the Yukon, so too did the military construction workers and defenders. As the Japanese were dislodged from the Aleutian chain and the fears of invasion of North America receded, the scene of military-naval activity moved away into the far Pacific, to the Asian mainland, the Philippines, and eventually Japan itself. Once again the North of Canada became remote and quiet. Despite the fact that the area was more or less dormant for another decade, the changes that had been wrought by the war remained. The airfields and roads could now be used for civilian and governmental purposes. At last there were ways to get in and out of the Canadian North.

During the 1950s, there was yet another important

strategic development in the Canadian Far North. This involved installation of DEW (Distant Early Warning) Line of the North American Air Defense. This "electric fence" is a radar system set up across the Canadian northern reaches to provide advance warning against possible attack by missiles or aircraft from the Soviet Union. It remains in place today, maintained and manned jointly by the Canadian and United States military.

Only in the past decade, however, has there come about a fuller realization of the potential of these Northern territories. Recent worldwide shortages of minerals and forest products, of hydroelectric power and petroleum—all of which are plentiful in Canada's northern lands—have speeded Canada's own interest in its Arctic backyard. Development of these areas, overcoming barriers of cold and distance, has been hastened by available and new communications mechanisms—the airplane, radio, and even satellites. This physical wilderness, containing more than 40 percent of Canada's land mass, is no longer a psychological wilderness.

On December 8, 1953—a historic day for Canada—Prime Minister Louis St. Laurent established, through Parliament, a Department of Northern Affairs and Natural Resources. (In 1966, the name was changed to Department of Indian Affairs and Northern Development.) This act established a new governmental structure designed to colonize, administer, and develop Canada's northland—including the Yukon and the Northwest Territories. In creating this new department, St. Laurent aptly noted: "It has been said that Great Britain acquired her Empire in a state of absence of mind. Apparently we [Canadians] have administered these vast territories [the North] in an almost continual absence . . . of mind."

The "vast territories" of which the prime minister was speaking were those lands in Canada's Far North that remained after the provinces to the south had been carved out and confederated. The northlands cover a total of 1.5 million square miles and comprise two territories: the

Yukon in the far northwest and the so-called Northwest
Territories lying east of the Yukon. Both are north of the
60th parallel. In 1953, when Prime Minister St. Laurent,
took steps to reactivate them, the territories together had
only twenty-five thousand people. Today, the population
has more than doubled, to about sixty-five thousand, and
in addition there are a great number of transients—
businessmen, developers, technicians, civil servants, and
tourists. In general, the North is a region of high infant
mortality and of low longevity. The social welfare and
living conditions of the indigenous peoples still require
improvement. Neither its transport nor its industries nor
its infrastructure are yet adequate. Basically, living
conditions remain difficult.

In historic terms, it could probably be said that a
combination of church, state, and business held these
lands for Canada. The church was represented by Catholic
and various Protestant sects, notably the Anglicans, performing yeoman work among the Indians and Eskimos.
The state was represented by the Royal Canadian
Mounted Police, of which more is said later. Business was
first represented by the Hudson's Bay Company, its activities dating from 1690. In addition to the fur-trapping and
"general store" enterprises of this company, there followed the early Yukon gold miner and, later, prospectors
seeking not only gold, but zinc, iron, lead and now petroleum. To this day, however, there remains a question as to
just how rich a storehouse of natural resources this region
may be. While the vast deposits of oil-rich tar sands,
ordinary petroleum, and various other minerals are surely
there, it remains to be determined just how much input of
capital and manpower would be necessary to get those
riches out, and whether such enterprises would be
profitable.

At long last the Canadian North is being developed—in
some respects like the American West, though nearly a
century behind. Yet, in contrast to the expansion of the
American West, developments in the Canadian North

involve the opening of a "corporate frontier" rather than an individualistic one. It is not a land for cowboys and prospectors—but rather a land that can only be fully developed by massive infusions of capital, skilled manpower, and technology. Also necessary is a massive infusion of government funds for roads, schools, administrative and health services, and civil servants. Today almost ten thousand persons are employed in these Northern regions by the federal government alone. This represents nearly one-fifth of the total population. Some have characterized this grouping as "Ottawa in the bush."

Both regions—the Yukon and the Northwest Territories—remain the constitutional responsibility of the federal government. It has sometimes been contended that the attitude of the latter toward these areas is too "colonialist." Nonetheless there is an ongoing effort by Ottawa to slowly transfer authority both to the indigenous inhabitants and to the territorial administration. Answerable only to the Canadian cabinet and the Parliament of Canada, both territories derive most of their revenues from the federal government and are governed by appointed commissioners and elected councils. The governments of these regions may thus be said to be "representative" but not "responsible." Thus far the federal government refuses to consider provincial status for these northern lands.

Canada's northern territories are ordinarily considered as including the Yukon and the Northwest Territories. They range from the sixtieth parallel of latitude northward to a triangular apex near the North Pole. The western boundary of the Yukon lies along the Alaskan border. The eastern boundary of the Northwest Territories is determined by Baffin Bay, Davis Strait, and the shores of Greenland, which is still owned by Denmark. The southern boundaries of the two are determined by the various provinces from British Columbia to Manitoba, and by the shore of Hudson Bay. Islands in the bay are considered part of the Northwest Territories. The Yukon and the Northwest Territories will now be discussed separately.

THE YUKON

Yukon is a Chilcotin Indian word meaning "the great river" and referring to the Yukon River. One of the longest in North America, the Yukon has its source at the junction of the Lewes and Pelly rivers near Fort Selkirk. It flows northwest some two thousand miles, traversing Alaska and emptying into the Bering Sea. In 1895 the Yukon area was created as a separate district of the Northwest Territories, and in 1898 the Canadian Parliament made the Yukon into a separate territory. It was the gold seekers who went first into the Yukon and then into Alaska who had the most profound original European influence on the area. This region served as the eastern gateway to the Alaskan Klondike and here, in 1896, the gold rush of the Far North actually began. Dawson City sprang up overnight and within a year became the largest Canadian community west of Winnipeg. Fortunes were made and lost quickly here during the next three years, but as yet richer finds in Alaska were reported, the gold seekers moved on to the west. The region once again fell into the doldrums and, by 1910, the population of the entire Yukon was less than six thousand. In the years between then and now, the search for gold extended itself into searches for other minerals—silver, lead, uranium, and now petroleum. The Yukon Territory is a triangular mass of some 207,000 square miles bordering Alaska to the west and British Columbia to the south. Its eastern boundary fronts on the Northwest Territories, and its northern tip touches the Arctic Ocean along a 135-mile coastline. It is a land of spectacular scenery—of massive mountains, great plateaus, and fertile valleys. At least twenty of its mountains exceed 10,000 feet elevation. Mount Logan, located in the southwestern section, is the highest in Canada (19,850 feet). Climatically the region is dry and cold, though slightly more moderate in the winter than the Northwest Territories. There is a frost-free period of about ten weeks with long hours of summer-night sunshine. As a result, there is a surprisingly rapid growth of crops. Yet Yukon holds the record for the coldest temperature in Canada—eighty-one degrees below zero Fahrenheit (February, 1947) at the settlement of Snag.

The capital city, Whitehorse, named for nearby Whitehorse Rapids, had its beginnings in the gold rush. However, it was not incorporated as a city until 1952, and it now has a population of six thousand. It is located on the Yukon River some nine hundred miles southeast of Dawson City and some one hundred miles north of the B.C. border. It is at Milepost 917 on the Alaska Highway. Whitehorse is the eastern terminus of a 110-mile railway running westward into Skagway, Alaska, and the Pacific Coast. District headquarters of the Mounties, Whitehorse is the main commercial and distribution center for all the Yukon.

By ethnic origin, the twenty five thousand inhabitants of the Yukon are composed of British, 53 percent; Indians and Metis, 20 percent; Eskimos, 10 percent; French-Canadians, 7 percent; Scandinavians, 6 percent; others, 4 percent. Religious affiliations are unrecorded.

The territorial economy is based wholly on natural resources—originally gold and silver, but now including lead, zinc, copper, asbestos, and petroleum. The total production of minerals from the region in 1970 alone exceeded $80 million; copper, lead, zinc, and asbestos were the most important. Though there are some indigenous forests, the cutting and use of the timber is localized and not highly developed. Hydroelectric production is only in the early stages, but there is great potential. While the road system has been developed fairly well in the wake of the construction of the Alaska Highway (which traverses the southern Yukon), travel mainly continues to be by airline and air charter.

The Yukon has one parliamentary representative in the House of Commons and one senator. The seat of the Yukon's territorial government is at Whitehorse. That government is headed by a commissioner appointed by the federal government at Ottawa. He is aided by a legislative council composed of fifteen elected members. (Further increases in the council's membership will be tied to the territory's increase in population.) The council, however, has no power over money bills, internal security, or major developments of natural resources. Thus, deriving most of its revenues from Ottawa, the Yukon remains the direct responsibility of the federal government.

THE NORTHWEST TERRITORIES

The Northwest Territories, having an area of 1.3 million square miles and a population of forty thousand, comprises over one-third of Canada. It covers as well the Arctic archipelago, which includes the great islands of Baffin, Victoria, and Ellesmere. The southern limits represent the extreme northern reaches of ordinary tree growth. Above this band of forests is the treeless tundra and muskeg, a region studded with immense lakes and a few great rivers, such as the Mackenzie. Almost all the continental mass of these territories is within the permafrost area, and, in the northern reaches, only two or three weeks during July may be frost free. In the lower reaches of the region, such as the area near the settlement of Yellowknife, the frost-free period may be somewhat longer, though seldom exceeding ten weeks.

The name Northwest Territories originated in the phrase "Rupert's Land and the North West Territory." The area had been a major part of the Rupert's Land charter granted by King Charles to the Hudson's Bay Company. (History of the region is detailed in earlier chapters of this book and indelibly inscribed in the exploits of Arctic adventurers ranging from Henry Hudson to Robert Peary, Richard Byrd, Roald Amundsen.) From this original vast royal grant were carved the Prairie Provinces (Manitoba, Saskatchewan, and Alberta) as well as large portions of Ontario and Quebec. The present boundaries of the Northwest Territories, only established in 1912, are as follows: On the western side, bounding Yukon; on the southern side, touching British Columbia, Alberta, Saskatchewan, Manitoba, and Hudson Bay and including the islands in that bay. On the eastern side, it reaches as far as Greenland waters, and it stretches north to eighty-three degrees latitude and the Arctic Ocean. The North Magnetic Pole, well known to all navigators, lies within this region at seventy-three degrees, thirty-five minutes north latitude and ninety-two degrees, twenty minutes longitude.

There is, of course, no question of Canada's ownership of the Arctic lands and islands. The problem, rather, is one of sovereignty in the waters and beneath the floating islands of ice. This question has been raised by recent conferences on the law of the sea as well as by environmental problems associated with development of the new Arctic oil and gas fields. The delicacy of the Arctic ecology and its future protection pose troubling long-range problems for Canada.

No consideration of these northern territories can be made without some reference to the important animal and bird life. There are the moose, the grizzly and polar bear, the mountain sheep, the white fox, the seal, the walrus, the whale, the wolf, and the Arctic hare. One of the oddest is the narwhal, a member of the porpoise family, which sports a single tusk. This may have been the animal that aroused stories of the fabled unicorn among European explorers. There is also a great variety of bird life, and this is the summer home of the Canadian geese. Most important of all fauna of the region, however, is the caribou, a cousin of the reindeer, which serves as the source of staple food, clothing, shelter, tools, and weapons for the nomads of the North. These caribou, ranging widely over all the northern territories, were at one time said to have numbered more than 2 million head. Today, however, they are down to no more than 350,000. Under intense conservation efforts, the Canadian government is now trying to increase the caribou supply as an adjunct to Eskimo and indigenous Indian diets.

The capital and metropolis of the Northwest Territories is Yellowknife, originally a gold-mining town established in 1934. It numbers some six thousand inhabitants and is located on the northern shores of Great Slave Lake. It is connected by road with Edmonton, some nine hundred fifty miles to the south. Yellowknife itself lies less than three hundred miles south of the Arctic Circle and thus shares the splendors of the "Midnight Sun."

Most northerly of all Canadian settlements—indeed of all the world's settlements—is that on Ellesmere Island. It is only five hundred miles from the North Pole. Here is located a joint Canadian-American weather station (and radar "alert"). Here live some two hundred men of both nationalities.

The settlement of Resolute, on Cornwallis Island, is considered an important center of Canadian Arctic life. Here is located a group of some five hundred persons who handle distribution of freight, mail, and personnel for the Arctic. This town is located some eighteen hundred miles north of Ottawa.

Another important Arctic center is Frobisher, on southern Baffin Island. This settlement is composed of about two thousand whites and Eskimos. It is being utilized as a "laboratory" for study of transference of the Eskimo from indigenous habitat to the modern industralized world. The town is built with careful planning, even to connecting dwellings with business concerns via covered and heated walkways.

Another major center of activity in the Northwest Territories is the port of Inuvik. This town of some three thousand is located near the mouth of the Mackenzie River.

The population of the Northwest Territories is estimated (1975) at forty thousand. This figure includes about twelve thousand Eskimos, eight thousand Amerindians and some twenty thousand whites and Metis. A breakdown of religious affiliations for these groups is not available.

The economy of the territories is dependent, in the main, on minerals. Today, mining represents 85 percent of the area's gross domestic production. Lead, zinc, gold, silver, copper, and petroleum are the most important minerals produced. Forestry, tourism, hunting, fishing, and the fur trade also produce considerable income.

While major oil finds have already been made at the mouth of the Mackenzie River, it is believed that there are even greater finds yet to come from the Arctic islands. The major problem, however, is to find economic ways of moving the Arctic oil and gas to industrial centers, Canadian and American, without destroying the environment or upsetting "native" land claims. Movement of the oil by tanker has not yet proved possible, because of ice and danger of spills. Shipments by pipeline are nearly prohibitive in cost and ecologically troublesome. Despite these difficulties, it is planned eventually to build a major oil and gas pipeline down the valley of the Mackenzie River, this to connect with existing pipelines to the eastern and midwestern United States and eastern Canada. (See Chapter 13.)

Like the Yukon, the Northwest Territories has one senator, but two parliamentary representatives in the House of Commons. The Northwest Territories also has a council composed of twenty elected members. This council is presided over by a commissioner appointed from Ottawa. Like that of the Yukon, this government is considered "representative" but not "responsible." The federal government retains control over all major operations such as taxes, security, appropriations, and development of natural resources. In spite of such continuing political colonialism, however, here in the Far North the Cambrian Age is learning to live with the Atomic Age. As one writer puts it, the Canadians may never learn to live in the Far North, but they are learning to live with it.

12

The Eskimo and the Indian

A s noted in pages just past, the Canadian government chooses to consider the problems of the northern territories and those of the aboriginal peoples, Eskimos and Indians, in tandem. Ever associated with the history and culture of the Canadian Northlands have been those twin lords of yesteryear. The skills of these peoples in living with their environment and the lessons they taught their European conquerors in the ways of nature have been briefly described in earlier, historical pages of this book. However, so important have been the contributions of these colorful peoples to present-day Canada, and especially the Far North, that it is imperative we spend more time with them. These are Canadians, too!

Thousands of years before the Europeans reached and resettled North America, the various regions of Canada were peopled by two types of aborigines—the various tribes we know today. It also created the group inhabiting the far northern shores of the Arctic Ocean and the dates, it now seems evident that Canada was subject to two or more separate waves of invasion from Siberia and other parts of the Asian mainland. The first of these may have begun as long ago as fifteen thousand years, continuing over many aeons until about two thousand years ago. These nomadic peoples swept from Asia across the Bering Strait into Alaska, Canada, and other parts of North and

Central America. This movement brought about the formation and settlement of various North American Indian tribes we know today. It also created the group inhabiting the far nothern shores of the Arctic Ocean and the adjacent Arctic islands. There, people became known as Eskimos.

THE ESKIMO

The term *Eskimo* apparently originated in the 1600s when the eastern Canadian-American tribe of Algonquins found themselves at odds over territorial claims with these more northerly people. The Algonquins, who cooked their meat, are said to have given to this enemy the derisive name *Eskimo* "eaters of raw meat." This name was subsequently adopted by French and English settlers, later becoming both an official and an unofficial appellation.

The name that Eskimos have given themselves, however, is *inuit*. This means "several people" or, in broader translation, "mankind" or "humanity"—similar in some respects to the term the Navajo Indians apply to themselves, meaning "the people." The Eskimos have a special group of words for their own. The word *inuk*, for example, means "one Eskimo," but the word *kabloona* means "one white man." As *inuit* denotes the Eskimo people, the word *gablunaag* denotes white people.

These Eskimo are people of short, stocky stature, yellowish brown complexion, with prominent cheekbones and Oriental eyes. They may well be a mixture of races. Both physical and cultural characteristics would seem to support the theory of a mixture of racial strains.

Today, the Eskimos are mainly settled in a great arc paralleling, but north of, the Arctic Circle. Their number worldwide is estimated at more than eighty thousand. There are in Canada some eighteen thousand; in Greenland, about twenty five thousand; in Alaska, thirty three thousand; and in Siberia, some four thousand. Of those Eskimos living in Canada, some three thousand reside in northern Quebec; one thousand in Labrador; four hundred in northern Manitoba; a few hundred in the Yukon; and over eleven thousand in the Northwest Territories. The remainder are dispersed through the other provinces. Most of these reside in small, clannish settlements ranging from a few families in camps to villages of two or three hundred inhabitants. There are two large settlements of note, however. One is at Frobisher Bay on Baffin Island, where twelve hundred Eskimos reside. The other is the town of Inuvik, near the mouth of the Mackenzie River on the Arctic Ocean.

These are people whose Canadian habitat has been, till now, the Arctic coastline and the islands of the Far North. As nomads in that desolate and harsh land, the Eskimos had depended wholly on hunting and fishing for their existence. For that livelihood, they hunted caribou, small Arctic animals, and wildfowl. In fishing they sought the seal, the walrus, and the whale. The hunter with the harpoon is now the hunter with the rifle. From their favored caribou they managed to secure skins for clothing, for shelter, and for bedding. From the caribou, the whale, and the walrus, they found their food and fuel. They first depended for transport on their sleds and huskie dog teams, and their walrus and sealskin boats, the umiak and kayak. Today, as well, they have learned to use the snowmobile and the airplane. For their housing, the early Eskimos used skin wigwams or made domed huts from blocks of snow and ice, these the well-known igloos. Today, however, that sort of housing is almost anachronistic. More likely, Eskimos may live in a simple wooden-framed house or in prefab buildings maintained by their corporate or government employers.

Today, as with his Indian cousins, the Eskimo is hard put to maintain even a semblance of his earlier culture. Here, too, diseases and other ravages of the European intrusions have done their work. Yet, unlike the other aborigines of Canada, many Eskimos have more easily made the transition. While remaining in the Arctic, they have found it possible to adapt their ways to the new type of economy, education, and white culture. Yet, in some ways, they have been able to retain their own culture and their own way of life.

Eskimos are now engaged in commercial fishing, in boatbuilding, in logging, and construction. They are developing mechanical skills and are now employed in mines, factories, and machine shops. Many Eskimos have found employment in governmental activities ranging from RCMP constabulary to nursing.

There are a number of Eskimo cooperatives associated with creating and selling Eskimo art and crafts. Products of their arts—sculptures in soapstone ivory and whalebone; etchings, drawings and stone-cut prints—are world famous. Today, this arts production is valued in millions of dollars annually.

Prior to World War II, less than 15 percent of the Eskimo children of Canada attended school. Few of these passed beyond the sixth grade. Today it is estimated that 90 percent of all Eskimo children receive an eighth-grade education, and a few are going on through a university. There is also considerable emphasis now being given to vocational training for the Eskimos.

Since Canada's confederation, the Eskimos, like the Indians, have generally been wards of the central government. Only in 1960 were they given the franchise, but in the northern territories, this is still a qualified vote since those regions, unlike provinces, have only partial internal self-government. In 1969, the territorial council of the Northwest Territories gained its first Eskimo member.

The Eskimos receive the usual social service, family welfare and unemployment grants accorded to other Canadian citizens. Today, however, the Eskimos are becoming more militant politically, associating directly with the Canadian Indian tribal groups. Together they are seeking from federal and provincial governments a redefinition and repossession of indigenous tribal rights and lands. In effect, they are seeking to resuscitate their own cultures. In fact, the Eskimos have formed a citizens' organization of their own—*Inuit Tapirisat*—the national organization representing all of Canada's Arctic inhabitants. This group is even seeking official sanction for elimination of the word *Eskimo* and its replacement by the more favored word *inuit*. It also seeks, with little hope, a separate Eskimo province in the Far North.

The Eskimo language appears unrelated to any other world linguistic group. It appears to be a composite of several dialects (including Alaskan Aleut), and its grammar is complicated. Many words can be modified by adding suffixes. For example, *tuktoo* means "a caribou." *Tuktoojuak* means "a big caribou." The language seems to make little distinction between nouns and verbs, but rather is built upon the phrase "to be." It seems to flow out of actions. For example, the Eskimo has many words for snow, each denoting fine distinctions thereof and each denoting actions that the snow precipitates—falling, sledding, igloo-building, blowing, freezing. It is a conglomerate of thoughts that are living—not a tidy, dead syntax. Another example: "the house is yellow" would be in Eskimo "the house is bright (like the midnight sun)"; "the house is red" is "the house is looking like blood."

The Eskimo is not governed by the eye alone. When looking at a picture, the Eskimo will not necessarily look at it right side up, but just as likely from the side or upside down. He is not governed by ordinary concepts but keeps his concepts lively. Thus he is not bound by our own rigid ideas of vertical and horizontal rules and enclosed space. He is also apparently unused to straight lines. He disregards such determinants and, instead, opens himself and his imagination to space much more than does the rigidly acculturated European. He regards space as movable in visual terms, not static. His carvings show this so well.

One interesting illustration of this idea is that often the Eskimo sculpture is made with no base. A carved seal, for example, is not destined to stand still. It was not intended to be set in a single place, but rather to be handled, turned, and rolled about without constriction. Thus it is that carvings are not considered things but rather actions, like songs. A piece of ivory deftly and beautifully carved from a whale's tooth is thus sung—and thus released. And the words of the Eskimo are like the knife of the carver—they free the idea—releasing form and bringing it into open consciousness. Even the word for poetry is associated with the word for "to breathe." Thus poetry and song and art, including sculpture, all come from the individual, the personalized depths. Their history is oral, recorded for their folklore in song, poetry, and dance combined. These individualized song-stories belong to the composer alone and may only be enacted by him or with his permission.

The following bits of poetry quoted from the reputable book on Canadian life, *A Guide to Canada the Peaceable Kingdom*, exemplify the Eskimo's identification with actions of nature:

> *The great sea has set me adrift*
> *it moves me*
> *earth and the great weather move*
> *they have carried me away*
> *and moved me inwardly with joy.*
>
> *And yet there is only one great thing,*
> *the only thing to live,*
> *to see in huts and our dreams,*
> *the great day that dawns and the light fills the world.*

Governed by the monotony of ice and cold, the long winter nights and long summer days, the Eskimo learns to think in this fashion—satisfied with the actions and flow of nature in harmony with humans. He concentrates on the essentials of existence, merging these with nature—scenery, climate, and all. He concentrates on his main needs. He inculcates into each action—whether story, song, or art creation—a philosophy that recognizes man as the actionable receptacle through which life's forces flow.

The Eskimo's philosophy of life is reportedly summed up in a single word, *ajornarmat*, which means "that's life" or *c'est la vie.* It incorporates a fatalism, studied equanimity, composure, and ability to bear the vicissitudes of life without flinching.

The Eskimos are generally introverted, deeply emotional but not outwardly so. Devotees of the harsh life of their environment, they are people of great courage. Against their enemies, the Eskimos are addicted to scorn and the use of mockery. In turn, they dislike mockery and insist on saving face. Their social life is governed by a broad series of taboos. The *angakkoq*—"shaman"—is believed to be the only person possessed of those supernatural powers that can overcome such taboos and restore good fortune.

Today the Eskimo is turning faster and faster toward the white man's culture. The picture of the happy hunter, clad in fur parka and riding behind his faithful dog team toward his igloo, is almost dead. That way of life has now nearly vanished—but, given the new accent on environment and how to live with nature, that is a tragic loss.

THE INDIAN

The number of "status" or "registered" North American Indians in Canada today approximates three hundred thousand. Of these some hundred and forty-five thousand live on more than two thousand reserves covering more than 6 million acres. The remaining hundred thousand not in reserves are either urbanized or live on small farms in white communities. Most of the Indians are concentrated in a few provinces. Quebec has some twenty-five thousand; Ontario, fifty-two thousand. Some thirty-two thousand live in Manitoba, and Saskatchewan has about the same number. Alberta is the home of twenty-six thousand and British Columbia has forty-five thousand. The Northwest Territories contains some twenty-five hundred and the Yukon, six thousand. Newfoundland, which has about ten thousand Indians, controls its own Indian affairs. (In the other provinces, the Indians are wards of the federal government.)

The *Metis* (from the French word *miscere*, meaning "to

mix") represent a separate facet of any study of Canada's Indians. Numbering some three-quarters of a million today, these European and Indian half-castes are not resident on reservations but are generally urbanized. Nor are they under jurisdiction of existing Indian treaties and related federal-provincial legislation covering the full-blooded Indians. Most of the *Metis* are concentrated in Saskatchewan, Manitoba, Alberta, and British Columbia.

As every schoolchild will recall, the name *Indian* was (inaccurately) applied to the inhabitants of the New World by Columbus, who assumed that he had reached India. These first inhabitants of the New World, like their cousins, the Eskimo, are believed to have come from Asia, crossing the Bering Strait in several waves of migration that originated from two thousand to fifteen thousand years ago. Some of these settled in what is present-day Canada; others went eastward to the Atlantic shores or southward into the American plains, Mexico, and Central America. Probably the heaviest concentration of Canadian Indians settled along the St. Lawrence River and along the British Columbia coastline.

Virtually all the Indians were great hunters and trappers. Many were skilled fishermen. They lived on the available fish, fowl, and land animals; using wood for their huts and wigwams; using skins for clothing, shelter, for tools and weapons. They invented the snowshoe as well as the fabulous birchbark canoe and cedar dugout. They lived for intertribal warfare and for the prestige attendant upon their bravery and strength of arms. Some contended with the Eskimo for the prized caribou; others contested with neighboring tribes for the buffalo. Only a few of the Indian tribes took to farming, these raising corn, beans, gourds, and tobacco. One of their most important food staples was pemmican. This was dried meat, pounded and mixed with fat and berries, then stored in skin bags for future use.

One of the most important sources of food and clothing was the buffalo of the plains; these were easily hunted and soon almost exterminated after the arrival of the white man and the advent of the horse. Those fleet-footed animals were an import of the Spanish conquistadores who brought them into Mexico and California in the sixteenth century. Eventually the horse appeared on America's Great Plains and in Canada.

The lives of these Indian tribes were partially nomadic, partially settled, but always hard. The uneasiness and occasional violence of Indian life were enhanced by the increased pressures accompanying the coming of the white—explorers, trappers, missionaries, and settlers. These newcomers introduced startling commercial ideas of barter and money. They took over the hunting and fishing lands for their agricultural pursuits. They introduced new gods. As well, they introduced new dangers to the tranquility of the Indian life—whisky, firearms, and disease. (Before the coming of the white man, the Indians had never known smallpox, influenza, or venereal diseases.) All these factors provided new dangers to the Indian and his environment. The Indians had taught the European newcomers all they had known of their land and their environment. In payment, the Indians were enslaved, almost destroyed, by the civilization of the newcomers. That incoming white man's culture had robbed the Indian of his caste and codes—stripped him of his self-assurance and his dignity. Even the most devoted of the Christian missionaries incoming could not substitute a real new world for that old and self-contained world of the Indian. That had been destroyed.

Apart from the Eskimos (Indians of the Arctic), the Canadian Indians were classified in five main groups: (1) the Pacific Coast Indians, such as the Haida, Nootka, Salishan, and Kootenayan; (2) the mountain and plains Indians, such as the Cree, Ojibway, Blackfoot, Assiniboine, and Sioux; (3) the Indians of the Great Lakes and the St. Lawrence valley, such as the Algonquin (also known as the Algonkian), Iroquois, Huron, and Mohawk; (4) the Micmac and Montagnais of the Maritimes and Quebec; and (5) the Athabaskan Indians, those tribes of the great northern forests and tundra.

Each of these tribes devised a particular way of life. The Pacific Coast Indians lived on berries, roots, fish, and game. They were great fishermen and lived in boxlike huts carved from wooden planks. These tribes developed the totem pole, a form of family and tribal veneration, carved from giant trees. They were also specialists in stonework, metal work, and basketry. They developed a unique and sophisticated system of tribal government.

The plains Indians, especially the Blackfoot and Cree, were heavily dependent on the buffalo for their subsistence—food and clothing. They were devotees of basketry and beadwork, featherwork and pottery. The Cree were also involved in quillwork, in the highly efficient use of skins, and in the making of boxes and containers.

The Algonquin and Athabaskan were great hunters and fishermen, using so effectively their birchbark canoes. Both these and the plains Indians lived in wigwams. The Algonquin, however, also devised the longhouses of timber as dormitory-type residences for many families. The Algonquin were involved in basketmaking, stonework, weaving, and woodwork.

The Hurons were members of the famous six-nation group of the Iroquois Confederation, but, at times, were also enemies of the Iroquois. The Hurons were also important allies of France during the early years of that nation's colonization of the St. Lawrence region. The Hurons were skilled in bonework, pottery, and quillwork. They were also the great middlemen in the beaver pelt business.

The Micmac of the Maritimes and related tribes were specialists in beadwork, bonework, and woodwork. They were also experts in making canoes of the regular birchbark variety. Another Atlantic Coast tribe, now almost extinct, the Beothuk, close relatives of the Eskimo, built a unique high-prowed and high-sterned canoe.

When the Europeans arrived in Canada, they found the Indians in total control of that environment. Ever since 1500 A.D., there has been erosion of the Indian position. Over the following four and a half centuries, the Indians thus moved from an autonomous position to one where all facets of their lives have been either seriously affected or utterly destroyed. In all elements of their own habitat, they have suffered loss of control of their own affairs. Their entire survival as "Indians" has been so harmed that it became necessary for them to make their culture, their religion, their traditions survive only within the bounds of the family—almost "Underground."

As the new settlers took over aboriginal hunting and fishing grounds and turned them into white-owned farms, the Indians became excess to the national life. They were no longer needed as pathfinders for the explorers, as allies in the wars that beset North America in the seventeenth, eighteenth, and nineteenth centuries. Indian affairs were then made totally subservient to the interests of the whites. The Indians were forced into reserves and became foreigners in the lands of which they were formerly liege lords.

Land has ever been of prime importance to the Indians. This was as true of the aboriginal peoples in Canada as elsewhere. Most Canadian Indian lands were lost by treaty and much of the remainder was given up by forced sale. Government reservations were created for the Indians in areas not desired by the whites. (The Indians of the northern territories, like the Eskimos, do not have land set aside for them.) For the Indians, even today, the traditional hunger for land—and for rights to fish and hunt—still lingers. In many areas of Canada in recent years, there has been a resurgence in the demands of the Indians for recovery of their original fiefdoms. As a result, lawsuits and protests, organized and unorganized, have been mounted by Indians from British Columbia to the Maritimes.

The question of land for the Indians is extremely complicated. There are two groups of Indians involved. The first of these is the group that has signed treaties. There are also the nontreaty Indians, these mainly in British Columbia, the Yukon, the Northwest Territories, and northern

Quebec. The Canadian government apparently accepts that treaty commitments should be lived up to, but it will not renegotiate these treaties. The contrasting Indian Brotherhood position, however, is that, if the Indians are not satisfied with these treaties, they must be renegotiated. The government appears to be agreeable to dealing with claims of Indians on the basis of a 1763 British royal proclamation—but that does not apply to nontreaty Indians. However, the Canadian courts seem inclined to contest this view. A recent judicial decision holds that the 1763 proclamation did apply to British Columbia, since it was a British statute and therefore applied to all territory later ceded to the crown. That proclamation stated that tribes with whom the crown had not signed treaties should not be disturbed in the possession of traditional hunting lands or lands traditionally used by the Indians for other purposes. Carried to the extreme, this would mean that the Indian tribes living therein would have a valid claim to most of all of British Columbia.

It can thus be seen that there has been a resurgence of chauvinistic Indian aspirations in Canada. This drive has been sparked in part by a growing Indian population; in part by worldwide attention to nationalism; in part by the civil rights drive; in part by libertarian themes favoring minorities. The urbanization of many Indians and their resultant academic and technical education have also begotten new and more vital leadership within the Indian community. Once again the Canadian Indians seek to regain control of their own lives and lands.

Much of this new energy stems from Indian determination to revive their own culture. Rather than undergo total assimilation by the white-supremacy society, Indian leaders seek to fit their own culture into the Canadian racial and ethnic "mosaic." As some young Indian leaders characterize it, they wish to become a part of the mainstream of Canadian society without losing their own identity. They do not wish to turn back the clock— they wish only to survive as Indians.

Full Indian control of the various departments of Indian affairs, national and provincial, has been suggested as one means of accomplishing these Indian aims. More public knowledge and white understanding is also required. The Indians wish it widely broadcast that they plan to regain control of their own political, economic, and social affairs; their own education, traditions, and mores. Today, however, there seems to be a breakdown between Indian peoples and the leaders of the white bureaucracies of Canada, national, provincial, and local. The Indians seem to be fully aware of the issues; only a few of the whites may fully comprehend them. The imperative, however, is now to discuss and resolve these issues intelligently. The Indians expect solutions—not merely a rehash of their problems. These they already know. Some of the white leaders seem willing to undertake discussions, but they are often reluctant to put forward solutions, especially if these solutions fly in the face of the white world. In talking about the Indian problems, some aboriginal leaders claim, the whites speak only in divisive terms—either up or down. The Indians, instead, speak of things as a whole— all facets of a problem as one. In the case of housing programs for Indians, for example, there are related problems of construction, of water, of sewage, of costs, even employment. Full and proper resolution of these housing problems for the Indians naturally means siphoning away of money and manpower from white needs which, presumably, may have higher priority. The whites' solutions for Indian problems, thus, may be only half-hearted and incomplete.

There has, for example, been great pressure from white-ruled governments, especially the provinces, to force the Indians to sell their tribal lands. The James Bay hydroelectric development, eight hundred miles north of Montreal in northern Quebec, is a case in point. This project destroyed traditional Indian hunting lands and diverted or damaged Indian fishing streams. Its aim is massive waterpower production and associated industrial and mining development. Here the Indians recently sold off the greater part of their birthright and were relegated to a much smaller reserve. In general, however, the response of many Indians has been rejection of offers to buy their lands on grounds that this would violate the basic rights of the Indian people and eventually would be nothing less than racial genocide. The National Indian Brotherhood is now in the process of researching these Indian rights and the means whereby they can best be protected.

It should be realized that the full-blooded Indian, protected by treaty, who lives on his reserves, has some defense of his own community life. Governmental efforts to translate the way of life of these Indians from quasi-nomadic cultures into the semi-urbanized or farm tenant situation simply loosen close-knit family ties and social defenses. Indian leaders contend it is essential, as well, to cut down the death rate of preschool Indian children, which is now eight times that of white children. It is essential to raise the life expectancy of all Indians. This is now only thirty-six years—a figure close to half that of white longevity in Canada. Eighty percent of Canadian Indians have substandard housing. Only 60 percent of Indian children ever attain to grade eight, though 95 percent of white children surpass that scholastic level.

The family is the essential Indian unit; more leisure, more money, and more breaching of their own social order can only compound their problems. Education, technical training, and truly effective social welfare programs are their first essentials. Whites' misunderstanding of Indians' needs is the root of the trouble. To students of American history, this story of the Canadian Indians provides a sad parallel. There are similar stories to be told in South Dakota and in British Columbia, in the state of Washington and in Quebec, in Maine and in Manitoba. In Canada, as in the United States, the future of the Indians, given the pressures of history, can only be fraught with difficulty and despair.

13

The Economy

Pages foregoing have described in some detail those facets of Canada's story that have materially influenced that nation's economy and brought it such riches. There were the intrusions of the immigrants upon the prairie lands formerly ruled by Indians and their buffalo herds. Those prairies today supply the granaries of the world. There were the intrusions of the geologist and the miner into the uninhabited, even uncharted, regions of the Northlands. From those exploits have come some of the world's most precious minerals—including petroleum—for the treasure chest of this kingdom of Canada and for the coffers of other nations. There have been the loggers, the lumbermen, the timber tycoons who have brought forth from Canada's great forests much of the world's plywood, pulp, and paper. There are the fishermen who have found on the Grand Banks of the eastern shores and in the salmon runs of the west coast their own kinds of riches. There are the men and women of commerce and industry who have brought Canada into its prime position as a resource country and as a leading world trader. They have made their land into America's best customer and in turn America's foremost supplier. All these, and more, are responsible for making Canada into one of the most highly developed and diverse and richest among all the nations of the earth.

It will be recalled that Canada is the second largest nation of the world in terms of land area, coming only after the Soviet Union. Inhabiting the Canadian land mass, however, are less than 24 million persons, thus ranking it only twenty-sixth in population among all nations of the world.

Canada is extraordinarily rich in natural resources, both in diversity and in volume. Many of those resources are still untapped, and their extent is still relatively unknown or only partially measured. Canada, along with the Soviet Union, is one of the two industrialized nations on earth that can fully meet their own energy needs in terms of petroleum, natural gas, uranium, water, and coal. As a result of this abundance of riches, Canada today ranks ninth among the economic powers of the world. Furthermore, the country ranks sixth in the world in terms of foreign trade, coming only after the United States, West Germany, Japan, the United Kingdom, and France. Canada is also one of the world's prime timber producers and manufactures 40 percent of the world's newsprint. With a gross national product of $214 billion (1977) and a federal budget above $44 billion, average family income now exceeds $16,250 yearly, and the per capita income is $8,410.

Mining, including petroleum production, ranks second only to agriculture among Canada's resource industries in net value of output. The country produces more than sixty commercially exploitable minerals. She is the world's largest producer of asbestos, zinc, silver, nickel. She ranks second worldwide in production of potash, gypsum, molybdenum, and sulfur. She ranks among the leading producers of uranium, titanium, aluminum, cobalt, gold, lead, platinum, copper, iron ore, and coal. The value of annual production of minerals (excluding petroleum) in Canada exceeds $11.6 billion, with more than sixty thousand workers employed in that area. The United States is increasingly dependent on Canada for necessary supplies of nickel, iron ore, lead, zinc, silver, gold, and platinum. While Canada seeks expansion of her minerals production and diversification of her markets, she also seeks an increase in the domestic processing of her minerals. Most important of all is her firm determination that Canada's own minerals needs be met first.

Today, crude petroleum ranks as the largest single item in Canada's extensive minerals output. The country's annual production of crude oil is estimated at 1.2 billion barrels, with an annual value approaching $4.9 billion in 1977. Proven reserves of petroleum have been estimated at 9 billion barrels. It is expected that the recently discovered Arctic reserves, plus petroleum extractable from Athabaska tar sands in Alberta (see Chapter 8) may be in excess of 500 billion barrels of oil. Canada today ranks twelfth in the world in oil production and twelfth in terms of her known reserves. She has more than forty refineries in operation. Recent exploration developments are expected to triple oil supplies. Sixty percent of oil operations are American owned. Canada's petroleum exports to the United States have been about eight hundred thousand barrels daily, but, as Canada's own needs have increased, these exports are being swiftly scaled down. On November 20, 1975, Energy Minister Alastair Gillespie announced that all oil exports are expected to end in 1981, two years earlier than forecast in a National Energy Board report.

Canada's production of natural gas is estimated at 2.5 trillion cubic feet yearly. Her reserves of natural gas are reckoned at 65 trillion cubic feet. The value of natural gas production in 1977 was $3.4 billion. This figure is likely to rise sharply in coming years, however, as Canada is in process of imposing sharp price increases step by step on all natural gas exported to the United States. At present, Canada sells a trillion cubic feet of natural gas to the United States annually. This amounts to 40 percent of all her production.

It is clear from the foregoing statistics that the United States has been heavily dependent on Canada for much of her petroleum and natural gas imports. At present Canada is supplying some 6 percent of U.S. crude oil demands plus some 4 percent of American natural gas needs. Unfortunately, these exports to the United States are on a swift downward spiral as Canada first satisfies her own vital needs.

One of the world's longest pipeline systems (2,023 miles) moves more than six hundred thousand barrels of crude daily from Edmonton, Alberta, to Port Credit, Ontario. There are, as well, other major pipelines in Canada: from Edmonton to Vancouver; from Taylor to Kamloops, B.C.; from Sarnia to Toronto; and from Montreal to Ottawa.

Another important petroleum line that operates in the reverse direction takes crude oil from Portland, Maine, to Montreal. This pipeline carries oil produced in the Caribbean and Venezuela and shipped to Portland. This is a price-saving offset for Canadian supplies to the American West. Thereby Canada makes up for roughly the same amounts of oil that she exports to the American West Coast. Thus Canada avoids the necessity of transporting her Western petroleum long distances to her Eastern cities either via the Panama Canal by tanker or via transcontinental train, truck, or alternate pipeline. It is assumed that pipelines now in planning stages will alleviate this offsetting process.

The growth of natural gas lines for gathering and transmission has been swift. The most important of these now carry natural gas from Canadian fields to the American West Coast, to the American Midwest, and Canada's East. There are about seventy-five hundred miles of such gathering and transmission lines. The longest of these stretches some twenty-three hundred miles from Alberta to Montreal, with branch lines delivering gas to United States markets. A thirteen-hundred-mile line carries Alberta gas to markets in California. An eight-hundred-mile line delivers gas from the Peace River district of British Columbia to Vancouver; Seattle, Washington; Portland, Oregon, and adjacent cities.

Today Alberta produces about 85 percent of all Canada's gas and oil. British Columbia produces about 10 percent. Provinces of Saskatchewan and Ontario, and the North west Territories produce the remainder. Several dozen exploration companies are searching for additional supplies in Western Canada, in the Arctic, and offshore along both Atlantic and Pacific coasts.

As has been true with the finds in Alaska, a major problem remains, the question of the best means of transporting oil and gas out of the Canadian Far North at effective price levels and without major harm to the environment. There has been some consideration and effort to move such finds by ship tanker. Because of the problems of ecology, of ice floes, and of the shortness of the summer season in the North, this idea has thus far been largely discounted. There is now intense consideration of associating natural gas finds in the Canadian North with those in the Alaskan Prudhoe Bay region. This would involve building a gas line from Prudhoe Bay southeastward through the Yukon and Northwest territories. This combined effort would proceed down the Mackenzie Valley through Alberta to Calgary, then east and west as demand dictated. (This proposal was based upon the abandonment of the idea that a gas pipeline would be built to parallel the present Alaskan petroleum pipeline route from Prudhoe Bay to Valdez.) About half the projected flow (4.5 billion cubic feet daily) from this combined effort would be from Alaskan fields, the rest from Canada's Mackenzie Delta. Midwesterners considered this longer Mackenzie Valley project more advantageous.

A three-year study for Ottawa conducted by British Columbia's Supreme Court Justice Thomas Berger concluded that no gas line should be built across the northern Yukon connecting Alaskan oil fields with the Mackenzie Valley project. He favored a route which would follow the Alcan Highway (described in paragraph following). Berger's conclusions were based on major environmental concerns and the need first to settle existing land claims of some three thousand Indians and Inuits.

This Alaska Highway Route proposal has been less well developed than the others, thus taking more time for engineering studies. However, construction time would be shorter and transportation costs less. This plan would bring Alaskan natural gas directly through the Yukon, British Columbia, and Alberta along the Alcan Highway. Then at Calgary (the same as the Mackenzie Valley route),

one leg of the pipeline would serve the western part of the
United States, running through central Oregon and ending
in California; the other leg of the pipeline would carry
natural gas as far east as Chicago. Scheduled for completion in about 1983, the pipeline would be expected to carry
up to 2.6 billion cubic feet of natural gas a day, or 5 percent
of the total United States consumption. The cost is to be
$10 billion.

Possible Pipeline Routes for Northern Gas

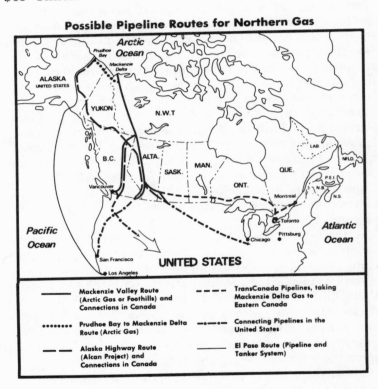

This 4,800-mile pipeline (48 inches in diameter) would
cross 2,700 miles in Canada. Prime Minister Trudeau wants
the pipeline; the United States wants the gas. (Canada
withdrew its proposal that a 125-mile smaller gauge

pipeline be built along the Dempster Highway to allow the Mackenzie Delta gas line to connect with the Alcan Project at Dawson City.) Leaders of Canada and the United States have given their approval of the Alaska Highway Route.

Until the ratio of oil production to proven reserves stops declining, Canada has little alternative but to severely limit or turn off the export spigots to the neighboring United States. Since nearly 90 percent of the Canadian oil industry is in the hands of foreigners, this problem becomes even more difficult to solve. The related problems of costs and environmental concerns over transmission of that Alaskan oil to west coast ports via tanker, with attendant dangers of marine spills along the Pacific coast-line of Canada, continue to build up. To meet these prob-lems, there is now some consideration of putting oil dis-charge facilities on the western shores of the Olympic Peninsula in Washington State, in order to avoid possible oil spillage in the Strait of Juan de Fuca and in the waters off lower British Columbia. There is also some considera-tion of establishment of a new oil refinery in British Columbia, this to use Alaskan oil, thus reversing the flow of Canadian oil on the West Coast. All this boils down to the idea of the Canadian man in the street, who insists on his government conserving Canadian oil for his own use. After all, says the Canadian, "We live in a cold country—colder than the United States. Just because the Americans want to buy our natural gas and oil doesn't mean that we should sell it to them. If we sell, what will we do to keep warm or to drive our machines?" (It should be recognized that Canada generously exported ad-ditional emergency supplies of natural gas and oil to the United States during recent severe winters.)

Canada has about one-third of the world's fresh water supply and one-sixth of the world's waterpower resources. In harnessing that waterpower, it is second only to the United States. With assets in excess of $10 billion, this industry employs more than forty-thousand Canadians. Much of the country's hydroelectric power is fed into

power grids serving America's northeastern states. While
hydroelectric plants are being expanded or newly con-
structed at massive installations in Labrador (Churchill
Falls), in Quebec (James Bay), and in British Columbia, this
source of power is far from being fully utilized. There has
been some consideration of associating the hydropower
development at James Bay with nearby uranium deposits
to produce enriched uranium for nuclear reactors. (See
pp. 250 , 251.) The Canadians are talking with the French

government on this matter. The new process would require
expenditures of some $2 billion and intake of some seven-
teen thousand tons of uranium ore. Canada's present annual
production of uranium is only sixteen thousand tons, but
she remains the world's largest exporter of that mineral.
The entire venture would thus require massive new capital
as well as additional exploitation of uranium resources.
The new plant would also require an immense amount of
electrical energy. Nevertheless it appears that both nuclear
and thermal power sources will be increasingly utilized in
Canada. It is likely that thermal and nuclear power capacity
in Canada will even overtake hydro capacity.

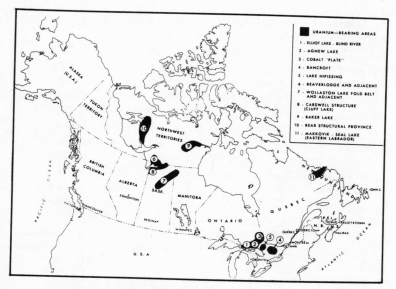

As mentioned earlier, Canada is one of the prime food producers of the world, specializing in grains, livestock, and dairy products. Unfortunately, only half a million workers remain in farming and animal husbandry. Family farms are being replaced by agribusiness enterprises as rural populations drift into cities. Given the fact that Canada, like other industrialized countries, has suffered a major loss in farm population, it has been essential to mechanize and commercialize most farming activities.

Annually the value of all field crops exceeds $2.5 billion; the value of livestock marketed and on farms exceeds $3.5 billion. The annual value of dairy production exceeds $1 billion; the value of poultry production amounts to $600 million. Tobacco, fruits, and vegetables earn more than $100 million each. Maple products—sugar and syrup— exceed $20 million annually. Total agricultural production now exceeds $12 billion annually from a land that is only 8 percent arable.

Canada shares with three other nations—the United States, Australia, and Argentina—the lion's share of the world wheat market; the Canadians actually hold a third of the total market. Exports of all Canadian grains now exceed 800 million bushels annually. Wheat alone accounts for about 10 percent of the value of all Canadian exports. Excluding wheat, more than 90 percent of all Canada's foodstuff production is consumed within the country. However it is interesting to note that livestock production, accentuating the foreign sale of cattle and poultry products, also brings a major return to the Canadian farmer. Livestock now is said to account for about two-thirds of the Canadian farmer's cash income, wheat about one-third.

Canada's nineteen thousand miles of coastal waters, her many rivers and lakes, all contribute materially to Canada's food production through commercial fisheries. Much of this production, both fresh and canned, is exported to the United States. Total production from fisheries exceeds $750 million annually from catches surpassing 2 billion pounds. This fishing industry provides a livelihood for more than fifty thousand workers. All this makes Canada rank third among the world's fishing nations.

Canada contains more than a million square miles of valuable forests. Ninety percent of Canada's forests stand on publicly owned crown lands. Her timber products create about one-fifth of all her exports. Half of the Free World's newspapers are published on Canadian newsprint. Canada is also the world's largest exporter of softwood lumber and allied wood products such as plywood. The forestry industry employs more than two hundred seventy-five thousand persons, and their production is valued in excess of $4 billion annually. A number of products ranging from plastics to explosives, from alcohol to yeast, come from the wood fiber industry. Pulp and paper alone is the largest single creator of wealth in Canada—standing first among all Canadian industries in value of production, employment, and capital investment.

Historically, in Canada, manufacturing became a matter of necessity. Isolation, Indian and European wars, tariff walls, and economic needs made it imperative that the Canadian "colonists" live on the land, develop their own cottage industries, and become self-sufficient. As a result, Canada has moved from its rural agrarian situation into a highly industrialized society. The twentieth century has witnessed development of an entire industrial economy in Canada, much of this dependent on investment of foreign capital and the working of multinational or conglomerate organizations. Many of these capital-intensive efforts brought about swift expansion in resource industries— pulp and paper; smelters and refineries; chemicals and petrochemicals; automotive plants and associated factories. Allied with these developments came a broad expansion of secondary industries—metals fabrication; textiles and clothing; beverages, breweries, and food processing plants.

Manufacturing is now the paramount economic component in Canada, making the nation sixth among the world's industrial countries. Industry is now said to employ about one in every four working Canadians—about the same proportion as in the United States. Largest manufacturing groupings in value terms are pulp and paper mills; motor vehicles; meat packing; petroleum refineries; iron and steel mills; dairy processing; sawmills; and general industrial machinery. Total value of all industrial production is estimated to be well in excess of $45 billion annually. In 1976 the net income of the top five industrial firms was $1 billion.

A special word is required on Canadian participation in the automobile industry. Historically, that production has spanned the past seventy years in Canada and thus is closely associated with American automotive developments. American Motors, Chrysler, Ford, General Motors, International Harvester, Kaiser, Renault-Somo, Volvo, and White are the principal producers. Today, these nine leading manufacturers of autos, trucks, and parts in Canada employ over fifty thousand workers with an annual payroll in excess of $500 million. In addition, there are over a hundred thousand people engaged in selling, servicing, and repair of autos and trucks.

In January, 1965, Canada and the United States signed a special agreement that provided for removal of tariffs and other impediments to trade between the two countries in motor vehicles and original equipment. One purpose of that automotive trade pact was to provide Canadian vehicle and parts manufacturers (several of which have American ownership or control) with easier access to North American markets outside Canada. It was hoped that this pact would bring about increased productivity and expanded employment in the auto world on both sides of the Canadian—United States border. It is interesting to note that, partly as a result of this agreement, finished automobiles and chassis became one of Canada's most valuable exports in 1968 and after.

With fifty-nine thousand miles of rail lines, Canada today has more railroad mileage per capita than any other country of the world. It will be recalled from the discussion in earlier pages of this book how the history of Canada was so changed by the completion of its first transcontinental rail line. Today she depends not alone on two transcontinental rail networks (Canadian Pacific Railway and Canadian National Railway), but, as well, has important north and south arms. All this is essential for carrying the products of farm and forest, mill and mines to market.

In addition to its rail network, Canada has more than half a million miles of roads. Some four hundred thousand miles of these are hard surfaced. The most important part of this highway network—one well known to many American visitors—is the four thousand eight hundred sixty-mile Trans-Canada Highway, which extends from the Atlantic to the Pacific. Important too is the famous Alaska Highway described in earlier pages of this book.

Canada's inland waterway system, which brought on her early exploration and colonization, remains important even today. Heart of this system is the combination of the Great Lakes, the St. Lawrence River, and the St. Lawrence Seaway. This seaway, opened in 1959, brings ocean ship-

ping from the Gulf of St. Lawrence onto the midwestern
doorsteps of Canadian industry. The seaway is essentially a system of locks and channels that overcomes the
falls and rapids in the upper St. Lawrence River and
between Lake Ontario and Lake Erie. Between Montreal
and Lake Ontario alone there is a series of seven major
locks. Five of these were built by Canada, two by the
United States. The Welland Ship Canal, twenty-seven
miles long, built between Lakes Erie and Ontario on the
Canadian side, bypassing Niagara Falls, is an important
adjunct of the entire seaway. Today this ship channel
upstream from Montreal has a twenty-seven-foot depth.
Downstream from Montreal to the Atlantic—a total of a
thousand miles—a thirty-five-foot channel exists. Thus
from the Atlantic to the head of the Great Lakes at the end
of Lake Superior, a distance of two thousand three
hundred miles, there exists a channel for ocean shipping. A
total of 57 million tons of cargo was moved through the
seaway in 1975. More than six thousand ships—Canadian,
United States and foreign-flag vessels—moved through the
seaway in that year. (See Fig. 1, page 256 for a St. Lawrence
Seaway profile view.)

The airplane has played a vital role in developing
Canada, especially in opening up the resources of her Far
North. It is easily understandable how this is true if one
simply recalls the vastness of Canada. The bush pilots who
have played such an important role in providing access to
Canada's mining regions led to the beginnings of the transcontinental airlines in existence today. However, the bush
pilots continue to be important, too.

The two major transcontinental and transoceanic airlines
operating within and without Canada today are Air
Canada, a government-owned corporation, and Canadian
Pacific Airways, a private subsidiary of Canadian Pacific
Railways. Air Canada now spans half the globe, providing
service to all major communities in Canada plus more than
twenty foreign nations. Canadian Pacific Airways, with
more than seventy-five thousand miles of air routes, links

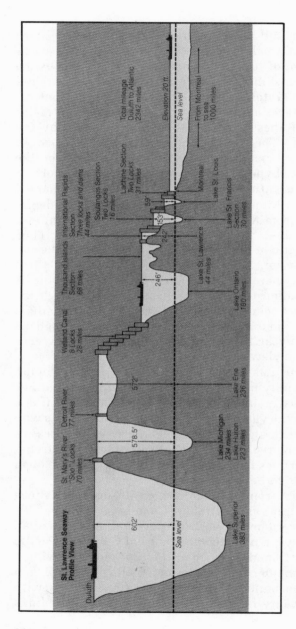

Figure 1. Profile of the St. Lawrence Seaway

many Canadian communities with some fifteen foreign countries. Canadian Pacific Airways is one of the few transoceanic air carriers that has service ranging from the Equator to the Arctic Circle as well as across the international date line. Both carriers—Air Canada and Canadian Pacific Airlines—serve a number of cities within the United States.

Like all heavily industrialized countries, Canada has a vast network of telecommunications. In per capita ownership of telephones, few countries are ahead of Canada, which has one telephone for every two persons. Ninety-seven percent of all Canadian households have radios; 96 percent have a television; 93 percent have telephones. Telegraph and telex services are provided by joint operation of the two transcontinental railway companies— CPR and CNR. The world's first geo-stationary communications satellite for domestic commercial use was put into operation by Telesat Canada in 1973. This installation provides augmented television and telephone service throughout Canada, especially in the Far North.

Communications buffs will be interested to learn that both Alexander Graham Bell and the Italian wizard Guglielmo Marconi conducted some of their most important experiments on Canadian soil. In the summer of 1874, Bell completed his basic work on his telephone invention at his father's home in Brantford, Ontario. Although he first successfully transmitted the human voice by telephone in the city of Boston in 1876, the first long-distance call was made from Brantford to Paris, Ontario, later the same year. Marconi in 1901 received his first trans-Atlantic wireless message at St. John's, Newfoundland, thus beginning his important radio communications work.

The publicly owned Canadian Broadcasting Corporation dominates the country's radio and television services. There are also privately owned television and radio stations as well as an expanding cablevision. There are some 270 private radio stations and 60 private TV stations in operation. CBC operates 158 radio stations and 184 TV broadcast and rebroadcast stations. Many of these broadcast both in English and in French. It also operates shortwave facilities broadcasting to the northern territories in Eskimo and Indian dialects. Radio Canada International maintains daily scheduled service in eleven different languages.

Canada's cultural enterprises, particularly publishing and films, will be discussed in later chapters of this book. In the face of the American cultural flood, these enterprises have special problems. Some statistics and background, however, are important here. There are three principal newspaper chains in Canada (see Chapter 14). Over one hundred daily newspapers are published in English and about twelve in French. There are, as well, more than eight hundred weekly newspapers. The first newspaper in Canada, the Halifax *Gazette,* was established in 1752, by a former Bostonian, John Bushell. This paper is still published as the *Provincial Government Gazette.* The first newspaper published in the province of Quebec was the Quebec *Gazette,* originating in 1764. It survives today as the Quebec *Chronicle-Telegraph*—the oldest continuing private newspaper in North America.

Two top press services—Canadian Press and United Press International—supply news to the press of Canada. Canadian Press, established in 1917, is a cooperative association of which most daily newspapers are members.

Some eight hundred magazines—consumer, trade, professional and ethnic—are published in Canada. Only four or five of these-*Maclean's, Chatelaine, Saturday Night, Homemakers Magazine,* and the *Star Weekly*—are of national consequence. For some time past, this arena has been dominated by many American magazines, including *Time* and *Reader's Digest.* These two have had so-called Canadian editions with special tax benefits for Canadian advertisers. These special rights are being eliminated under recently enacted Canadian government legislation.

Motion picture production in Canada has been, until recently, heavily dependent on American sources. In late years, however, there has been a strong effort to produce feature films, documentaries, and TV film sequences. Revenue for private firms from all these types of films, for public and private use, is about $25 million yearly. The federal government, through its National Film Board, is actively encouraging Canadian film production. In 1978, there were some fourteen hundred theaters in Canada, with attendance running about 90 million yearly.

Canada ranks eighth among nations in earnings from tourism, with a gross income of nearly $2 billion yearly. Tourist traffic through Canadian ports of entry totals over 40 million persons annually. Of these, nearly half are returning Canadians, while some 20 million are American visitors. Visits by Canadians to the United States number about 10 million yearly. Some 95 percent of all persons entering Canada travel by automobile, the remaining 5 percent by various modes of common carrier. Canadians traveling overseas number more than half a million yearly. Canada's international tourism expenditures exceed $3 billion yearly—a figure that makes Canadians among the most traveled of peoples.

Canada has some twenty-five national parks, many of these well known to American tourists. Park attendance exceeds 20 million persons yearly. The oldest and largest national park is Banff, which attracts more than 2.5 million sightseers, skiers, and campers annually. Prince Edward Island National Park, with its more than three hundred thousand visitors each year, ranks second in attendance. The Citadels of Quebec City and Halifax and Signal Hill at St. John's, Newfoundland, all national historic sites, each attract a quarter million visitors annually.

Annual events that attract thousands of foreign and domestic visitors in Canada each year include the Shakespearean Festival at Stratford, Ontario, the Shaw Festival at Niagara-on-the-Lake, Ontario; the Calgary Stampede; the Winter Carnival at Quebec City; the Klondike Days at Edmonton; and the Canadian National Exhibition in Toronto.

Despite political and building problems, the city of Montreal successfully hosted the 1976 summer Olypmic

Games. This internationally celebrated event welcomed 10 million visitors, including seven hundred thousand Americans. Costs of preparation were $1.2 billion. Though plans for the games had been plagued by labor strikes and civic disputes, the mayor of Montreal, Jean Drapeau, and his citizenry proved themselves more than adequate hosts. Montreal has also been the venue of the highly successful 1967 Expo, which celebrated the one hundredth year of Canadian confederation. As the country's gastronomic capital, and with a large number of hotels, night clubs, and tourist attractions, the city of Montreal is well suited to host such spectaculars.

Canada ranks sixth among all nations in terms of foreign trade. She comes after the United States, West Germany, Japan, the United Kingdom, and France. Even more important, however, in American eyes, is the fact that Canada is both the best customer and the largest provider for Uncle Sam. This makes the United States and Canada the world's greatest trading partners. Some 21 percent of all United States exports went to Canada in 1976—an amount more than double that which went to the next-best American customer, Japan. In turn, Canada supplies 25 percent of all United States imports.

Dollar figures for trade between the two nations are now much higher than in previous years, reflecting inflationary trends and the energy crisis. Canada's exports in 1977 totaled $44.131 billion, up 15.7 percent from a year earlier, while imports increased 12.2 percent to $42.053 billion. Exports to the United States in 1977 were a record $30.88 billion, while imports from the United States were $29.542 billion. The United States provided for 70 percent of all Canada's exports in 1977 and 1978.

Among other important customers of Canada are Japan, the United Kingdom, and West Germany. To these she exports forest products, motor vehicles, agricultural products, and minerals. Her most valued import partners after the United States are Japan, the United Kingdom, West Germany, Venezuela, and France. From these she takes industrial machinery, petroleum, automobiles and parts, electrical equipment, trucks, and aircraft.

A word needs to be said about Canadian labor organizations. These are increasingly important in the life of that nation. Today there are more than 10 million employed in Canada's work force. More than one-quarter of these, male and female, are members of trade unions. About two-thirds are members of international unions, most of which are American led. The Canadian Labour Congress (equivalent to and associated with the American AFL-CIO) alone represents 1.8 million members. Of these some one hundred and sixty-five thousand are steelworkers; a hundred and two thousand are united auto workers; sixty-seven thousand are woodworkers, and fifty-nine thousand are mineworkers. Other important unions include the printers, construction tradesmen, transportation workers, fishermen, and longshoremen.

It is especially interesting to note that Canadian trade unions are putting more distance between themselves and their American trade union counterparts. Most of the Canadian unions are demanding greater autonomy and a larger share of international offices. They are also insisting that Canadian unions set their own policies, rather than receiving dictates from the international bodies. Labor bargaining and political orientation are already under Canadian control. Some Canadian groups, such as the paper workers, have split completely from their American affiliates, now forming a wholly separate union. Here again is revealed the extent and depth of Canadian nationalism.

Today the Canadian trade union movement is important for yet another reason: its extraordinary influence in at least one national political party. This is the New Democratic Party, a party of Socialist-populist orientation. It was an outgrowth of unions of earlier postdepression political parties, the Labour Congress and the CCF. The NDP came into being only in 1961 and now controls provincial government in Saskatchewan as well as a number of parliamentary seats. Since 1970 many trade unions have agreed to pay per capita levies from their workers' treasuries to help finance the party activity.

Governmental programs, including social security benefits, represent an important segment of personal income in Canada. As in other industrialized countries, fiscal and economic controls are utilized to level off price fluctuations—booms and depressions. There are many consumer subsidies and agricultural controls designed to influence production. Labor-management agreements are in wide use, but federal-provincial legislation thereon is in conflict. Social security schemes are extensive, ranging from retirement benefits to health insurance and medicare coverage. Family allowances, veterans benefits, and unemployment compensation schemes are also very broad. Public welfare programs and pensions for the handicapped are extensive and expensive. The various social services are administered at three levels of government—federal, provincial and municipal. Most of these benefits are paid from relatively high income and sales taxes.

Canada has been considered as one of the most hospitable and profitable of climates for foreign investors. As a result of the huge inflow of foreign capital, especially since World War II, more than one-fourth of all Canada's nonfinancial industry and commerce is now in the hands of foreign owners. More than 80 percent of the grouping is owned or controlled by United States interests. Canadian investors, on the other hand, own only half of one percent of United States corporate investment. Japanese, West German, and British investments are also extensive and growing. The United States investments are primarily in petroleum, rubber, transportation equipment (including autos), electrical products, chemicals, and extractive minerals. It has been estimated that some 35 billion U.S. dollars—or nearly 40 percent of all United States foreign investments—are now placed in Canada. By comparison, Canadians have only $12 billion of their own funds invested worldwide. Some 60 percent of Canada's manufacturing industries, half of her mining and smelting, and three-quarters of her petroleum and natural gas industries are controlled abroad, chiefly from the United States. In chemicals, autos, and computers, foreign control runs up to Allan MacEachen, minister of external affairs when ness in Canada is much higher than in any other industrialized country. Traditionally, Canadians have encouraged that foreign investment, recognizing that it was imperative to the country's development. Today, however, Canadians are both more aware of, and more skeptical of, the troubles and benefits of such investments. In general, however, and within certain limits, ongoing foreign investment will be essential for Canada's continued economic growth.

It was against this background of questioning of foreign investment in Canada that the Foreign Investment Review Act of 1973 was passed by the Canadian Parliament. That act has now been implemented. It represents an effort to obtain better Canadian control over the economic environment and to obtain increased financial benefits for Canadians. Under this act, Canada has the authority (1) to control further acquisition of Canadian businesses by foreigners; (2) to control investment from abroad that is seeking to enter into new businesses; (3) to oversee expansion of foreign firms already operating in Canada but seeking to diversify into unrelated businesses. According to Allan MacEachen, minister of external affairs, when the act was passed, these five criteria govern five aspects of foreign investment: (1) impact on general economic activity, such as employment and exports; (2) the degree of participation of Canadians in ownership and management; (3) the effect on productivity and technical development; (4) the effect on existing competition; (5) compatibility with other Canadian economic policies. The final test of all these factors will be whether new or expanded foreign enterprises are likely to be of real benefit to Canada.

A few financial comments are both important and timely

to this chapter. It should be mentioned that Canada's currency is based on the Canadian dollar with its subparts of 100 cents. This Canadian dollar fluctuates or "floats" against the United States dollar and other foreign currencies daily, depending on the strength of Canada's economy and financial and trade markets. In ordinary circumstances, the Canadian dollar is usually within two or three cents of parity, or equality, with the U.S. dollar. In recent years, the value of the Canadian dollar has usually been slightly higher than its U.S. counterpart. However, as a result of the November, 1976, Quebec election, the Canadian dollar dropped eight cents in ten days. It reached a forty-five-year low of $83.92 on October 2, 1978, but hovered around ten to fifteen cents off the U.S. dollar in 1978.

It should be noted that both the banking system and the equivalent of the American savings and loan companies (the trust companies and the *caisses populaires*) are highly competitive. In fact, in very few countries of the world is the banking-savings system so violently competitive and so subject to quick change as in Canada. In general, too, Canadian banks and trust companies pay higher interest rates than those that have prevailed in the United States in recent years.

It is precisely Canada's long and arduous economic role as "hewer of wood and drawer of water" that will make that nation increasingly important to the rest of the world during the remainder of the twentieth century. Canada remains a highly important provider of raw materials, not alone for the United States, but for Western Europe and Pacific Rim lands. Since Canada is one of the few industrialized nations on earth with her own adequate supplies of oil, natural gas, electric power, and water, and with sufficient foodstuffs for her essential needs, she is more protected than most against the worst shocks of unemployment and inflation. There is a real resilience in this Canadian economy, which can only be destroyed by internecine wars between capital and labor, between the French and the English, or between provincial fiefdoms and Ottawa. Even more difficult for Canada, however, may be the requirement to maintain her markets, her culture and character, her full national identity in the shadow of the American behemoth.

Canadians are often inclined to cry "wolf" as regards the condition of their economy. In fact, however, it is generally stronger than they may admit. As Prime Minister Trudeau has succinctly, even ironically, summarized his nation's real potential: "Everything is not perfect with the Canadian economy—but it is not bad to be the best in the world!"

14
The Power Elite

The claim is made that Canadians have a classless society—that theirs is entirely a middle class. The idea of a single-level social image is carried further with the contention that most Canadians are relatively equal in their incomes, in their possessions, in their educations, and in their social standing. This claim is not true. One can admit that Canada has no truly aristocratic society, titles having been outlawed in 1919. There is no nobility other than the British monarchy and the royal family. The questions are whether money values transcend egalitarian values and whether corporate, family, and "old boy" relationships still carry great weight. In Canada they do. There is indeed a power structure—an elite that constitutes a definite upper class.

It may have been that, during the colonial centuries, Canada's rural society of the prairies and the pioneers was not differentiated as to caste. However, this rural, frontier society has been entirely outdated by Canada's urbanization, industrialization, broadening political, economic, and familial ties. There may well be a middle-level classlessness—but there is also a ruling group. Yet, the writer believes that this power elite may, in fact, number only one or two thousand "principals." With their families, this leadership group may number no more than ten thousand.

It could be that the concept of a middle-level classlessness so commonly attributed by Canadians to themselves is partly a product of advertising. It could result from American cultural intrusions via the media—TV, radio, and magazines. It may be that, as the middle class is both principal producer and principal consumer in the Canadian system, the image not only goes unchallenged, but is actually fostered. It must surely result in part from the industrial control and growth of trade unions that are modeled on the American cultural pattern. All this may tend to mislead Canadians regarding their own identities and social natures. The economic elite of Canada does not intend to overthrow that image of classlessness, but rather to sustain it. Indeed, as they also control that image through their media connections, they are likely to feed it.

It will be admitted that there is not a large number of desperately poor people in Canada. These will be helped by government, subsidized by broad social welfare schemes. Although it is claimed there are five thousand millionaires in Canada, only a few of these can be considered multi-millionaires. It is also admitted that there are few barriers to opportunity. In Canada today, individual economic and social advance can be made to a certain level—say the upper middle class—by resourcefulness, imagination, ambition, and a little bit of luck. To this extent, and quite superficially then, the image of a complete middle class society in Canada may appear plausible. But is it?

In developing the ideas of this chapter, the author assumes that the word *power* means the capability of making effective decisions on behalf of large groups of Canadians. The power elite is therefore that grouping which, by such decisions, directly or indirectly affects the lives of many or most Canadians. Such decisions may lie within local or provincial milieu—or be even nationwide. The buying public may be affected through actions of an industrial or commercial complex. These economic decisions may well have political and social determinants—just as, in reverse, political decisions may have economic and social repercussions. Here is where the real authority of a power elite is centered. Some will contend that use of such strength by a power elite—whether that be oligarchic or democratic leadership—is essential for a stable society. In any event, Canada surely appears to have such a power elite—its determinations spilling from economic into political or from political into economic arenas.

With respect to Canada, it is also important to remember that economic, cultural, and ideological power systems are broader than the national boundaries. There are spillovers into other parts of North America—and vice versa. American influences are pervasive in Canada. In turn, Canadian influences (especially in the wake of the energy crisis) are now becoming important in Alaska, in the Caribbean, and within the United States itself. There are even tendencies toward continental integration in some fields. The pervasiveness of American culture in the Canadian media; talk of a North American common market; activities of the North American Air Defense; and the broad influences of multi-national corporations—all show these tendencies. In effect there is a kind of ongoing synthesis with action in both directions, north and south. American doctors move into Canada and Canadian doctors move into the United States. Journalists, academics, artists, movie stars, sports personalities—and corporate directors—move back and forth across the forty-ninth parallel. Powerful Canadian businessmen move into governmental positions in Ottawa and Canadian civil servants move out into industry. Given this interchange, the power elite may become international as well as national, its influence extended rather than diluted.

It is the purpose of this chapter to make a further analysis of the Canadian society and leadership. Let's find out whether it is truly democratic; whether it is solely a middle-class meld; or whether there is a real oligarchy.

For Canada today, there is indeed an increasing affluence. This is based in part on availability of credit, in part on increasingly higher wages. The hourly wage rate in

certain fields, especially the trades, surpasses wage levels
in the United States. There are extensive social services,
including health plans and unemployment compensation,
available to all Canadians. These programs, more extensive than in the United States, are underwritten by
government and the Canadian taxpayer. This makes for
some classlessness.

Yet in Canada today there are also persons and families
of great wealth and influence. These may not be so numerous or ostentatious as in New York or Texas or Paris.
Furthermore, Canada has no real cafe society or celebrity
world competing with Hollywood or Las Vegas, though
Montreal, Toronto and Vancouver are coming close. Nonetheless, the wealth, the power, the financial and political
influence, the "old boy" ties of club, of school, of family,
are indeed there. Members of the power elite are inter-
locked and very powerful even though they are few.

This structure of power is reinforced by ethnic, religious, and vocational backgrounds; by business, social,
and political institutions; by family and educational ties.
The elite group seeks to perpetuate its status, avoiding at
all costs the dilution or destruction of its own authority
and wealth. Distinctions of rank in Canada, of course, are
much more difficult to perceive than in older European or
Asian societies. There, aristocracies—with their ac-
couterments of precedence, heraldry, professional and
political monopolies—are more common. Nevertheless,
there is a broad understanding of rank in Canada, which is
based, in very large part, on corporate directorships; on
wealth and status of families long- and well-known in the
community; and, of course, on academic or political position, even club and church affiliations. A reconstruction
and analysis of this power elite group must, of course, be
relative. This involves a kind of gamesmanship. These
class distinctions may look artificial—but in everyday life
they are real. Here occupational ranks become important
too. Doctors and lawyers are at the highest levels, along
with industrialists and corporate presidents. Teachers and

civil servants would rank somewhat lower. Clerks and blue-collar workers come in at still lower levels. All these distinctions measure social distances between the poor and the middle class and between the middle and upper classes. The "across-the-tracks" concept is as real today in Canada as it was twenty-five years ago in small-town America.

Almost every major city of Canada has its few families of great wealth and great social prominence. These may be measured in several generations. They usually have their own social life—their clubs and friendship circles, their academic associations, their favorite charities and churches. This grouping of first families—this real upper class—generally supplies far more than its proportionate share to the composition of big-business boardrooms. As well, it controls membership of a majority of cabinet and judicial posts, national and provincial. It contributes more than its share, also, to parliamentary, especially Senate, seats. There is, as well, first-family control of media resources—publishing, television, and radio. There is great power exerted by this group over university presidencies and chancellorships, over learned societies and cultural associations. With all this power, they also have more money, earned or inherited. The top 1 percent of income recipients in Canada receives 40 percent of its income from dividends. This first-family grouping, together with a very few nouveaux riches, exerts a control in Canada far in excess of its proportionate numbers.

Just as in every other developing society emanating from European colonialism, it was true in Canada that certain ethnic groups of immigrants established a special place for themselves. This was true of the English and the Scots in Upper Canada and of the French in Lower Canada. These social positions of primacy were cemented into place throughout Canada during the nineteenth and early twentieth centuries. As a result, lesser social status was accorded to newer immigrant groups. First affected were the Irish, the Scandinavians, and the Ukrainians; later on, the southern Europeans and the Orientals had similar problems. Furthermore, the English and Scottish tended to lord it over the French—and in some Canadian communities still do so. Often, as in the case of the French-Canadians, the lower-echelon status was accepted unflinchingly. Today, at long last, such class or social differentiations based on ethnicity are being challenged—but they are not yet destroyed. It should be recognized, too, that the two-class social system of Eastern Canada—English above French—is being overtaken by economic as well as political pressures. The fact that the present prime minister of Canada is a French-Canadian, and the third such, is indicative of change. In the case of the French-Canadians, the objection to being given a lower social status has also become a major precept of their separatism and their "quiet revolution."

In view of the foregoing historical facts it is not surprising that the Anglo-Canadians, mainly Protestant English and Scottish, had created for themselves a very special status in Canadian political, economic, and social sectors. In this process, efforts to establish a landed gentry in Canada—this modeled along the strict lines of the English class society—broke down first in the rural areas. This breakdown resulted from the environment, from the great distances, from widespread poverty sometimes resulting from farming failures, and from the tendency to attain only to the lowest common denominator of gentility.

At the time of Canadian confederation in 1867 and shortly thereafter, the combination of Anglos and French made up about 90 percent of the total population of the country. Germans made up some 7 percent, with other ethnic groupings fragmentary. Later came massive migration from central and southern Europe. By the 1930s, the proportion of the Canadian populace of British and French origin had dropped to 80 percent. Diverse other European and Asian groupings then totalled 18 percent. By the late 1960s, the total of Anglos and French had dropped to about 72 percent, with various European and Asian groupings nearing 30 percent.

One important international thesis greatly influenced the stratification of Canadian immigration. This was a development in the field of political sociology that encouraged the concept that races were not equal. Worldwide, there has been a hierarchy of caste built on race—the blacks on the bottom. Ascending one or more rungs therefrom were the American Indians and the Orientals, including Chinese, Japanese, and East Indians. At the top of the social ladder were members of the white race, especially northern Europeans. Thus it was that races and nations had acceptance in a hierarchy of presumed superiority. This concept is dying today, but in the past century it had great influence and many proponents in Canada as elsewhere. The consequences of this doctrine still linger on, unfortunately, even though it is now generally conceded that there is no scientific basis for—or proof of—such a hierarchy of races. There were distinctions along religious lines as well—the Anglicans at the top; Methodists and Presbyterians and members of the United Church in the middle; Roman Catholics, Jews, and members of Eastern Orthodox rites at the bottom. These religious differences thus reinforced racial and nationality divisions.

Many Canadian political leaders have built their power base on diatribes against immigrants of certain ethnic groups or vocational classes. They have insisted on "the right kind of immigrants" and the "right" man for the job. Even as late as the 1920s, J. S. Woodsworth, father of the CCF party emanating from Manitoba, wrote and preached ideas of ethnic superiority of the Britisher and northern European over the central and especially the southern European. In a contradictory book tinged with both humanity and racism, *Strangers Within Our Gates*, Woodsworth tried to prove that biological and ethnic differentiation supports social and racial stratification. He insisted on the primacy of position and social values of those with British backgrounds. He characterized those immigrants from the Mediterranean area as being distinctly lower class. He contended, as well, that the Orientals should not be assimilated into Canadian society and those then in Canada should only be used for the most menial of tasks.

Today, though there is no obvious policy of restrictive immigration, it appears that, during the past two decades, special preference has been given to immigrants of commonwealth and northern European extraction. Today, too, there is considerable complaint from various sectors of Canada, especially trade union officials, demanding prohibitions on further immigration. These complaints stem in large part from the fact that Canada has been suffering from the effects of worldwide recession and massive unemployment.

It has been true that the heaviest immigration into Canada has occurred during the regimes of the three French-Canadian prime ministers, Laurier, St. Laurent, and Trudeau. This is a very interesting commentary on the attitudes of Anglo-Canadian nationals towards the touchy subject of immigration. Offsetting this attitude, however, has been the rather constant high level of British immigration. It is self-evident that the predominance of the two basic nationalities—French and English—has never been seriously challenged. They have only challenged each other.

In fact, it has taken nearly two decades for the Canadian economy to absorb the heavy immigration and population increase of the first postwar years. Upgrading of any modern society is accomplished, in part, by increases in educational opportunity, by specialized training, by new emphasis on professionalism, and by general enrichment of the economy. The labor force is thus placed in upward mobility, and some of that group are bound to find places in the power elite—particularly if the ceiling and the "rules" for such upward mobility are not clamped on too tightly. In Canada this would appear to remain a question. Both immigrants and native-born Canadians of lower social levels still find it difficult to crack the barriers into the real power elite. Not unless they happen to become very wealthy and well educated can they attain to that stratosphere. Even then, they may have to combat the rigid and ultraconservative attitudes of the "old families" and "old school ties."

In Canada today, the field of industry and commerce will serve to show both the extent of control of that power elite and the small number of individuals in such control. A relatively small number of firms is responsible for an extraordinary amount of activity and power. The principal directors of these few firms not only have power over their own corporations, but also have tentacles and interlocking directorates spreading into other firms, into other countries, and even into academic, cultural, and media activities. Until recent years, there has been very little actual policing by the Canadian government of these interlocking relationships. Lately, there has been some investigation by government of restraints of trade and the extent of international (especially American) ownership-control of various sectors of the Canadian economy. There is one single determinant on the part of government—that is to protect Canadian industry against outside competition. (This has been detailed in the preceding chapter on Canada's economy.)

Within the Canadian corporate community today, there are about fifty so-called giants. The activities of these corporations—mainly multinationals—are so extensive that they are not even publicly known. Highly important is the extent of foreign, especially American, control of these giants. These corporations manage the largest proportion of industrial output in Canada. As well, they own about 38 percent of all Canadian property. This includes land, factories, business buildings and inventories. In short, these corporate giants control at least 15 percent—per haps even 20 percent—of all Canadian business and commerce. This concentration of corporate power under foreign ownership has brought about much more secrecy and lack of public accounting than might otherwise have been true. What now, therefore, in political terms is the course of action that is best for the public good? Canadian nationalists may soon determine a new course for these corporate giants.

For some unexplained reason, the Canadian investor, for a long time after World War II, was reluctant to develop or take over his own corporations. This may have been the result of extensive timorousness—some call it the "Scottish mentality." In any event, it encouraged outside risk capital which came into Canada to take the dives—and to reap the rich rewards. Only now do Canadians generally recognize the social and political results that have followed on the economic effects of these outside takeovers and continuing outside ownership. In sum then, until recently, the middle-level Canadian investor has not been ready to share broadly in the development and riches of his own land.

By tacit consent and by their inaction, they have allowed foreign capital to enter. As a result, dispersal of ownership—meaning a wide number of stockholders—is not common in Canada. Many corporate giants nominally in Canada retain majority or even full control of their operation in the United States, the United Kingdom, or elsewhere. Two of the few corporations with broad Canadian ownership are the Canadian Pacific Railway and Bell Telephone of Canada. On the other hand, T. Eaton Company (a department store chain) and General Motors of Canada do not have public participation. Even for Bell Telephone of Canada, American Bell remains the largest single stockholder. It is understandable that American, British, and other foreign owners have been reluctant to relinquish control of their Canadian subsidiaries, largely because of the excellent profit margins, the political stability of the nation, and the great potential of the future Canadian market. However Canadian nationalism at long last is forcing a slowdown and a backtracking to provide fuller Canadian corporate participation and control.

In 1950 there were in Canada only eighteen corporations

with assets in excess of $100 million. By 1960 there were thirty-four more such. Five of these were in petroleum, three in pulp and paper, one in iron ore; one in chemicals; three in automotive products, two in food; two in meat packing. These were active as well in a variety of other, secondary, activities. For example, the large firm Canada Packers is not alone active in meat packing. As well, it is heavily engaged in tanning of leather and production of soaps, feeds, and canned fruits and vegetables.

For the past two decades, there has been marked expansion—growth, merger, and takeover—among Canadian corporate giants. This corporate matrimony has enhanced the power of the corporate elite with respect to all sectors of Canadian life. Yet it must be constantly kept in mind that Canada is unique among industrial societies. Much of its economy is not really owned by Canadians, but by owners and managers located outside its borders. One of the more historic Canadian commercial institutions, Hudson's Bay Company, still heavily British in ownership, was first a fur-trading and later a mercantile chain. Today as well, it is associated with petroleum development and real estate. The great Canadian Pacific Railway Company also has a number of subsidiaries, ranging from realty and hotels to mining, shipping, and airlines. Many of the largest Canadian firms have associations with European or Japanese as well as American multi-national affiliates. Aluminum of Canada (ALCAN), for example, is an associate of Alcoa. Iron Ore Company of Canada (U.S. owned) has associations with British and South African interests. Bowaters Paper Company has British and American backing. The retail dry goods chain, Simpson-Sears, has Canadian and United States interests converging.

By 1960 there appeared to be some 175 dominant corporations in Canada. At that time, only 907 individuals residing in Canada shared between them over 80 percent of the directorships in those dominant corporations. The members of the same group also shared between themselves over half the directorships in the nationally char-

tered banks. They also shared half the directorates in the
national life insurance companies. These people even held
a large number of directorships in smaller companies not
considered to be "dominant." Thus these men and women
are sensed to be the core of the economic elite of Canada.

Further illustration of the widespread power of the
above mentioned group is shown by a recent analysis of
the Canadian banking community. This study showed that
the 30 directors of the Bank of Montreal, Canada's largest,
held more than 220 directorates between them. Similarly
the 25 directors of the Royal Bank of Canada held some 240
other directorships.

In recent years, Canada, like other nations, has been influenced by the intrusions of, or creation of, great holding
companies. Perhaps the most famous of these is the Argus
Corporation of Toronto. This group was created by a man
reputed to be the richest in Canada, Edward Plunkett
Taylor, now retired.

Operating from a single financial center, Argus began,
shortly after World War II, its takeover and domination of
major Canadian corporations. Today it controls at least
ten of these, including Massey-Ferguson, Dominion Tar and
Chemical, the St. Lawrence Corporation, B.C. Forest
Products, Dominion Stores, and Standard Broadcasting
Corporation. It also has control of Hollinger Enterprises,
Noranda Mining, and Kerr-Addison, three of Canada's
premier gold producers.

The Argus conglomerate is now directed by John A.
(Bud) McDougald, who has been labeled by *Maclean's*
editor Peter Newman as Canada's "grand master" of business. McDougald is a transnationalist par excellence,
doing business everywhere, from his home base in Toronto
to Palm Beach to London and Palm Springs. He is reputed
to be the stereotype of a Hollywood tycoon—secretive,
tough, arrogant, conservative, and highly successful—
with a fortune now estimated in excess of a quarter billion
dollars.

As Chairman of the board of the Argus empire (succeeding E. P. Taylor), McDougald has a personal empire that extends even beyond Argus and into such diverse directorships as General Bakeries; Canadian Imperial Bank of Commerce; Avco Corporation; Crown Trust, and First National Bank of Palm Beach (Florida).

A competing conglomerate—the Montreal-based Power Corporation of Canada, directed by Paul Desmarais—several years ago made an unsuccessful bid to take over control of the Argus group. Desmarais, through his holding companies, Gelco and Nordex, along with Power Corporation, controls investments in companies specializing in oil, water, electric power, and transport. Desmarais's net worth is estimated at several hundred million dollars; total assets of his majority ownership companies run into billions. He is said to control more than seventy companies in all. The more established "old boy" tycoons, such as Taylor and McDougald, class Desmarais as a financial "Johnny come lately"—and a corporate gambler whose bona fides are not yet fully accepted. Nonetheless, Desmarais is a power to be reckoned with even beyond his own conglomerate. He is considered unique in both Anglo- and French-Canadian financial worlds. Today, Desmarais has close working relationships with top officials of the Bank of America and holds about 14 percent of Argus Corporation's nonvoting stock.

Yet another interesting industrial complex is the Molson conglomerate. Head of this grouping is Honourable Hartland Molson. He and his associates, notably Donald G. Willmot, are involved in breweries, banking, insurance, real estate, and various industrial enterprises.

One of the most historic—and powerful—of all Canadian corporations today is the Canadian Pacific Railway. It is a conglomerate, with a net income estimated to exceed $100 million yearly. This was the original transcontinental rail line heavily favored by the country's first prime minister, Sir John A. Macdonald. With American engineering and British and United States financial backing, the company completed Canada's first transcontinental rail line in 1885.

Today, this company has a diversity of activities extending far beyond the passenger and freight business. Extensive government subsidies of cash and real estate (more than 50 million acres along its mainline) made it one of the country's largest landlords. Through its subsidiary, Marathon Realty, CPR still owns extensive shopping centers in Montreal, Vancouver, Calgary, Edmonton, Sudbury, and other Canadian cities. It has giant logging interests in British Columbia. It operates hotels, steamship companies, airlines. Its Canadian Pacific Air subsidiary—the largest private air operation in Canada, second only to government-owned Air Canada—has global air routes east and west.

The CPR has retained extensive mineral rights, despite the fact that it has sold off much of its original land grants. It holds a conglomerate of mining interests in British Columbia, including a large smelter at Trail. That giant Consolidated Mining Company is 63 percent owned by CPR. The railroad also operates sulfur, potash, and petroleum interests. It is a heavy stockholder in Pan Arctic Oils, Ltd., and has been a heavy investor in North Sea oil. It also has extensive interests in Japan, India, and the United States.

The most "Canadian" corporation of all is T. Eaton Company. Founder of this mercantile chain was Timothy Eaton, a dour Methodist who arrived in Toronto as an immigrant in 1869. Beginning with a single retail store, now extended into one of Canada's prime mercantile chains, Eaton's led Canadian commerce in development of fair working practices and employee benefits. Eaton could not, however, abide labor unions. Intensely paternalistic and authoritarian, Timothy Eaton sought to base his operations on the idea of a single price system and cash only— with satisfaction guaranteed. He established a store catalog for his rural clientele even ahead of Sears, Roebuck. Eaton died in 1907, but his family power elite was secure on the Canadian scene.

Timothy's son, Sir John Eaton, took over the firm, and

from 1901 to 1922, when he died, he and his wife were the leaders of Canadian society. Exceedingly rich, regal and reactionary, they considered themselves as Canada's real "first family." The founder's grandson, John David Eaton, "ran the store" from the time of his father's death until his own death in 1973. Today the department store chain is managed by John Craig Eaton and his brother Fred, members of the fourth generation.

Under the Eatons, the store chain became the fourth-largest corporate entity in Canada, smaller only than the federal government and the two railroads. Today the store chain has fifty thousand full-time and fifteen thousand part-time employees. It includes about 50 department stores, many warehouses, and until recently 250 catalog outlets. It also holds massive parcels of downtown real estate in the principal cities, particularly Toronto, Winnipeg, and Vancouver. Its total value is said to be in excess of $500 million, much of which is held in a family trust. Though considered by many still to have reactionary, paternalistic leadership, it has great power in provinces and municipalities. As a commercial and political influence, Eaton's and its family owners have thus had a profound influence on Canadian life.

One of the most powerful of Canadian family fortunes centers about the name Bassett. John Bassett, Sr., built his fortune out of the now-defunct *Toronto Telegram*. In this he was associated with the Eaton family. J. Bassett, Sr., also owned the majority interest in the Toronto Maple Leaf Gardens, home of the famous hockey team. He has also been associated with the Toronto Argonauts, one of the best of Canada's pro football teams. He even owns a Toronto TV station. His son, John Bassett, Jr., is now perhaps the most important of Canadian film producers and impresarios. He is owner of Toronto's World Hockey League franchise, the Toros. The connection between the families Bassett and Eaton is even more extensive than was noted in joint ownership of the *Toronto Telegram*. Today, the Eatons have a piece of the action of the Toronto

Toros as well as some stock in the Bassett film companies. Both these families have extensive and similar academic and social interests. Male members of both families, for example, attended the influential, old-boy tie, Upper Canada College. Many financial interests of both families are now in a joint family trust.

James A. Richardson III—MP from Winnipeg and former minister of defence—is one of Canada's wealthiest men. He is also considered to be one of the most enigmatic of Canadian politicians. "The Silent Minister," he was called. He is considered an "outsider" in Liberal hierarchy. He attended Queens, where his father was chancellor of the university. He is married to a member of the great British shipping family, the Cunards. An extremely capable and financially versatile Winnipeg businessman, he is the inheritor of wealth and creator of more wealth. Some estimate his fortune at $700 million—comprising brokerage, insurance, grain terminals, livestock, and real estate, including one of the tallest buildings in Winnipeg. He can hardly be called the parliamentary voice of the populist West. Nonetheless, Richardson has been highly successful in decentralizing governmental activity away from Ontario—some of this being relocated in his home town. As a result of his politicking, Winnipeg has acquired a branch of the Canadian Mint. It has the repair facilities for Air Canada. It has received defense and aerospace contracts. It is said that Richardson would like to be prime minister someday but probably will not make it, since he is so ardently antibilingual (and by implication, anti-French-Canadian).

The telephone book of St. John's, capital of Newfoundland, lists some thirty companies associated with the name of the Crosbie family. Leaders of this powerful clan today are brothers, John and Andrew. John is a lawyer, the intellectual of the family with strong political ambitions. He has been a cabinet minister in both Conservative and Liberal provincial regimes. He was first a friend and is now a foe of the father figure of Newfoundland politics,

Joey Smallwood. Andrew, the younger brother, is an industrial tycoon, a man of vision and energy. He runs the Crosbie business empire. The *Globe and Mail* has reported that brother Andrew holds seventy-seven company directorships. A sometime supporter of Joey Smallwood, Andrew, like his brother John, is reported to have secret ambitions to become premier of Newfoundland. The Crosbies are grandsons of Sir John Crosbie, minister of finance in Newfoundland's preconfederation days. The boys' father, Ches, financed Smallwood's early political ventures. The family fortune was developed from margarine; from heavy construction ($50 million in government contracts); from ownership of Eastern Provincial Airways (fourth largest in Canada); from insurance; from shipowning and freight services; from hotels and tourism. Today the Crosbie group of companies employs twenty-five hundred persons, and its business volume exceeds $100 million annually.

The foregoing are only illustrative of the extent and interaction of family power in business and commercial Canada. Others who might be similarly mentioned would include scions of the H. R. MacMillan family, pioneer in Canada's western timber industry; Jake Moore Labatt, head of a brewery fortune; Leonard Hynes, chairman of Canadian Industries, Ltd.; Donald G. Campbell, publisher; the Honourable Louis-Philippe Beaubien, holder of extensive company directorates; John Aird, lawyer, also with extensive company holdings; the Honourable Paul Desruisseaux, who concentrates on TV, cinema, and publishing; the Honourable Louis P. Gelinas, who has varied interests, industrial and financial; the Honourable Salter Hayden, lawyer, whose holdings range from restaurants to paper mills; the Honourable Allan MacNaughton, lawyer, with directorates ranging from insurance to construction; the Honourable Lazarus Phillips, lawyer, whose interests run from real estate to bridge building.

Some further discussion should be made concerning the concentration of ownership and control of mass media in

Canada. Here, with very few exceptions, both operation and capital of the firms are exclusively Canadian. This is in direct contrast to the high degree of foreign ownership and control seen in Canadian industry, manufacture, and commerce. It could mean that operation of this media group brings in only a small margin of profit and thus is not of real interest to foreign owners. More likely, however, is the prospect that they are profitable but in the hands of a few old families who are not willing to let them go. They may thus be viewed not alone as economic instruments but also as social institutions that must be preserved as distinctly Canadian.

Prestige and power may thus attach to them in an unusual way. Southam, Thomson, Sifton, Bassett, Atkinson, McDonnell, Hindmarsh, Cromie, Hunter—all are newspaper families and all are members of the power elite, the Canadian upper class. Their scions are graduates of the same private schools and members of the same metropolitan social clubs, charitable endeavors, university boards.

One of the largest of Canadian family enterprises is the Southam Company. Among other newspapers, it controls the Ottawa *Citizen*, the Montreal *Gazette*, the *Calgary Herald*, the Winnipeg *Tribune*. The Vancouver *Province* is half owned by the Southam Company and half owned by Pacific Press Limited. Southam also has important interests in Hugh C. Maclean Publications Limited and in radio and TV stations in a number of major cities of the nation. The Southam family group began its operation in 1877, when it took over the Hamilton *Spectator*. Prime control of all the enterprises still rests with members of the Southam family.

Yet another influential family enterprise is Thomson Newspapers Limited. This group has forty newspapers ranging from Newfoundland to British Columbia. It also has extensive holdings in the United Kingdom and is considered one of the largest newspaper chains in the world. It operates a broadcast sector—radio and TV—as well. Its Canadian-born founder, Lord Thomson of the

Fleet, died in London in 1976, aged eighty-two. Major control of the company is lodged with the founder's son K. R. Thomson.

Another powerful grouping is the Free Press Publications Limited. It has majority control over the Toronto *Globe and Mail*, the *Winnipeg Free Press*, the *Vancouver Sun*, the *London Free Press*, the *Ottawa Journal*, the *Calgary Albertan*, the *Victoria Colonist*, and others. It, too, is involved with radio and TV stations. Today the group is headed by Richard S. Malone.

In terms of both circulation and advertising, the greatest newspaper in Canada is the *Toronto Star*. Its circulation is in excess of half a million, and its weekly associate, the *Star Weekly*, has a circulation of 1 million. Both form part of the Hawthorne Foundation. Two single families—Atkinson and Hindmarsh—still provide full family control and direction.

There are both similarities and differences to be found when the French-Canadian publishers are compared with their English-speaking counterparts. Largest of the Quebec dailies is the French-language Montreal *La Presse*. Others of consequence are the *Montreal Star* (English), the Montreal *Gazette* (English), the Montreal *Le Devoir*, the *Montreal-Matin*, the Quebec *Le Soleil*, the Ottawa *Le Droit*. Several of the newspaper-publishing concerns also own radio stations. The Montreal *La Presse* and the *Montreal Star*, like others in this group, have had generations of single-family ownership. Among the more notable and ubiquitous names in this arena of management are those of Bassett, McDonnell, and Bourassa. Among the more influential of the French-language publications mentioned here is *Le Droit* of Ottawa. *Le Soleil* of Quebec City is considered to be the most powerful paper in French Canada—locally as effective as the *New York Times* or the *Guardian* in Britain.

The pattern of concentration of newspaper control within a few hands is thus clear. A similar pattern of control is evident in the publishing of periodicals. These form three main groups: (1) Canadian consumer magazines such as *Macleans, Homemakers Magazine* and *Chatelaine;* (2) consumer magazines published outside Canada but possibly having special Canadian editions—such as the controversiial *Time* and *Reader's Digest;* (3) trade and professional magazines published, for the most part, in Canada. Both domestic consumer and trade publications in Canada are concentrated in the hands of Maclean-Hunter Publishers, Ltd., or Hugh C. Maclean Publications, Ltd. The latter is controlled by the Southam newspaper group. Maclean-Hunter, publishing *Macleans* and *Chatelaine,* is by all odds the dominant consumer magazine publisher, while Hugh C. Maclean is predominant in the trade journal field. Maclean-Hunter also publishes the *Financial Post,* the highly influential Canadian equivalent of the *Wall Street Journal.*

The "old school tie" concept in the Canadian upper class is both widespread and complex. Canadian thinking admits that a modern industrial economy insists on a free and upwardly mobile labor force, one essentially egalitarian; but there is also general recognition in Canada that there must be an elite leadership of that force. In most Western nations, sponsors of the egalitarian idea believe that members of the labor force should be allowed to move upward through the system to the very top. In Canada, that concept is not yet fully accepted: there is a ceiling of precedent and privilege above which the worker may find it exceedingly difficult to ascend. Anglo control of industry in French Canada has been a classic example of this situation. Thus, in Canada, the upgraded worker may meet social barriers in matters of income and position, in education, even in religion. In the circumstances, then, it becomes increasingly clear that educational opportunity must be a major goal of the children of lower-class families in Canada. Private school education and university training, especially for the principal professions, have long been particular reserves of higher-income families, and these barriers are breaking down only slowly.

The private school system in Canada, as in Britain, thus has been the backbone of the educated elite. Purism in educational training, especially that of the "classical college system," continues to have great weight. Canada today has some eighty private elementary-secondary schools enrolling about twenty thousand students. It has been estimated that two-thirds of the recognized Canadian elite has attended such schools. These institutions create shared manners and mores, "establishment values," and "presumptions" of leadership. They even set patterns of speech, mannerism, and custom. From the major boys' schools have come one-third of all Canada's important corporate directors. Half of these are said to come from one school alone—Upper Canada College, which is considered to be the Groton or Eton of Canada. Nearly as important, however, are Lower Canada College and Bishop's College in Quebec; St. Andrew's College and Ridley College of Ontario; St. George's and Shawnigan Lake schools in British Columbia. For girls, perhaps the most outstanding are Bishop Strachan School in Toronto and Crofton House in Vancouver.

The same elite groups tend to center their scions' collegiate training about the Universities of Toronto and British Columbia, McGill University, and Queens University at Kingston (Ontario). For postgraduate study, they favor Harvard Law and Business schools in the United States and Oxford and Cambridge in Britain.

The French-Canadian establishment group, numbering no more than five hundred to a thousand in all, likewise has a cohesive relationship through family, university, religious, and business ties. Like the Angles, these French-Canadians appear to concentrate on particular schools and universities. The University of Montreal and Laval University of Quebec City are in special favor. At the secondary level, College Sainte-Marie and Le Petit Seminaire of Quebec are especially important.

Commissions, corporate boards, universities, churches, family links –all these bring Canada's leaders together. So, too, do clubs, particularly golf clubs and metropolitan social clubs. The club life of the larger cities has been extraordinarily important in providing social and business contacts for the elite groups. Many of these are similar to the famous and traditional British clubs. Most prominent among these Canadian institutions are the Mount Royal and St. James' Clubs of Montreal and the Garrison Club of Quebec City. In Ottawa, power centers in the Rideau Club; in Toronto in the York and Toronto clubs. In Winnipeg, the "in" institution is the Manitoba Club; in Calgary, the Ranchman's Club. In Vancouver, it is the Vancouver Club, and in Halifax, it is the Halifax Club. These clubs have long been important status symbols in business and professional circles. The membership thereof is jealously passed on, first to members of the elite families, and only thereafter to newcomers to the elite circles. Status may derive from other situations, but, in Canada, clubs help.

It is generally acknowledged that certain of the clergy, in association with academicians and other intellectuals, have some leadership role. The well-known Toronto intellectual Marshall McLuhan and the famous Catholic Cardinal Leger are illustrative of this caste. Formerly primate of the Roman Catholic Church in Canada (and brother of the present governor-general), Cardinal Leger has now retired from his Canadian post to become a worker among the lepers in Africa. Mention has already been made of the interchange of relationships and roles, academics moving into government service, government servants into business or back to academia. However, it is generally conceded that, in Canada, the role of the intellectual has never been allowed to become too powerful—too critical—too "far out." The Royal Society of Canada, a learned group formed in 1882, is one of the few intellectual groups that take in all the major fields of higher learning, including humanities and sciences. Election as a fellow of this body is accorded by the existing membership. The social snobbery attached to attainment of membership therein is pronounced.

It is virtually impossible to assess the position of the clergy today in reinforcing the power structure. In the Province of Quebec, up to a decade ago, the hierarchy of the Catholic Church held places unchallenged as to both recognized social leadership and political power. Today, however, in the wake of secularism and separatism, these roles have been considerably diminished. Today, with some 40 percent of all Canadians Catholic, there are some sixty or more bishops and archbishops in religious command. These are gathered into an association known as the Catholic Conference. The group is said to hold disparate views on the major social questions of Canada. Thus it does not appear to exert a major leadership role. Since Cardinal Leger's departure, too, there has been no single outstanding personality of his fame and achievement within the Catholic hierarchy.

Similar to the position of the Catholic hierarchy in Quebec, though not quite so pronounced, has been the position of the Anglican hierarchy in Ontario and the Maritimes. Of lesser consequence has been the position of the Presbyterian, the Methodist, and the United clergy. The Anglican church, more than the other Protestant denominations, appears to come to an apex in terms of leadership of both clergy and laity. The Anglican Synod is presided over by the archbishop primate of Canada. He is thus the titular head of a group of some 30 bishops and some 300 presiding laymen.

While it is difficult to select a true labor elite in the field of trade union leadership, this area is becoming increasingly important. It seems certain that, in any future basic social studies of Canadian leaders, it cannot long be overlooked. Prestigious positions in the growing Canadian trade union field were originally held by American officials of affiliated unions. Today, however, more than two-thirds of Canadian trade union leaders are Canadian born. While it is not yet important in social and educational fields, Canadian labor does have economic and political power. Labor's involvement in formation of political parties like the CCF and the NDP has been demonstrated elsewhere in these pages. This kind of power is only bound to grow as the total membership of Canadian trade unions increases. Organized membership in Canadian trade unions now totals more than two and a half million.

The political-bureaucratic elite in Canada is considered to number about two hundred and fifty senior officials in the federal government and provincial governments. A few of these are in Parliament. The Senate, composed of honorific appointees with corporate connections, merits special attention in enumeration of any such elite corps. Other members of the elite are found in the fields of trade and commerce; in finance and external affairs. In any discussion of Canada's political elite must be included prime ministers and cabinet ministers; provincial premiers; justices of the Supreme Court of Canada and provincial chief justices. Any of these may have an elite role at a given point in time. Senior officials in certain of the more important crown corporations and boards may also be included. It is generally conceded that this political elite is the best educated of any other group in Canada. More than one-quarter of them will have taught in university at one stage in their varying careers, and about a third have advanced academic degrees. There is also considerable rapport between this group and corporate leaders, and between this group and academic or social leaders of the larger Canadian communities. Here both family and political party connections may also be important.

Illustrative of the interaction—social, educational, and familial—that ties members of the political elite together are the following members of Canada's top echelon today: Ex-governor-general, Jules Leger, is a member of an illustrious Quebec family and the brother of the former Roman Catholic cardinal primate of all Canada. Jules Leger was earlier a career diplomat, serving as Canadian ambassador to Belgium, France, Italy, and Mexico.

Prime Minister Pierre Trudeau, scion of a wealthy and socially elect Quebec family with both French and English connections, is a graduate of the University of Montreal as well as a select private secondary school. He had an illustrious academic career before entering politics and continues to maintain important connections in academic circles.

The late Prime Minister Lester Pearson aptly illustrated the "old school tie" relationship, intermeshed with political power. Pearson had been a Rhodes Scholar, then a professor, then a diplomat. Later, as minister of external affairs and as prime minister, he openly helped a coterie of old school chums and diplomatic colleagues. As Pearson ascended into the political and social stratosphere, he carried some of these old school friends with him—including Norman Robertson, high commissioner to London; Hume Wrong and Charles Ritchie, both former Canadian ambassadors to the United States. Pearson's son Geoffrey is related by marriage to the principal owners of Labatt's Breweries.

Prime Minister Trudeau, like his mentor-predecessor, Lester Pearson, seems to have developed a political elite out of confidantes and cronies. He has built this grouping out of the secretariat of the prime minister's office and that of the cabinet. From that elite corps have come many of his major cabinet appointments. Furthermore, in an effort to weld his underlings into a unit totally at his beck and call, he has adopted a certain rule of flexibility. In fact, during the past eight years, he has shifted or removed at least forty of his cabinet ministers. In addition, he has sought to limit his parliamentary secretaries to terms no longer than two years, thus giving them a chance to broaden with varied experience. Today it appears that his ministerial cronies of greatest influence are Donald Macdonald, minister of finance; Marc Lalonde, formerly press secretary to Trudeau and now minister of health and welfare; Gerard Pelletier, ambassador to France and long-time friend of Trudeau; and Allan MacEachen, leader of the House of Commons. The last appears to be a real "comer." He was earlier minister of external affairs and minister of labour.

One recent study concluded that, of 157 people included in a presumed "political elite," 79 had served in the federal cabinet, 30 as provincial premiers, 39 as members of the judiciary. Several had served both as provincial premiers and as cabinet ministers.

So far as the author can determine, there is today no up-to-date and deeply analytical study of Canadian social life extant. However, some valued views are contained in the excellent book The Vertical Mosaic by John Porter. The book attempts to develop both the themes and the contrasts of a specific power elite. A second, more popular and lively work on the subject of the Canadian power elite is Peter C. Newman's The Canadian Establishment. This book takes a look at the vanities, the foibles and fancies of Canadian captains of commerce, of dowagers and dauphins in a highly entertaining way. These works, plus other tangential materials available to the author, support the thesis that there is indeed in Canada today an effective oligarchy. This grouping—based on family, business, social, educational, intellectual, and political ties—surely creates an upper crust of power and social primacy. There also appears to be a certain collegiality of that membership even in an acceptance of social responsibility and a certain paternalism. This is a kind of minority rule operated by a sense of collective judgment. This group also appears to have its roots in Canadian tradition and familyhood, measuring its actions in a spirit of patriotism, of Canadianness. Action and control by this small group are aided by bureaucracies and by corporate or family ties.

Ordinarily this view of Canadian society and power might not be considered as terribly important. It would not be cause for much concern, for example, in Scandinavian society—though more so in Britain. While there is always considerable claim of a single powerful "establishment" in the United States, even that view is questioned on grounds that the American body politic and social structure are so vast—and so inert—that no single group can control them all. In Canada, however, things are slightly different. The fact of existence of this single, partially integrated, and powerful elite means that the concept of Canadian "equality" is challenged. These clear class differences, the author contends, stand in the way of implementation of a true democracy—even of cohesive nationhood. This theme will be addressed again in the concluding chapter.

15
Entertainment and the Arts

C anada's uneasy cultural relationship with its down-stairs neighbor, the United States, has been aptly characterized by Prime Minister Trudeau. Said he: "Living next to the United States is, in some ways, like sleeping with an elephant. . . . No matter how friendly and even-tempered is the beast, one is afflicted by every twitch and grunt."

Until recent years, Canada's cultural situation was bound up more with its colonial mentors—Britain and France—than with its southern neighbor. Today, however, as a result of the persuasiveness and pervasiveness of all forms of American culture, Canadians are, more and more, being forced to look at the world—even at their own Canada—through American eyes. No matter whether one considers the field of TV and radio, films, books, maga-zines, or sports, the problem for Canada is much the same. The United States cultural behemoth dominates the North American scene.

This problem appears to have two main facets, reflecting into and mirrored from one another. One is the matter of culture—that which measures a nation's character through its art forms—its television, movies, literature, paintings, and all. The second is the matter of character emanating from those cultural forms—a nation's drives and goals measured in the attitudes, the emotions, the spirit of its people. In the case of Canada, both matters are complex and somewhat confusing to the casual observer. Both matters require detailed scrutiny. This chapter considers the problems of the Canadian culture, its arts and entertainments. The concluding chapter considers the question, "What is a Canadian?"

A recent American CBS telecast (Mike Wallace's "Sixty Minutes") made the contention that, for Canadians, America casts an oppressive giant shadow across their country—affecting both their culture and their character. Now, after 110 years of nationhood within that shadow, the Canadians are doing something about it. Their feeling is not just empty nationalism—Yankee-go-homism—it is much more complicated. The Canadians would like the Americans to view Canada as being different and not to be taken for granted.

A good part of this problem stems from the odd proximity to the United States of such a high proportion of Canada's population. As noted earlier in this book, almost 80 percent of Canada's people reside within 100—yes 100—miles of the American border. The diffusion of American airwaves—TV and radio—across the border cannot be stopped. In fact, it is helped by many direct links. Some Canadian stations buy time, advertising and programs, from the great American networks. Cablevision promoters push their product from American stations into Canadian homes. American magazines and books flood Canadian newstands and bookstores. American films dominate Canadian theater screens. American football stars perform on Canadian gridirons while Canadian athletes, singers, writers and movie stars find fame in the United States.

The problem of the sameness—the depth and all-pervading power of the American cultural influences on the Canadian entertainment scene—is especially noticeable in Canadian television. The Canadian government has become so prickly about this matter that it has introduced a law insisting that 60 percent of all TV (or radio) content broadcast from Canada be of Canadian origin. As exceptional as some of that Canadian content may be—

especially in documentaries, House of Commons coverage, and news analysis—it is no match for the audience appeal gained by the American situation comedies. "All in the Family" today, like "Leave It to Beaver" a decade past, is the big hit of the Canadian airwaves. On the French-Canadian side, such American productions as "Hawaii Five-O" receive specialized treatment with dubbed-in French dialogue.

In 1936 the Canadian Broadcasting Corporation (CBC) was developed to control content, advertising and programming, of all Canadian broadcast operations. This was at the time American radio was in full flower. The Canadians preferred a kind of noncompetitive British Broadcasting Corporation (BBC) rather than the highly competitive commercialized American networks. In 1958 the Broadcast Board of Governors became the dominant regulatory agency for all radio and television broadcasting in Canada. The previously established government-owned chain—the CBC—became relegated to the position of operator only. Thereafter, the government chain was forced to compete with private commercial operators and eventually to cooperate with them. (See Chapter 5 for House of Commons T.V. coverage.)

The state-owned CBC today operates 31 radio and 17 television stations. Its services are now available to more than 99 percent of the country's population, through either TV facilities or radio diffusion facilities. Privately owned companies operate 270 radio stations and 60 TV stations. There are 80 FM stations. The most important private TV network is Canadian Television. Other important private holdings include Canadian Marconi, Canadian Westinghouse, and West Coast Transmissions. As noted in the earlier chapter on The Power Elite, there are links between private broadcasting and certain newspaper chains or corporate conglomerates. Among the most powerful of these are the Southam Newspaper Chain and Rogers Radio Broadcasting, the latter being a subsidiary of the Argus group.

CBC provides programming in both French and English for its own use and for some of its commercial links. With more than ten thousand employees, CBC also operates international shortwave facilities in eleven languages as well as in various Indian and Eskimo dialects.

In 1968 new broadcast legislation became effective in Canada. The Broadcast Board of Governors was replaced by the Canadian Radio-Television Commission (CR-TC), which has five full-time government and ten part-time public members. It was hoped to make this organization more free of political influence than was its predecessor. It has much broader powers to enforce programming standards on both CBC and private broadcasters. The main purpose of CR-TC, as stated in its legislative origins, is to "safeguard, enrich and strengthen the cultural, political, social and economic fabric of Canada" for the entire industry.

To move toward that stated goal, from 1970 onward, it was required that 60 percent of prime time on all TV stations in the land be filled with Canadian content. Shortly thereafter, CR-TC required that 30 percent of all music on AM radio be performed, written, or composed by Canadians or, at least, recorded in Canada. The commission has also said that it will cancel the licenses of any station that does not provide adequate domestic news coverage or that is foreign owned. In the cablevision field, the commission has granted monopoly franchises in certain areas; the beneficiaries are required to give priority programming to Canadian material.

One of the few developments in the radio programming field that appears to be of Canadian origin—and that American radio stations later picked up—is the so-called hot line. This is the system of listener-announcer conversation with both ends of the conversation broadcast live. This type of broadcast has been in use and highly popular in Canada for at least a dozen years. American productions were subsequently patterned on the Canadian style. The extent and popularity of this kind of program in Canada is best illustrated by the fact that three prime ministers—Trudeau, Pearson, and Diefenbaker—as well as a number of cabinet ministers and provincial premiers have participated therein.

Officials of the governing CR-TC and the government-owned CBC often find themselves at loggerheads. The main issue seems to be the quality of programming, which, by some Canadians, is considered too highbrow and therefore too limited. The second problem has been the running feud over just how much foreign, especially American, content (including both programming and advertising) should be allowed. It appears that the goals of Canadian broadcasting are to be structured so as to defend against further American intrusion. They are also aimed at achieving a kind of "excellence" in contrast to "mass" appeal.

CBC officials, fighting back, contend that they would be delighted to replace "M*A*S*H" and "Maude," "but you can't do that until you have Canadian programs to replace them." The need is for time and money. It seems clear that Canadians are moving away from the idea that they ride on the back of American programs; but they must develop their own format and metier. Obviously the fight is for resuscitation—even survival—of a very important part of Canadian culture.

Yet another major cultural concern for Canadians is the matter of the movies. As noted in the chapter on economics, there are some fourteen hundred movie theaters in Canada. These annually cater to 90 million-plus viewers. Most of the theaters are dependent on American or other foreign films. The federal government's National Film Board, with nearly a thousand employees, produces documentaries and pushes for more Canadian feature-length films. This, too, is an effort to reverse the foreign, predominantly American, cultural tide.

Some of these efforts to develop a distinctly "Canadian" movie industry appear to be paying off. In 1973, a Canadian product, *Kamouraska*, won international acclaim at the Cannes Film Festival for the first time. This story of

Quebec of 1839 portrayed the attitudes that French-Canadians have towards themselves.

Even Hollywood is paying more attention to the Canadian film product. The National Film Board of Canada received Oscars for *Churchill's Island* in 1949, *Neighbours* in 1952, and *I'll Find a Way* and *Sand Castle* in 1978. In 1976, Budge Crawley won an Oscar for his documentary *The Man Who Skied Down Everest*. The Film Board has received forty-nine nominations for Oscars and special acclaims for such works as *The Apprenticeship of Duddy Kravitz*. Other films given special mention were *The Violin, The Family That Dwelt Apart,* and *Hunger*. Associated with tributes to Canadian films were the industry's tribute to Canadian-born film stars who have made names in Hollywood. A partial list of stars includes Norma Shearer, Mary Pickford, Deanna Durbin, Mack Sennett, Walter Pidgeon, Marie Dressler, Alexis Smith, Walter Huston, Anthony Perkins, Lorne Green, Raymond Burr, and Raymond Massey. All this is a far cry from Rudolph Friml's *Rose Marie* which set out an anachronistic concept of Canada inhabited only by trappers, Mounties, and Indians.

Prior to World War II, Canada depended heavily on American and British stars for satisfaction of her own repertory, concert, and ballet needs. Those few Canadian stars who managed to become famous in their homeland had, in general, first established their reputations on the London or New York stage. The real breakthrough for Canadian artists came with the spread of their names throughout Canada via radio and TV. The work of singing groups like the Irish Rovers and of individual folk singers like Joni Mitchell, Gordon Lightfoot, and Paul Anka is illustrative. So, too, are the careers of such musical stars as Maureen Forrester, Giselle Mackenzie, Robert Goulet, Percy Faith, and Guy Lombardo.

Today, the epic and internationally celebrated work of the Shakespearean Festival at Stratford, the Shaw Festival at Niagara-on-the-Lake, and the Royal Winnipeg Ballet have won worldwide fame. The CBC must be credited with providing the first effective training ground for these and allied Canadian theatrical arts.

Yet another kind of celebrity has been the sports figure. This group must include the 1948 Olympic figure-skating champion, Barabar Ann Scott, and the hockey players Gordie Howe, Rocket Richard, and Guy La Fleur. Here too, however, the pull of the American purse is phenomenal. It is said that nearly every major star on the National Hockey League circuit (including all the first-string players of the 1975 championship Philadelphia Flyers) came from Canada. And not to be forgotten in the sports world is the famed Canadian racehorse Northern Dancer, winner of the 1964 Kentucky Derby.

Sports may be considered among the more ephemeral and intangible cultural pursuits of any nation, including Canada. While it must be stated that Canadians have not brought home many world championships, nevertheless, there have been some outstanding successes. Canada has produced at least one heavyweight boxing champion, Tommy Burns, who held the title from 1906 to 1908. Another Canadian, Ned Hanlan, was the world's foremost sculling figure. There have been a number of Olympic medalists in a variety of sports. The Montreal Canadiens, with more than twenty Stanley Cup championships to their credit, have dominated North American hockey.

Canada must also be given special credit for developing certain sports besides hockey, including lacrosse, soccer, and her own brand of football. Professional Canadian football, very similar to the American game, utilizes a number of former American college stars. For the sheer number of Canadians who participate in any sport, curling is the game. Some eight hundred thousand Canadians are involved with this sport. Curling is an ancient Scottish game, played on ice with curling-stones and brooms. This game is popular among all ages in all regions of Canada.

It was a Canadian, James Naismith, who invented the game of basketball. A native of Ontario and an outstand-

ing athlete for McGill University, Dr. Naismith, was a
YMCA worker in Springfield, Massachusetts, in 1891,
when he created this game for his charges as a stopgap
between football and baseball seasons. In what is now a
worldwide sport, Dr. Naismith's basic rules for basketball
still apply.

Canadians have always appeared to have a joyful zest
for competition and sports. As well, they are both avid
bettors and rabid rooters. Relating this joy of competition
to other patterns of Canadian life finds some comparison
in the field of commerce—leading back into organized
sports. In this connection it is interesting to note that
Montreal, long a cosmopolitan capital of Canada, served as
the host for an Olympic-type competition in 1844 and
again served as host to the international Olympic Games
in 1976.

Canada's visual artists—painters, sculptors, and
photographers—have never yet managed to produce a
"national school" or special "national style." Though occasionally portraying regional characteristics, as in landscapes of the Far North, they have usually managed to
follow a kind of international trend. There was the Victorian canvas of the nineteenth century. There was the
impressionism of the early twentieth century. There is the
pop art and the so-called electronic art of the present day.
It has been contended by a reputable art critic that in
recent years, Canadian artists have been released from
their so-called closet culture, and a new vitality has come
upon the scene—again international rather than national.
There have developed new modes of experimental styles of
understanding and of social motifs. The so-called New
York style is now prominent—and, some critics say, again
shows the "imperialist" influence of America.

As regards Canadian art generally, the most popular
subject has always been the landscape. This is
understandable in a terrain so dominant in its vastness
and its power and its lighting. Many artists divide their
work between rural summer scenes, which emphasize

flora and fauna, and the wintery urban canvases in which people are central.

A few of the most important Canadian artists are Jack Shadbolt, David Milne, Alfred Pellan, Mary Pratt, Toni Onley, and Claude Tousignant. John Boyle is a noted painter of historic scenes, and Jack Wise is one of the most imaginative iconic painters. Now deceased, Emily Carr, Paul-Emile Borduas, and Clarence Gagnon were painters of distinction. From the notable schools of Indian painting is a group of Cree/Ojibway artists. Norval Morrisseau was one of the group's founders. Youthful Carl Ray is one of the most traditional artists of the group.

By all odds the most prominent Canadian painter was A. Y. Jackson, now considered the "Grand Old Man" of Canadian art. One of the leaders of the so-called Group of Seven, Jackson specialized in landscapes. He is said to have pictured Canada of the early twentieth century in much the same way as Thoreau and Emerson depicted nineteenth-century New England via their writings. Jackson and the rest of the Group of Seven (Carmichael, Johnston, Lismer, Macdonald, Varley, and Harris) worked mainly in oils. They were sometimes condemned as too provincial or too militant, but they did indeed produce a body of painting that has been central in the evolution of Canadian art.

In yet another area of the arts, Canada has been able to produce a world-renowned figure. In the field of portrait photography, Yousuf Karsh, Turkish born and now a citizen of Ottawa, stands preeminent. He has photographed the world's great—from Churchill to Einstein, from Schweitzer to Sibelius. Here is one Canadian figure who does not fear competition from the American cultural scene.

Among the most important of Canadian works of visual art are aboriginal artifacts of Indians and Eskimos. Eskimo sculptures, done mainly in stone or whalebone, are both fashionable and expensive. The ceremonial artifacts and costumes of the various Indian tribes are highly prized by museum curators. The Canadian government has spent several millions in recent years to repatriate bits of Canada's ancient indigenous heritage from private holders. It is now illegal to sell aboriginal artifacts outside Canada until the National Museum of Man has had a chance to buy them.

One of the most problematical aspects of Canadian culture lies in the field of writing and publishing. Here again, the elephantine American cultural influence is discerned—and almost overwhelming. Despite valiant efforts by the Canadian government to foster Canadian literary works, only 5 percent of book sales are recorded as being truly Canadian. Best-selling American books are best sellers in Canada as well. Many American publishers have branch houses in Canada. So, too, do the largest British publishers. There are only a few strictly Canadian publishers. Most important of these are probably Maclean-Hunter, Ltd., of Toronto; Chateau Books Company of Montreal; Edition Fides of Montreal; McClelland and Stewart, Ltd., of Toronto.

It is generally accepted that few Canadian authors can amass wealth by their writings alone. Advances are small, and there are few film rights. Free-lance writers must depend on other professions, such as TV or newspaper journalism, for their livelihood. The provinces are attempting to encourage writers by grants; the federal government, by scholarships and exhibits of "Canadiana" in the post offices of the nation. Every writer in Canada is said to lust after the annual Governor General's Literary Award. This involves a large cash prize in addition to publicity. Comparable prizes are given by the Province of Quebec and the Canadian Council.

Among important preconfederation writers have been the explorer Sir Alexander Mackenzie and the geographer David Thompson. The exploits of these have been detailed in historical sections of this book. More recent writers of note have been Lucy Montgomery, author of the children's classic *Anne of Green Gables;* Mazo de la Roche, author of the well-known *Jalna* series; Stephen Leacock, the famed humorist; Marshall McLuhan, philosopher and critic (*The Media Is the Message*).

Winners of the 1976 Governor-General's Literary Award for fiction were Marian Engle (author of *Bear*) and Andre Major (author of *Les Rescapes*, meaning "*The Survivors*"). Other Canadian authors familiar to the American reading public include Margaret Atwood, author of the 1976 best seller *Lady Oracle* and *Survival* (an important analysis of Canadian nationalism in literature); Margaret Laurence, author of *A Jest of God* (from which the movie *Rachel, Rachel* was made) and a receipient of the 1974 Governor-General's Award for *The Diviners*; Hugh MacLennan, who gained fame as author of *Two Solitudes* (a superb exposition of the conflict between French and English in Canada). The former ambassador to the United States, Charles Ritchie, recently won the governor-general's award for his best-selling biography, *The Siren Years*. Farley Mowat, specialist on Arctic life; Ernest Seton; and Eric Nicole are also authors of consequence. Three Canadian writers who have made names for themselves in the United States are Saul Bellow, 1976 Nobel Prize winner in Literature; Arthur Hailey (author of *Airport* and *The Moneychangers*); and John Kenneth Galbraith, the famous Harvard economist.

A novelist who has received considerable attention recently is Richard Rohmer, author of two Canadian best sellers, *Ultimatum* and *Exoneration*. Rohmer is a Canadian Reserve Air Force general and a specialist on the Far North. His books tell of a 1980 effort by the United States, first to annex, and later to invade, Canada. The invading Americans are defeated by the courageous Canadians. Both these imaginative works, catering to current nationalist trends, were best sellers on both sides of the border.

Perhaps the most famous of current Canadian novelists is Mordecai Richler. He developed his reputation first in New York and London, more recently in Hollywood. There a feature film made from his novel of the same name, *The Apprenticeship of Duddy Kravitz* recently received acclaim. Another work of Richler's, *St. Urbain's Horseman,* won the governor-general's award in 1971.

Yet another well-known Canadian author, Pierre Berton, has developed a reputation in both fiction and nonfiction. He is best known for his work on the history of the building of Canada's transcontinental railways, including both books and such TV documentaries as "The Last Spike" and "The National Dream." Berton is reputed to be Canada's richest author, earning more than $400,000 yearly.

One author who has made himself a considerable reputation both in newspaper editing and in nonfiction is Bruce Hutchison. Perhaps his best-known nonfiction works are *The Unknown Country* (quoted in the Preface of this book) and his excellent biography of Prime Minister Mackenzie King, titled *The Incredible Canadian.* Hutchinson has been editor of the Victoria (B.C.) *Colonist* and presently serves as editorial director of the *Vancouver Sun.*

It appears that, in the French-Canadian sector of the country's literature, there is still a long way to go to attain national and international honors. By far the best known of the output of French-Canadian writers is the novel *Maria Chapdelaine,* written by Louis Hemon some sixty years ago. This, a novel of Quebec habitant farm life, became an international classic. A novel of Montreal's urban life, Gabriel Roy's *Tin Flute,* published in 1946, is also of consequence. Another French-Canadian author of note is Victor-Levy Beaulieu, whose novel *Don Quichotte de la Demanche* won a 1974 governor-general's prize.

The situation of the Canadian novelist Morley Callaghan best demonstrates the past isolation of Canada from the rest of the literary world. The famous American critic Edmund Wilson characterized Callaghan as the "Turgenev of Toronto" (Callaghan's home) and said that he was the most unjustly neglected novelist in the English-speaking world. Callaghan first gained prominence in exile in Paris and New York. Among his best works were *The Loved and the Lost* and *The Many-Coloured Coat.* He was friend of

Ernest Hemingway and Ezra Pound in the 1920's. Despite the efforts of American publisher friends at Scribners and the *New Yorker*, Callaghan never gained a wide-ranging audience in Britain, the United States, or Canada—and today is almost forgotten.

During the past two decades, there has been something of a renaissance in Canadian poetry. Much of this has centered about the so-called Poets' Corner of the University of New Brunswick in Fredericton. Perhaps the best known of this group, who established an international reputation for himself, was Bliss Carman. Others of the group were Sir Charles G. D. Roberts and Archibald Lampman, Canada's foremost nature poet. Other widely known poets of recent consequence are E. J. Pratt of Newfoundland; Pauline Johnson, who wrote of her own Indians and of nature; and Ralph Gustafson, who, with his collection *Fire on Stone*, won a Governor-General's Literary Award. A well-known French-Canadian poet, Nicole Brossard, won a comparable governor-general's award of 1974 for her collection *Mechanique Jongleuse*. A poet of distinction is Rina Lasnier who in 1974 won Quebec's highest literary award, the Prix David.

It has been said by some observers of the Canadian literary scene that, in both Canadian fiction and poetry, there is a kind of melancholia, the recognizing of forces beyond one's control. Unlike the deep optimism or the deep sensitivity to social forces in American or British literature, Canadian literary themes have, thus far, had little relevance to the great social movements. They have concentrated instead on personal difficulties, even withdrawal. Apart from one or two major works, such as Hugh MacLennan's *Two Solitudes*, there is even little discussion of the fact that there are two Canadas—one French, the other English. Furthermore, truly indigenous Canadian literature appears to have readership among only a small proportion of the populace. Most Canadians are voraciously consuming American or British or French best sellers rather than the efforts of their own Canadian authors. This tidal wave of foreign cultural influences is well-nigh overriding.

It is not that Canadians are illiterate—not at all. They are, in fact, reported to import and to read more outside publications than does any other nation in the world. At one time, this import figure was said to have reached some 70 million periodicals yearly. Many more magazines are imported than are published in Canada. Some 80 percent of all magazines sold off the newsstands in Canada are now produced in the United States or have American editorial backgrounds. Among the most popular American publications are *Ladies' Home Journal, McCall's, Good House-keeping, Family Circle, Newsweek, U.S. News & World Report,* and *Playboy.*

Two of the most popular periodicals, *Time* and *Reader's Digest,* until recently published Canadian editions that provided for insertion of advertising into a periodical specifically designed for the Canadian market. In this latter effort—so-called split runs—American publishers were able to build up their advertising incomes without incurring editorial expenses in Canada and, more important, without encouraging Canadian authors. Members of the Canadian Parliament have long considered this as unfair cultural-economic warfare, and they have recently legislated against it.

The Canadians have been determined to throw the Canadian editions of *Time* and *Reader's Digest* out of Canada or to take them over. The case of *Time* has been particularly difficult. Today it is the largest weekly circulating in Canada, with more than five hundred and fifty thousand copies distributed. Its nearest competitor on the weekly circuit is the American *Newsweek.* The Canadian editions. All this made Time Canada one of the most pages of distinctly Canadian news, and its ads were all Canadian. The remainder of the magazine—international news, cinema, etc.—was taken from the parent magazine—the same as that which Americans read in their own editions. All this made *Time* Canada one of the most profitable arms of Time, Inc., of New York. Time Canada ceased publication with its edition of December 29, 1975, and Canadian subscribers are now receiving the regular American edition. (At this writing, it appears that Reader's Digest, with much the same problem, will attempt to continue its Canadian edition under a "charitable trust.")

It is thus clear that Canadians not only resent the fact that Canadians are seeing the world—even their own Canada—through American eyes. They also resent the loss of Canadian advertising dollars to American publishers' pockets. Time and Reader's Digest were not Canadian enough. By parliamentary action, Ottawa has now determined to improve the economic climate for Canadian magazines. Canadian advertisers in American publications like Time can no longer write off as business expenses their advertising costs in American journals. In order to qualify for the privilege of Canadian advertising tax write-offs, any American magazine would need to put within its covers more than 80 percent Canadian news or authorship and must be 75 percent Canadian owned. This kind of action would make the end results substantially different from its American parent publication. The Canadians claim this is not censorship. Time and other United States periodicals can still be imported and read by Canadians. The idea is only to deprive these publications—notably Time and Reader's Digest—of their Canadian advertising revenues. By this action, it is estimated, more than sixteen million Canadian dollars would be freed for advertising in strictly Canadian magazines. Thereby Canadian authors would also benefit. Said Cabinet Minister J. Hugh Faulkner, "I have no intention of giving up my subscription to Time . . . [but] Time should not be expected to explain to Canadians what's going on in Canada."

Because of cultural infiltration and economic domination from the south, Canadian periodicals have suffered materially. Ten years ago, there were at least eight major weekly or monthly indigenous Canadian magazines designed for general hearthside reading. Today there are only three majors—the women's fashion-cum-homemaking publication *Chatelaine, Homemakers Magazine,* and the monthly general interst *Macleans.* (The latter magazine, founded in 1905 as a monthly and converted to a biweekly in 1975, became a weekly newsmagazine in September, 1978, fulfilling a promise made to the federal government when restrictions were imposed on *Time* magazine's Canadian edition). Two others, both associated with Canadian newspaper efforts, might be considered important—*The Star Weekly* (published by the Toronto Star) and *Saturday Night.* Of the French publications, *Le Revue Populaire* and *Samedi* are most important. These compete with the French language edition of *Chatelaine (La Revue Moderne)* and with *Le Magazine Maclean's.* With only a few Canadian magazines remaining profitable, and with the continuing floodtide of American journals, these Canadian home products look like saplings in a forest of American trees.

There are in Canada some outstanding literary and scholarly periodicals. Among these, the *Canadian Forum, Arts Canada,* the *Canadian Review,* and publications of the Canadian Institute of International Affairs are exemplary. So, too, are certain of the professional journals emanating from university, legal, and scientific societies. There are also a number of good trade publications. Nonetheless, the fact that there are so few Canadian general interest journals that will pay adequately for the work of Canadian authors makes it difficult for young Canadian literary lights to subsist. And thus they are faced with the alternatives of chancing fame in Canada or of exporting their person and their product to London or New York. As a result, there is a tendency to argue for much more extensive governmental subsidies for writers as well as other artists.

It is also the intention of the Canadian government to eliminate tax deduction provisos for Canadian businesses advertising on United States cablevision outlets and border radio and TV stations that are heard and seen in Canadian homes. It is not intended to put this plan into effect until sufficient time and programs are available on Canadian stations to satisfy Canadian needs. It is estimated that Canadian firms are now spending $20 million yearly advertising on United States border stations. Some of these exist only to serve the Canadian market. The new tax setup will make Canadian stations more viable and Canadian programming more self-sufficient. All this should improve the quality and strength of the Canadian TV and radio systems.

In a speech delivered before American publishers recently, Canada's minister for cultural affairs, J. Hugh Faulkner, said that it was essential for a country to have its own searching and enlightened network of communications. On TV, radio, and feature films, Canadian products must be given an opportunity to compete. The Canadian government has given material assistance in production of Canadian feature films. The problem now is to obtain sufficient exhibition space (much of which is controlled by Americans). The Canadian government, henceforth, will be asking exhibitors, distributors, and theater owners to improve their percentile performance in exhibiting feature films from Canada. If this does not happen, the Canadian government will legislate to make such opportunities for Canadian products.

The minister of culture also insisted on greater opportunities for Canadian writers and encouragement of Canadian books. He insisted that there must be special incentives in the realms of Canadian fiction, criticism, letters, and poetry. Faulkner contended that foreign publishers must change their perception of Canada: "Canada is not simply an extension of the American market. . . . You [American publishers] are operating in a sovereign country. . . . We must insure that the Canadian-owned book publishing industry does not fall . . . and has room to grow. We shall be taking measures to protect our indigenous publishing industry."

Books and writers, playwrights and poets, artists and their pictorial themes, even musicians and their music—all reflect the kind of society in which they are rooted. They depict the kinds of ideals and interests, the moral and social values to which their nation aspires. They depict the pains and pleasures, the joys and sorrows of their society. They find, develop, and later protect their national traditions. They exhibit the variety and color in their national mosaic. It is obvious that Canadian authors and artists are essential factors, not alone in reflecting their country's values and conflicts, but in binding their country together.

According to one reputable Canadian writer, the key word for Canadian authors is "survival." She contends that novelists, poets, and playwrights especially are influenced by the environment in which they live and write. The work they turn out thus reflects the influence of the country itself. Products of certain great authors—for example, Steinbeck, Tolstoy, or Shakespeare—would be considered as very American, very Russian, or very English. For Canadians, the pressures may range from nature (cold and isolation) to colonialism and separatism. The intrusions and competition of the United States are obviously highly influential. In the face of these, the key word is "survival." That survival is measured in the defenses of 24 millions against the encroachment of 217 millions. In the words of Canada's Cultural Minister Faulkner, "For Canada—America's biggest sin is 'it's there!'"

16

Foreign Affairs

J ust as has been true with their economy and culture, leaders of Canada have been much concerned in recent years over what they consider to be the vexing problem of American intrusions into Canada's foreign affairs. In a speech on the subject, delivered before an American audience, Canada's then external affairs minister Allan MacEachen spelled out this problem. As he put it, until now, Canada has "puritanically opted for strict monogamy in a polygamous world." He has reminded the Americans that Canada can no longer put all her economic eggs in one basket. Canada recognizes the export opportunities in the Common Market and with Japan. There is a determination to strengthen commercial relationships with Eastern Europe and with the developing countries of the Pacific Basin. As well as securing greater control over her own economic destiny, Canada seeks to diversify her interests.

In recent years, Canada's foreign policy has actually been a kind of four-legged stool. One of the legs, considerably longer and heavier than the rest has been that complex geopolitical relationship involving the United States. The other three legs have been commonwealth links (including those with the British), the relationships with the United Nations, and those with NATO.

In 1970, a royal commission made a thorough study of the obviously lopsided state of Canadian foreign affairs. From that study it was concluded that three major options existed for Canada. She could (1) continue the status quo situation of partial domination by the United States; (2) opt for complete economic integration—and perhaps even later political association—with the United States in a kind of North American common market; (3) diffuse and supplement, even replace, some of her existing relations with the United States. Led by Prime Minister Trudeau, Canadian officials opted for the third course. They were determined to curtail American influence and to avoid further dependence on a single country by diversifying their external relationships. Thus Canada rejected her monogamous state and joined the polygamous world.

In the wake of her 1970 foreign policy review and her choice of that third option, Canada has already modified her relationships with the United States and with NATO. She has strengthened and diversified her relations with Eastern Europe, with Pacific Rim lands (especially China and Japan), and with Latin America. She now ends up with a septagonal stool. The seven legs make it somewhat less lopsided than before. Each of her foreign policy "legs" or major relationships, old and new, demands more scrutiny.

In the real geopolitical sense—in trade, defense, cultural affairs, environmental problems—Canada cannot escape her North American identity and her close and complex relations with the United States. The Honourable Allan MacEachen has admitted that one of the great success stories of diplomacy is the peaceful development of this relationship extending over the last century. Everyone has heard the cliche of the Canadian-American "longest undefended border." It is much more than that. Each has been a best customer for the other—Canadians for Americans, Americans for Canadians. Both Americans and Canadians now concede that these neighborly relations are going through a very difficult time. Our knowledge of each other has not kept pace with the growth of our myriad relationships. There are many irritants. There are also some important lubricants—as with the continuing mutually beneficial trade. There is a day-to-day interplay that is smooth and free flowing. When issues prove abrasive, they obviously require greater consultation and negotiation. For the Americans, too, there must be a tolerant understanding that some of these current abrasions come from the Canadians' own effort at national redefinition and reassessment of just what their national interests are. Both Canadian and American officials are becoming more aware that there must be broader understanding that decisions made either in the United States or in Canada almost invariably have an impact—sometimes major—upon the other neighbor.

The bilateral relationship that Canada has with the United States continues to be, by all odds, its most important. This relationship lies in three main areas. First of these is the global political-security area, which affects both the United States and Canada. American involvement in Korea, the Middle East, and Vietnam, and both nations' involvement as allies in two world wars are illustrative of this. The second is the range of multinational issues on which Canada and the United States may either diverge or coincide. An example of this is the law of the sea problem, on which the two nations diverge. The third is the range of problems of strictly bilateral interest, such as trade and energy matters. The latter includes the current headache over diminishing oil and gas exports from Canada to the United States.

For both the United States and Canada, this range of issues is shifting in this increasingly interdependent world. There are, for example, the new alignments coming out of detente and the SALT talks. There is the matter of increases in the number of nations that have joined the so-called nuclear arms club and that, in the process, make new alignments as well as international controls essential. There is also the range of environmental, financial, trade, and tariff relationships that can only be attacked by multinational action. There was the continuing hemispheric debate over such problems as the United States trade embargo against Cuba. This ban Canada refused to recognize. Canada is also much concerned with the various United States interventions into Latin America's internal affairs, such as the coups in Chile and in the Dominican Republic. All these matters continue to affect Canada almost as vitally as they do the United States.

It is interesting to note that, on many of these matters, Canada has taken action different from and in advance of the United States. There were the early efforts by Canada to open her own dialogues with both China and the USSR. In fact, Canada gently urged the United States to follow that lead. On matters such as control of marine oil pollution in the Far North, Canada also has been somewhat in advance of American interest—and action. Illustrative, too, have been Canadian actions to protect and to husband her own oil and gas reserves against external depredation. On the highly important law of the sea negotiations, Canada (with boundaries on the three oceans and with nineteen thousand miles of coastline) has been far ahead of the United States and again divergent. It was Canada that first insisted on implementing the two-hundred-mile territorial limit for offshore economic controls. This idea was originally objectionable to the United States, which insisted on the concept of "freedom of the seas" beyond the twelve-mile limit. Both Canada and the U.S. have now invoked the two-hundred-mile territorial limit with respect to commercial fishing. A temporary interim reciprocal fishing agreement between the two nations was suspended in June, 1978. Commercial fishing boats from each country were ordered to leave. A long-term solution is now sought regarding sports fishing. The issue is bound to provoke further bi-national abrasions.

Overall, in taking these and other independent actions, the Canadians' objective has been two-fold: (1) to strengthen their own economy and environment; (2) to enhance their own national identity. In this connection, Minister MacEachen is again worth quoting. Said he: "We do not propose to ignore United States needs or to take unfair advantage of the United States, but to enhance our own goals—to satisfy our own requirements—and, thereafter, to seek mutual advantage. We can only do this by . . . consultation and negotiation . . . not through domination." The minister's message is thus made "perfectly clear." It is now a matter of Canada first and Canadian–United States relations second.

As of this writing, there appear to be at least eight main problems complicating Canadian-American relations. First is the resolution of questions involving the $36-billion American ownership and control of businesses in Canada. (This matter has been given special attention in the chapters on the economy and the power elite.) Second, and most immediately troublesome, is the reduction of Canadian exports of petroleum and natural gas to the United States because of Canada's own internal needs. (This matter is further complicated by delays in building of the new natural gas pipeline from Alaskan Arctic fields as described in Chapter 13.) Third is the upcoming, and certainly protracted, review of the North American Air Defense relationships. Fourth is the reduction of pollutants in the Great Lakes. (It will be recalled that, in 1972, President Nixon signed an agreement with the Canadians to help clean up Lake Erie. He later impounded the essential United States funds, and that country has subsequently taken only minor action.) Fifth is the West Coast oil pollution problem, this stemming in part from development of the Alaskan fields, with associated transport difficulties. Petroleum is being transferred by tanker from Alaska to the continental United States, with attendant threats of marine pollution along the Canadian west coast. Sixth is the question of the flooding of the Skagit Valley in the State of Washington for hydroelectric purposes. This would result in a backup of water that would flood Canadian farmlands. Seventh is a similar water diversion problem at Garrison, North Dakota, which threatens Canadian lands. And, eighth, is an ongoing problem (including the question of toll charges) regarding the St. Lawrence Seaway. (A revised joint seaway tariff of tolls commenced January, 1978.)

To meet these and similar problems upcoming, Canadian cabinet ministers constantly emphasize the theme of consultation and bilateral talks. They admit that ministerial committees have not been too successful in recent years—and that more adequate ongoing consultative machinery must be maintained. They stress that there can no longer be domination of one partner by the other.

An International Joint Commission (IJC), a binational advisory and regulatory body, was established by treaty some seventy years ago. This body is composed of equal numbers of Canadian and American representatives. While it has made major contributions to Canadian-American amity at times, it appears in recent years to have become inadequate to its tasks. Perhaps leaders of both nations are now prepared to seek its revitalization.

Recalling Canada's past vulnerability to the United States, MacEachen restated Prime Minister Trudeau's earlier reference to the American elephant. He continued, "If the Canadian mouse finds herself so crowded in bed by the American elephant it is largely because she has failed to seek out other bed partners." In stating Canada's problems vis-a-vis the United States, the then external affairs minister, in yet another speech, showed that the two economies—Canadian and American—are not of the same magnitude. Certain facts reveal the imbalance between the two nations. (1) The United States outweighs Canada ten to one in terms of both population and GNP. (2) The United States provides markets for about 70 percent of Canadian exports, but these make up only 25 percent of American imports. (3) The United States supplies about 69 percent of Canadian imports, but that is only 15 percent of overall United States exports. (4) The United States absorbs about 35 percent of all goods produced in Canada, but Canada, in turn, buys only 2 percent of America's output. (5) The United States accounts for 80 percent of total foreign investment in Canada, while Canada's investors own only one-half of one percent of foreign investment in the United States. (Increased investment southward took place in 1978.)

While Canada continues to emphasize her north-south links with the United States, she now insists on expanding her east-west links, to diversify these and, in the process, to sustain her paramount national interests. Foremost among these east-west links is Canada's long-time love affair with the commonwealth.

A colony of Britain from 1763 until 1867 and an essential part of the British Empire (and later Commonwealth) until the present, Canada keeps a close historic-ethnic relationship with the United Kingdom. The special position of the British monarch as sovereign head of Canada symbolizes and cements this relationship. Today, however, this association is one of equality between the two nations rather than domination by Britain over Canada.

Political, cultural, and especially defense relationships between the two nations have been very deep. For example, the involvement of Britain in World Wars I and II immediately brought Canada into those conflicts as a full military ally of the United Kingdom. Some four hundred thousand Canadians served overseas during World War I. More than a million Canadians served in World War II. In both conflicts, Canada's soldiery took heavy losses.

It will be recalled that Canada did not receive full autonomy in foreign affairs and defense until 1926. (The first Canadian diplomat to the United States was accredited only in 1927.) The subsequent and highly important 1931 Statute of Westminster created the commonwealth, began to dissolve the empire, and made Canada a full partner with Britain in that commonwealth. Henceforth the two countries were bound together only by common allegiance to the crown—the British monarchy—and the commonwealth.

Under imperial and later commonwealth trade preferences, Canada gave and received preferential treatment to and from Britain. Overall, however, during the past twenty years, the balance of trade has run heavily in Canada's favor. Britain now takes less than 10 percent of Canada's exports. In turn, Britain provides only 5 percent of Canada's imports. Furthermore, Britain held over 40 percent of all foreign funds invested in Canada during the 1930s, but holds less than 10 percent of that investment today.

The Canadians, in a definite sense, have considered themselves as architects of the modern commonwealth. They enjoy their central role in that loose association, hold onto their membership tenaciously, and use the multinational and multiracial "club" as a consultative body of real consequence. Illustrative of Canada's deep interest in the commonwealth has been the wide reaction of her citizenry to the commonwealth issues raised by the Nigerian (Biafran) war, the apartheid and arms embargo issues relating to South Africa, and the Rhodesian Unilateral Declaration of Independence (UDI). On all these issues, Canada's own views ran ahead of those of the mother country, Britain.

Thus, in Canada's eyes, the commonwealth, with its thirty-six member nations, is alive and well—flourishing throughout the globe. Support for the commonwealth remains a central element in Canadian foreign policy. Members share a common language and a common historical experience. These shared values transcend racial, religious, cultural, and geographic perimeters and enable the commonwealth to respond to challenges with great flexibility. The grouping represents a formidable repository of collective knowledge. Functional cooperation is being expanded beyond simple politics—extending into matters of science, health, environment, trade, finance, and justice. The 1975 Commonwealth Ministerial Meeting, convened in Jamaica, formalized this expansion, and Canada agreed to provide 15 percent of the funds for the new activities. All in all, the commonwealth is concerned with people, and Canada is much concerned with the commonwealth.

Associated with this great interest is the fact that the

first, and long-term, head of the Commonwealth Secretariat was Arnold Smith, a Canadian. Many of the nonwhite commonwealth members have even asked Canada to assume a position of central leadership of the group, inferentially replacing Britain. To this, Canada has always demurred in the belief that it is a community of partner nations—not a monolith. The Commonwealth Meeting of Prime Ministers of 1973, convening in Ottawa, illustrated the Canadian determination that the "club" be one of equals. After the conference, Prime Minister Trudeau characterized that meeting as "one of beautiful equality with no single star performers."

Closely allied with her commonwealth interests has been Canada's extensive economic aid program. This effort, beginning with her help to commonwealth partners in South Asia through the old Colombo Plan, has now extended itself to a number of commonweatlh members in Africa as well as to various African Francophon states. (Canada, with her own French-Canadian citizenry, feels a special kinship with these latter nations.) In these aid activities, Canada seeks to help shift world attention from the military to peace—from politics to economics. At the same time, she seeks again to expand her ties. She is not only altruistic in these efforts, but believes that, in the future, these developing nations may well become some of her major trading partners. In 1977 over 40 percent of her total of some $1.1 billion in bilateral and multilateral foreign aid went to Africa. About half of this was in the form of grants, the rest in low-interest loans. She also provided considerable food aid to the starving peoples of the Sahel region of the sub-Sahara. She has likewise provided considerable technical assistance to these African nations through her own Canadian version of the Peace Corps. This organization, known as the Canadian University Students Overseas (CUSO), has both English- and French-speaking subdivisions. As an adjunct of all this help, Canada admitted some five thousand Asians as immigrants in 1972 when these and other commonwealth nationals were expelled from Uganda by Gen. Idi Amin.

All in all, it is said that Canada now gives more than 0.8 percent of her GNP in overseas economic aid. This figure is more than double that supplied by the United States measured in per capita terms. The Canadians view their aid efforts as a moral requirement. "It is only right for those who *have* to share with those who *have not*," says the Honourable Allan MacEachen.

As a middle-level power, Canada has preferred to operate through international organizations whenever possible. She was a charter member of the United Nations and an ardent supporter of that body. This has been difficult because of the cold war with the resultant weakening of United Nations influence among the great powers. The balance-of-power tactics in diplomacy among those superpowers, and Canada's close association with the United States till now, have complicated Canadian troubles in the international sphere.

Nevertheless Canada has played a key role in various international disputes. Prime Minister (then Minister for External Affairs) Lester Pearson was instrumental in conciliating the 1956 Suez Canal crisis, for which he received a Nobel Peace Prize. Canada has also played key middleman roles in Korea, in the Congo, in Cyprus, in Southeast Asia, as well as in the Middle East. Today, her troops are stationed on the Golan Heights, in the Sinai, and in Lebanon. More than twelve thousand of Canada's military have served in the Cyprus peace-keeping effort alone.

Recent attempts to push world interdependence instead of balance-of-power concepts have been beneficial to the Canadian point of view. Canada has been especially concerned with problems of environment and with the law of the sea. Canada is the fourth-largest contributor to the United Nations Relief Fund and a heavy contributor to the World Bank. The UN development program has been given heavy backing by Canada both in money and in manpower. The city of Montreal serves as the home of an important UN specialized agency, the International Civil

Aviation Organization (ICAO). Canada has always believed in universality of membership for the United Nations and in that organization's usefulness in social and economic development as well as for peacekeeping.

As Canada is one of the original members of NATO, and because of her close defense relations with the United States, it is important to say something concerning her current military posture. Of late, Canada's total force strength has been 82,054—of whom some 6,600 were overseas. This latter grouping included some 3,000 (formerly 10,000) Canadians assigned to NATO and 3,600 assigned to various United Nations Emergency Task Forces in Cyprus and the Middle East. Canada's international role has been especially important in those United Nations peacekeeping efforts. This fact stems in part from Canada's deep commitment to collective security under UN aegis and in part from its determination to maintain an independent role separate both from Britain and from the United States. As Winston Churchill once stated it, "Canada is neither a 51st State nor a cub nuzzling up under the she-bear, Mother England."

Canada's prime purpose in going into NATO was one of necessity. In 1949, when NATO began, the situation of the middle and smaller powers faced with Russian adventurism was somewhat precarious. There was, as well, the necessity for Canada to expand her defense relationships beyond those bilateral arrangements she had with Britain, her colonial mentor, and the United States, her superpower neighbor. Canada thus placed herself on a multilateral, rather than a bilateral, path—and she has continued along that path in most of her current foreign policy relationships.

The value of NATO, however, is now being seriously questioned by Canada. She has withdrawn more than half of her NATO contingent from Europe. In recognition of those Canadian doubts, the United States has insisted on divorcing NORAD from NATO, simply to reinsure her North American defense commitments with Canada. The reduction of Canadian forces in NATO is therefore due, not so much to her isolationism, but rather to her determination to cut down on defense commitments and, instead, to concentrate on broader economic and cultural ties with all nations. However, she continues under the nuclear umbrella supplied by the United States.

Creation and growth of the European Economic Community (Common Market), along with Canada's recent changes in trade patterns, has forced Canada to reevaluate and to seek closer ties with the major continental European nations, particularly France and West Germany. To this end, Prime Minister Trudeau made at least four journeys to Europe during 1976 alone. Canada has also joined the UN Economic Commission for Europe. In addition, Ottawa is seeking easier financial as well as trading relationships with the Common Market partners. To this end, an EEC office is being established in Ottawa. Reflecting this new interest in Western Europe, Canada's trade with the nine Common Market countries exceeded $2.5 billion in 1974—a jump of more than 30 percent over 1973.

In this arena, special problems continue to exist with France because of the sensitivity of Quebec separatism. The fact that Quebec is a French-speaking province, and so recognized by French authorities, continues to make foreign policy relationships between Ottawa and Paris extraordinarily delicate, though both Quebec authorities and French officials half-heartedly recognize that Ottawa continues to be the governmental superior of the Province of Quebec. This jurisdiction is restricted in Quebec's eyes, and pressure is constantly being exerted to further limit those spheres of superiority. The eventual aim of Quebec—and France—is to make Quebec a Francophon "state" *de facto* if not *de jure*.

It is obvious that the two governments—Ottawa and Paris—have buried the hatchet since the troubling day in 1967 when President de Gaulle outraged Anglo-Canadians with his shout from the steps of the Montreal city hall, "Vive le Quebec libre!" However, the people of Quebec, including present Premier Levesque, continue to look to France for fraternity and culture as well as for rhetoric. Yet, it may be said that, apart from the matter of Quebec and the French atomic bomb blasts in the South Pacific, the two nations are generally in agreement on international matters. In fact, Canada's recent trade with France has been booming in both directions.

Both France and West Germany are expanding their investments in Canada as well as their trade. In fact, Germany has now become Canada's third-best trading partner after the United States and Japan. West Germany is also said to have more than $2.5 billion invested in Canadian lands and business properties.

Canada was far ahead of the Western pack in opening relations, trade and cultural, with both the USSR and mainland China. Canada is selling considerable amounts of wheat to both nations and is broadening both sales and lines of credit to them. Most recent of the latter was a $500-million line of credit to the Soviets for technical equipment and know-how. This was concluded in 1975. Russia is sending raw cotton to Canada in payment of some of its trade debts. Since conclusion of the 1971 Canadian/USSR Agreement on Industrial Applications of Science and Technology, several hundred Canadian and Soviet officials have exchanged visits and information.

Prime Minister Trudeau's remark, in welcoming Premier Kosygin in Ottawa in 1971, raised eyebrows in Washington. Said Trudeau, "In its geographical position, Canada would like to have relations as friendly with the Soviet Union as they have been for many years with the United States." The political message was clear. The United States can no longer take Canadian friendship for granted. Even before the American steps toward detente, Canada was seeking to get out from the shadow of the American elephant—and was willing to hug the Russian bear.

Canada was long a defender of Peking's right to seats in the United Nations General Assembly and Security Council. In fact, she was somewhat ahead of the American

efforts to reopen relations with Peking. Illustrative is the
fact that, in the summer of 1972, at the very time President
Nixon made his memorable opening trip to China, some
five hundred Canadian businessmen led by Canada's external affairs minister, Mitchell Sharp, had opened a
massive trade fair in Canton. This, the largest trade fair
involving foreigners in China in recent years, was a two-
week, $2-million event completely underwritten by the
Canadian government. Sales by Canada to China are now
in excess of $200 million yearly, placing Canada among
China's top five trading partners. The high point in
expanding relations between Canada and China was Prime
Minister Trudeau's visit to Peking in October, 1973. There
he concluded a new trade and cultural agreement; a new
consular convention; and a special one-time admission of
ten thousand Chinese to Canada in an effort to reunite
families.

Japan is now Canada's second-best trading partner. In
addition to expanding trading relationships with that
nation, there is an effort to "politicize" those contacts.
There have been exchanges between parliamentarians of
Tokyo and Ottawa. The prime ministers of both countries
have exchanged visits. Tokyo is increasing its investment
in Canada. Those investments are now said to be in excess
of $600 million. Scientific accords have also been signed
between the two nations.

The effect of Canada's decision to broaden her foreign
affairs—including trade relationships—is clearly demonstrated by her 1974 foreign trade figures. Overseas
markets then showed a larger increase percentagewise
than did trade with the United States. Exports to Latin
America, especially Brazil, have shown the largest increase on a percentage basis, followed by exports to the
EEC and to commonwealth markets outside the United
Kingdom. Canada's exports to Britain continue to decline.
Imports from continental Europe are also increasing.

Although more than 40 percent of all Canadians are of
British background, the privileged status of incoming

Britons has been removed by recent legislation. Now citizens of all nations of the commonwealth, including Britons, are accorded equality.

One unusual aspect of foreign policy is Canada's attitude on immigration. For a nation of immigrants, like the United States, this has been a matter both of economic pressures and of political touchiness—dependent on the economic winds. Until very recent years, there have been more Canadian migrants to the United States than vice versa. Lately, however, that trend has been reversed. Today it is estimated that about twenty-six thousand Americans (or more than two-thirds of all Americans emigrating abroad) are annually going to Canada. In turn, the number of Canadians returning to Canada from America is just about in balance. This is a historic change, since large numbers of Canadians in the years prior to World War II found new homes in the United States.

There has been less immigration to Canada in the last two years, and the inflow is expected to dwindle to 140,000 annually. There were 142,156 immigrants in 1976. Canada admitted 218,000 immigrants in 1974. More than 38,000 of these came from Britain, 26,000 from the United States, 16,000 from Portugal, 12,000 from India, 12,000 from Hong Kong, and 11,000 from Jamaica. Others came from the Philippines, Greece, Guyana, Italy, and France in large numbers. In contrast to those of British and French immigrant background, the various other immigrant groups are sometimes called "The New Canadians."

The Province of Ontario continues to be the favorite haven for the immigrants: 106,000 went there in 1974. Some 34,000 went to British Columbia, 33,000 to Quebec, and 14,000 to Alberta. The majority of all immigrants are under thirty-five years of age. More than 10 percent of them are of professional categories—doctors, teachers, etc.

Summarizing, it may be assumed that Canada's first foreign policy objective is survival as a nation. Preservation of her independence of action will be her second goal. Insofar as the United States is concerned, Canada will insist on consultation and negotiation between equals. Thereafter—Canada will make her special contribution to an independent world. Here her aims appear to be prosperity and betterment of the human condition for all mankind. For her, international cooperation will be a moral imperative as well as a political necessity.

17
What Is a Canadian?

What is a Canadian? Is it the Ford factory worker in Windsor who is concerned with the size of his paycheck, his supply of Carlings beer, and the score of last night's hockey game between the Maple Leafs and the Flyers? Is it the French-Canadian housewife in Moncton whose favorite entertainment is the TV soap opera beamed at her from a New England station? Is it the Vancouver secretary who occasionally reads Canadian magazines but who much prefers the sexy American mag, *Cosmopolitan?* Is it the British-born architect in Halifax who finds his reading enjoyment in *Punch* and the London *Sunday Times?* Is it the Montreal textile magnate who banks in New York and winters in Jamaica? Is it the Ukrainian restauranteur in Winnipeg who, beset by labor troubles and inflation, is considering emigrating? Is it the young university student from Trois-Rivieres who venerates only General de Gaulle and Parti Quebecois? Is it the retired farmer in Regina, disciple of Diefenbaker and populism, who frets about the political leadership in Ottawa and thinks his country is going to hell in a basket?

It is all these who make up the composite photograph—the montage—of Canada. It is these and many more.

It is extremely difficult to sketch an accurate profile of any nation. It is especially challenging for a foreign writer to attempt such a distillation. What, after all, is the essence of a typical Dane, Australian, Greek, or Japanese?

Each of these is the product of his or her history, tradition, demography—the entire national heritage. So too
with the Canadian.

Pages foregoing have demonstrated the warp and woof
and rich texture of the colorful Canadian tapestry. It
remains now only to weave the variegated pieces together
to show the composite—the Canadianness—of this plural
society.

There is a paucity of studies delineating the nature of the
"typical" Canadian. The few writers who have made that
effort have been faced with a mass of material with
parameters ranging from a plural society to the vast landscape. Those who have attempted the task have used the
word *mosaic* freely to describe the Canadian nation. The
ethnic threads of this pluralistic society include French,
British, German, Scandinavian, central and eastern European, Amerindian, Eskimo, Asian, and Carib. Each new
nationality or racial grouping in turn has contributed its
color and its culture to the patterns composing Canada.
This mosaic or tapestry differs markedly from the homo-
genized culture of the United States. For, unlike Canada,
which thus far has sought to keep its diversity, the American cultural and ethnic colossus seeks to remould, to grind
up into "hamburger," all the diversities that exist in that
land. Even the few regional and racial divisions that do
exist are slowly being lost or sublimated in the homoge-
nizing process called Americanization. This is not yet true
of Canada. Urbanization, industrialization, and allied
cultural changes may bring this kind of homogeneity to
Canada one day. But today Canadians remain ethnocen-
tric—tribal. English, French, and "new" Canadians resist
the making of their nation into an amorphous state.

By comparison with their American neighbors, Canadians are also more conservative, more legalistic, probably
more consciously moral, more aware of social and economic class differences. The Americans are more egalitarian, free swinging, venturesome, and volatile. Both French
and English groups are earnest defenders of things
Canadian—less critical of their own land when talking

with outsiders than are the Americans. Canadians resent being considered as "just like Americans." They refuse any longer to be "taken for granted." In many respects Canada is an uncrowded society, with its diversities so clearly recognizable that it may be considered a nation still in process of formation.

For most Canadians, the land still dominates them. It is vast, disparate, often breathtaking—sometimes inspiring—sometimes melancholy. Much of the land remains untamed, some portions even uncharted. In some regions, there are more lakes than there are people. In other regions, there are more trees than fauna. The whole Canadian community is, in some ways, inhibited by its landscape. Survival in such a setting becomes not only a challenge but a must. Conquest of nature becomes a major personal triumph—and a loss to natural forces a personal or national tragedy. The Canadians, unlike peoples in more populous regions, have had to come to terms with nature. All these factors have helped to create within the Canadian an innate conservatism that is a central element of the individual Canadian character.

In addition, from pages past comes a distillation of at least five other major themes that meld with that conservatism to form the Canadian character. These themes have been implicit in the actions of Canada's prime ministers. They have recurred in statements and actions of her provincial premiers. They have been expressed in the works of the nation's writers and artists—and in the comments of the man on the street. These themes include (1) the question What do Canadians think of themselves? (2) the problem of separatism and its allied dangers of balkanization or breakup; (3) measurement of the force and direction of the "New Canadian Nationalism;" (4) the drive for a distinctive "Canadian" culture; (5) a restatement and redefining of Canada's prime national interests and goals. Each of these themes has been developed as a thread in certain pages of this book. These now require weaving together into the tapestry called Canada.

First of the ingredients deserving of our special attention is the peculiar proclivity of the individual Canadian, from time to time, to indulge in a bout of introspection. This embodies not alone a kind of "examination of personal conscience" but, as well, a searching analysis of his or her national identity. In essence, this examination seeks answers to two questions: What do Canadians think of themselves? and Where is their country going? These bouts of contemplation of the national navel seem to recur at intervals of five to ten years. In fact, when this mood of national self-doubt does occur, it becomes a veritable contagion. It even goes so deep as to question how many years of survival as a nation this Canada may have. A very few nervous nationalists may even go so far as to wonder whether Canada may soon by invaded—gobbled up—by a voracious, land- and resource-hungry United States of America.

Admittedly, this is a strange emotional and visceral ebb-and-flow mood. It ranges between a national preoccupation with despair and a feeling of national pride. There appears to be a wide difference between the two major ethnic groups on this matter. Members of the English-speaking community seem much more prone to self-doubt and concern over the nation's destiny than do their French-Canadian counterparts. This may stem from the fact that, over a very long period of time, the Anglo-Canadians have had a tendency to make denigrating comparisons of their nation's achievements as contrasted with those of Britain and the United States. This comparison, in turn, brings on a feeling of national inferiority, deserved or undeserved. In contrast, the French-Canadian may find protection from such comparisons in the very fact that his group is more cohesive and more insulated. Furthermore, the innate tendency toward separatism may lead those of French origin away from worrying much about the fate of Canada as a nation. The French-Canadian harbors no sense of cultural or ethnic inferiority. He is proud of his links with France—proud of his lineage from the land of the tricolor and the Marseillaise. A rank generalization some may call it—but do those of French background ever feel inferior about anything—their wine, their women, their food, their identity? *Alors!*

Each time this national mood of introspection and self-doubt seizes Canada, it seems, within some months, to be followed by a mood of national bouyancy. This latter mood shows up in a spate of intense nationalism, of preoccupation with culture and Canadiana, with renewed public determination to make of Canada an international showpiece. An example of this mood of bouyancy in recent years was the climate of high confidence inspired by the successful Montreal Expo of 1967. This was the glittering and widely acclaimed celebration of Canada's one hundredth birthday as a nation. Even more interesting was the fact that this particular mood of self-confidence was dispelled in the period 1970–1972, when Canada faced turmoil in new and violent pressures from Quebec's separatists. At the same time, Canadian leaders, under public pressure, occupied themselves with the task of "buying back" parts of Canadian business and industry from American ownership.

Surely Canada's increasingly firm position in a world so short of food, water, and other essential resources should, in the end, inspire more and longer periods of national optimism than of pessimism. The life and vitality of that national mood, however, may depend on answering two major questions. First of these is the vexing problem of separatism. Second is the allied question of regional and provincial inequities and federal-provincial quarrels.

How far can the central government of Canada go towards satisfying provincial demands without destroying national unity? Can ethnic, linguistic, social, economic, and political divisions be bridged? Earlier pages of this book have shown that the pulls of separatism, centered in the French-speaking Province of Quebec, and the parallel issue of federal-provincial relationships have together constituted an infection in the national bloodstream and body politic of Canada for a century past. This infectious drain on the nation's energies was apparent almost from the day of Canada's confederation, July 1, 1867. In fact, the aim of that very confederation was to meld Lower Canada (Quebec) into a larger grouping of colonies of predominantly Anglo-Saxon background. It was then, as now, hoped that French culture and allegiances would be submerged in a broader, specifically Canadian, character.

This dream of the Founding Fathers did not work out for several reasons. First and foremost were the built-in safeguards of the British North America Act and the earlier Quebec (1774) and Canada (1791) acts. These legislative enactments shored up French-Canada's special position vis-a-vis the nation as a whole. Tradition, religion, judicial decisions, and official approval of bilingualism increased the size of the chasm separating the two groups.

There were other reasons as well. Between 1851 and 1961, Canada is reported to have lost almost as many people through emigration as it gained through immigration. Only since 1961 has this outflow of population been reversed. It is important to recognize that it was generally the non–French-Canadians who were involved in using Canada merely as a transit stop and port of exit. The French-Canadians did not share in this general exodus. They stayed home and multiplied.

Perhaps as important as the foregoing, however, may have been the continuing weak economic situation of the French-Canadians of Quebec. That position, until very recently, has been in sharp contrast to that in most of the other provinces. This resulted in domination—economic, social, and political—by the Anglos over the French-Canadians. There grew up an attitude, not of inferiority alone, but of resentment among Quebecois toward other Canadians. Despite the massive recent expansion of Quebec's industrial base, this situation remains. Anglo-Canadians and Americans, in general, continue to dominate the corporate board rooms of Quebec. Furthermore, the largesse paid out by Ottawa to the government of Quebec in the form of subventions and equalization payments from the richer provinces to the poorer also has its psychological influence.

There are three options available for the French-Canadian: (1) He can remain an integral part of the confederation, keeping the status quo with all its abrasions. (2) He can seek total independence for Quebec and take the economic and political consequences, debilitating as those may be. (3) He can seek a looser confederation, possibly eliminating the political ties with Ottawa but retaining economic ties with the other provinces in a kind of "Canadian Common Market."

This boils down to the bare-bones question: Do the French-Canadians wish to become "Canadian" in the fullest sense? Or will they insist on preserving their own identity to the point of destroying the confederation as presently constituted? As pages foregoing will remind, some extreme separatists may say that this decision has already been made and the choice is for separation. Their only question is, When?

Yet another question that this matter of separatism brings up is, Could Canada survive as a viable nation in the event of Quebec's departure from the confederation? Furthermore, if Quebec goes, would this event in turn precipitate other fractures—other regional breakups? Unfortunately, this is not merely an academic question. For there is both sourness and friction between Ottawa and various provinces other than Quebec. Those problems too could bring about a dismemberment of Canada. Some, in fact, are so serious as to require constitutional solutions. In any event, devolution of power from Ottawa into provincial capitals seems inevitable. The question of whether Canadians want a bilingual nation is a subsidiary one. The main question is whether Canadians of all origins and all areas still want to be CANADIANS.

In his last address to Western Canada's leaders, just before he retired, Prime Minister Lester Pearson took special note of this disease of "separatism." Said he, "Canada is an awfully difficult nation to govern." He went on to spell out the fissions and fractures of his land—ethnic, geographic, economic, political, social. He emphasized that, in a country where political associations run east and west, there are geographic, economic, and cultural lines that run north and south. Thus there is a tendency to build up countervailing forces. In his discussion of the problem, Pearson admitted that, from his vantage point in Ottawa, he had never managed to get through to, or to fully understand, the people of the Canadian West.

Here is a situation that has plagued other prime ministers than Pearson. Indeed it has perplexed most of them. The misunderstandings between Ottawa and some provinces of the West, the Maritimes—and Quebec—are issues as relevant today as they were a quarter century ago. These are centrifugal forces that are economic as well as political, social as well as ethnic. The Western provinces are pulled toward the Pacific Rim lands. For the Maritimes, the pull is toward New England and Europe. Quebec is self-centered. Somehow these real or potential fractures must be constrained and mended.

A part of this problem may stem from the fact that there is underrepresentation of certain provinces in the House of Commons as well as in the Senate. Some of these provinces, too, have minority representation that carries no effective legislative voice. This situation in turn seems to create an unusual number of minority governments in Canada at critical times. To complete the vicious circle, that situation in turn creates new strains between Ottawa and the provinces in areas as wide-ranging as transport, social and labor legislation, and distribution of energy royalties. Obviously, political leaders of the more renegade provinces, by failing to send adequate numbers of representatives of major parties to seats in the House of Commons, are saying to the rest of Canada, "What is good enough for Ottawa is not necessarily good enough for us."

One way in which this situation could be alleviated would be to take the largely honorific membership of the Senate out of its anachronistic appointive cocoon. That body could be given both more equitable representational status and more legislative authority. This could possibly be done by giving the Senate of 102 members both elective and provincial casts. For example, 10 (or fewer) Senators could be elected from each of the provinces, with 1 senator each coming from the Yukon and the Northwest Territories. This would give to the Senate of Canada the same geographic and representational shape as that now seen in the Senate of the United States.

Yet another way in which these regional and federal-provincial frictions might be alleviated would be to develop a third major national "Natural Resources Party." This could reflect, for example, the interests of timber, fisheries, mining, and agriculture. Basing its strength on both capital and labor, such a grouping could provide at least a modicum of "political clout" in Ottawa. By consolidating the political and economic views of the Western and Maritime provinces on major issues, such a party might better be able to represent the needs of these regions. This kind of party might also be able to offset the big-business political cartels of Ontario and Quebec. It could even go some way to counterbalancing the divisiveness of separatism.

Related to these questions of separatism and of federal-provincial frictions is a single historical fact of Canadian life. That fact of life has not been tackled head-on. Actually it has been disregarded, even avoided, by most prime ministers and some premiers in recent years. Only a few courageous souls have alluded to it. This is the matter of central authority and of constitutional revision. At the outset of Canada's independence, the terms of confederation presumed a strong central authority in Ottawa. Geographic, economic, ethnic, linguistic, and political diversities defeated that aim. Over the past century, the governments of the provinces have grown progressively stronger while that of the central government has grown weaker. Various external influences, not alone American, have contributed to this strengthening of regional disparities and interprovincial pulls.

Perhaps now is the time for the people of Canada to bite

this constitutional bullet by clarifying these federal-provincial relationships. At the same time, the machinery of constitutional amendment and reform should be decided once and for all. If this comes to mean a looser confederation, which still hangs together for mutual advantage, would that not be better than this continual straining at the leash? Alternatively, would not stronger federal dominion and constitutional control over the provinces from Ottawa yet be the best means of preserving Canada as a single and viable nation? Here the country seems to have specific options, but for short-term political reasons, no option is being chosen. Someday that choice will be forced and painful. It would indeed be a great tragedy if Canada were ever to slide into major civil war to maintain its fragile unity. Surely some way can be found to preserve—and to enhance—allegiances to the *whole* nation rather than to its geographic or ethnic parts.

There is one element that is apparently contributing to Canada's internal strength and unity. In recent years, Canadians are showing themselves to be determined to "do their own thing." This attitude of nationalism—of confident assertion of their nationhood—had been directed toward London in the nineteenth century. Today, it is directed more specifically at Washington. For Canadians have long resented, and are finally beginning to fight back against, a certain condescension, arrogance, even indifference of Americans toward Canadians. They are also resenting the oft-stated dogmatic contention that "Canadians are just like Americans." They are not. Be these attitudes intentional or unintentional, friendly yet misguided, the Canadians are unwilling to be taken for granted any longer—by Americans or others.

They are insisting that their goods, their needs, their ideas, even their Canadian dollars be accepted on a par with things American. Indeed they insist on being accepted as coequals on this continent. Today the results of their introspection and their search for national goals, combined with their solid economic position, are giving them a new sense of equality—even of superiority, moral and economic. In fact that sense of new confidence is already being quietly demonstrated by Canadian generosity toward the Third World in fields of material aid and technical help. It is also being demonstrated in terms of Canada's willingness to provide men and money for United Nations peacekeeping activities. This attitude of self-confidence among Canadians is bound to increase, especially given the prospect of further shortages of resources on the world scene. For the most part, the Canadians will not be experiencing these shortages. Their own supplies of natural resources are enough to make them self-sufficient in the main. As a result, they will tolerate no further condescension—from Washington or elsewhere.

Given the strange set of unilateral actions taken by the United States during the last years of the Nixon administration against her best trading partner—Canada—it was no wonder that the latter thought she was being kicked out of her continental bed by her elephantine partner. In the wake of the energy crisis—and given the plethora of her own natural resources and foodstuffs—it may be that the Canadians now have the last laugh. Canada's curtailment and gradual elimination of shipments of natural gas and oil to American markets surely tell those Americans that the neighbor to the north is now thinking and acting for "Canada First." Canadians are determined to husband their scarce resources for their own needs. They will no longer unquestioningly do the bidding of the Americans. Their new foreign policy and trade doctrines show that Ottawa is beginning to diversify its external associations. In fact, Canada has decided to climb back into bed with a whole new set of bed partners. She is expressly, as her ministers put it, determined to be polygamous rather than monogamous. The decision has been clearly made to supplement rather than to supplant the United States relationship. As Prime Minister Trudeau himself has said, "Canada will no longer carry all its eggs in one basket."

Canada is declaring herself no longer a junior partner—

but an equal partner—on the North American continent as well as in the commonwealth. She is telling her American neighbor that she will be both nationalist and internationalist on her own terms and in line with her own best interests. In that process, she is proceeding to roll back the extensive American investment in Canada's own business and industry. She is determined not alone to show her sovereignty but to buy Canada back.

The United States will need to learn to live with this new sense of Canadian nationalism. Her best procedure, undoubtedly, is to foster mutual and continuing collaboration, consultation, discussion. Thereby she can restore mutual trust. The skeins of Canadian-American mutual interest are far too important to further knot up or to discard. These two nations need each other in this most interdependent of eras.

A part of Canada's introspective dreams has been devoted to measuring the standard of her own achievements against those of the British, the French, the Americans. As the last-named have become more and more burdened with domestic and international commitments, and as the American standards of life have declined or been deflected, the Canadians have come to believe that the quality of their life is ever more satisfactory. Emphasizing this very point were the prophetic words of the Canadian minister of energy. He recently told an American audience, "A part of the cause of the new Canadian nationalism and our determination to build something unique in Canada has been the malaise that exists in your land (America)." As the American dream turned into a nightmare, the Canadians were increasingly determined not to be a part of that nightmare. This is a tough assignment, given the mass of relationships—economic, cultural, and otherwise—that flow across the forty-ninth parallel in both directions.

Central to her dream is the problem of what to do about creating a distinctly "Canadian" culture. This matter has been doubly perplexing in the shadow of the American behemoth. Many Canadian writers and artists of the twenties and thirties characterized their native land as a "cultural bush league"—a literary and artistic vacuum. They looked at their Canada as a decent but gray society— a dullsville—a place to visit but not to live in. They acquired their reputations elsewhere or not at all. In fact, building a reputation in Canada was considered almost an embarrassment—elsewhere an achievement. In the years, when this cultural lag of Canada showed up most sharply, many of that country's talented young actors and writers migrated to New York, London, or Paris—to Burbank or the Left Bank. This was essentially true of the Anglo-Canadians. The young French men and women of talent were more inclined to stay at home among the habitants or to go only so far as Montreal or Quebec City. Thus the Anglo-Canadians, feeling unfulfilled, had the tendency to reject their cultural roots, while their confreres, the Quebecois, were accepting their own.

One of the more apt comparisons of this flight of the young "Canadian geese" southward comes from the well-known Canadian writer Hugh MacLennan. He compares this movement of cultural talent with the flight of young talent from Scotland southward into England in centuries past. It is important to note, however, that the movement of young Scots southward along the highroad of adventure from Edinburgh into London eventually helped to bring on political as well as economic domination by England over Scotland. The brain drain thus infused and helped to create the modern Britain. Many Canadians, MacLennan included, fear a similar end result—complete domination by the United States over Canada—if this southward movement to New York and Hollywood is not interrupted. It is such fears that inspire Canadians to revitalize their own culture. They hope thereby to reinsure their own independence.

There is, however, yet another reason. There is an increasing skepticism among Canadians about the tinsel, even tawdriness, of the intensely commercialized American cultural scene. The tube, the films, the entire American way of life is so infected. Many Canadians, therefore, no longer feel intimidated—or drawn—by the American glamor market. In fact, Canadians have taken very much to heart the lessons of their own Marshall McLuhan, that "The Media is the Message." Canadians seem determined to avoid that pitfall for themselves at all costs. The way in which they seek to reinvigorate and restore their own cultural scene has been spelled out by inauguration of grants, prizes, fellowships, and awards. Thus this home cultural scene at long last is becoming more enticing— more rewarding—for their youthful talented ones. Great strides have already been noted in sports, the arts, ballet, and theater. They have yet a way to go in literature and films. But they remain determined.

The final, and perhaps the most important, element in this depiction of "Canadianness" is the combined matter of national loyalties and of clear-cut national interests. Provincial loyalties seem to come first. Indeed, some provincial authorities are said to look upon Ottawa as the capital of a foreign nation. Is this nation of such disparate circumstances and geographic distances to be kept together only by allegiance to crown and commonwealth? Is it to be continually beset by linguistic, ethnic, cultural, and social divisions? Surely there are ways in which both geographic and ethnic differences can be moderated in favor of the interests of the nation as a whole. Some of these have already been set forth in paragraphs preceding.

"Abandonment" has been termed a controlling theme of Canadian life—one central to the nation's history and to development of her national character. This theme embodies rejections of previous loyalties—be they to Europe or America. As a result, newcomers to Canada, after escaping one tyranny or another, have been just a bit shy about giving their loyalties to a new, less tyrannical, national government. They have therefore held back some loyalties, retaining them for family or an ethnic grouping rather than subscribing full loyalty to Ottawa or to Canada itself. The peoples of the provinces, while gingerly accepting that they are Canadians, still sense that their first loyalty is to their province. They are fist of all Quebecois, Newfoundlanders, Albertans, British Columbians.

These attitudes of provincialism and nationalism in Canada today are trendy—fashionable. In some respects, they dovetail with the ups and downs of introspection. Nationalism means many things to many people. Prime Minister Trudeau would not quite characterize his version as "Canada First"—but it is pretty close to that. He prefers the term "national interest." However, many provincial premiers would disagree, placing their dukedoms first. Certain of the provincial premiers, fighting with federal cabinet ministers over distribution of oil royalties, might construe the federal attitude as "petty" nationalism. In turn, the attitudes of these provincial dukes and barons might, from Ottawa, be characterized as "xenophobic" and not to be tolerated by Ottawa. The business tycoon, challenged by the government on his presumptive or real monopoly, would characterize that bureaucratic intervention as "neo-nationalism." Finally, though that seems to be the aim of prime minister and cabinet, many Canadians cannot yet reconcile their new nationalism with their historic international role.

Throughout the course of Canada's history, her interests and international goals have not always been clearly defined. Some factions have favored isolationism, and others have promoted internationalism. There have been pulls between those who supported protectionism and those who advocated free trade. There has been controversy over the advantages of freer immigration or of closing Canada's doors to newcomers. Some factions worked to impede outside capital, and others wanted to encourage it. There have been those who favored closer association with the United States and those who preferred Canada to be less bound to her southern neighbor. There are even contradictory views on Canada's continuing association with the British monarchy and the commonwealth. These contradictions all seem to relate to the underlying periods of introversion versus extroversion—of national self-doubt and of recurrent self-assurance. Just what are Canada's most clearcut interests today?

Surely for Canada there must be the interest of independence—economic as well as political. As the shortage of natural resources becomes more acute for the rest of the world, Canada finds herself a "most favored nation." Both her economic and her environmental prospects are good—possibly even great. Here she needs only to husband her resources, to keep her eye peeled for new markets, as her ministers say, to supplement rather than to supplant the present superb trade relations with the United States. Given her sure economic base, Canada must continue to trade with the developed world and to aid the developing lands.

Canada has a special role to play in international affairs and this, too, is in her own national interest. She has a much-needed capability not only to support but to help strengthen instruments of international accord—especially in the United Nations, the commonwealth, and the field of disarmament. She has a mediating role to play among the great powers and Third World nations who have firm trust in her. She should also be able to play a pivotal role in future environmental matters. Her deep attachment to seeking solutions for the law of the sea and for ecological protection of the Arctic are indicative of her constructive attitude in an increasingly interdependent and ecologically conscious world. As one of the world's greatest trading nations, she is learning to walk the chalk line between nationalism and internationalism, between protectionism and free trade. Even her policy of immigration can be balanced between the need for new manpower and recurring pressures of unemployment. At the very same time she most needs new populations to fill her empty spaces and promote internal expansion, surely she will not close her doors to immigrants.

Her potential as an international leader has only begun.

Here her innate conservatism and her tendency toward isolation must be tempered with her great capacity for compromise, for conciliation, and for constructive international peace.

Finally there is the question of Canada's own unity. How can it best be preserved? We have offered suggestions concerning reduction of federal-provincial frictions. We have expressed hopes for elimination of ethnic, cultural, and social disparities or antagonism. It has been said by some that there is, in truth, only one underlying truly "Canadian" character—Anglo- or French-Canadian portions of the nation being only subcultural variants thereof, sometimes vexing but not really doomed to separation. Some will question this—especially those extremists on either side who are determined to see their country fracture. Perhaps, as former American Secretary of State Dean Rusk once commented, some countries become *states* in the legal sense before they become *nations* in the factual sense. That process takes time. Perhaps, too, the process of homogenization of Canada is proceeding all the while under cover of superficial disunity—by means of urbanization, industrialization, secularization, and common acculturation. There are, increasingly, common denominators, common traits, among the country's "tribes." Perhaps the acceptance of one national anthem, "O Canada," over the earlier much-argued "Maple Leaf Forever" and "God Save the Queen," is one indicator of such changes. Perhaps the recent (1965) acceptance of a new Canadian flag to replace the contested Union Jack is yet another. At long last, these may symbolize the realities of the unifying process. Possibly one day, Canada may even be ready to accept a single language—be that English, or French or Esperanto.

This idea of making Canada unilingual is understandably unpopular—surely controversial. If a single language were assured for all governmental, educational, business, and cultural activities, huge results would soon be seen. There would be financial as well as political benefits. In making this recommendation for unilingualism, one must recall that traumas of bilingualism or of multilingualism have embittered and seriously weakened other nations. Cyprus, Belgium, South Africa, Nigeria, and India are illustrative. Such traumas are to be avoided, not emulated. Is it not now time for Canada to reconsider the advantages of unilingualism? Would such a step not put a new vitality into Canadian nationhood—a new and happier spirit into the Canadian character?

Some sixty years ago, Prime Minister Laurier said that the twentieth century would belong to Canada. Somehow history mocked his words. The American "elephant" challenged Laurier's view. The turmoils of the various great and middle-sized world wars drained off Canadian energies and manpower. The Canadians' own sense of self-doubt and their internal squabblings also impeded attainment of Laurier's vision. It may be that Laurier was only premature. For, given her immense natural and human riches, her innate sense of values and constructive compromise, with her national neuroses overcome, Canada may still see Laurier's dream realized. The twenty-first century may yet belong to Canada.

Bibliography

BOOKS

Barr, John J., and Anderson, Owen, eds. *The Unfinished Revolt: Some Views on Western Independence.* Toronto: McClelland & Stewart, 1971.
Berton, Pierre. *The Last Spike.* Toronto: McClelland & Stewart, 1971.
   The National Dream. Toronto: McClelland & Stewart, 1970.
Beston, Henry. *The St. Lawrence: Story of a River.* New York: Farrar & Rinehart, 1942.
Blair, Neatby H. *William Lyon Mackenzie King.* Vols. 1, 2, 3. Toronto: University of Toronto Press, 1976.
Bloomfield, L.M., and Fitzgerald, Gerald. *Boundary Water Problems: Canada and the United States.* Toronto: Carswell Co., 1958.
Brebner, J. Barlet. *Canada: A Modern History.* Ann Arbor: University of Michigan Press, 1970.
Brown, Lorne, and Brown, Caroline. *Unauthorized History of the R.C.M.P.* Toronto: James Lewis & Samuels, 1973.
Careless, J. M. S. *Canada: A Story of Challenge.* 3d ed. Toronto: The Macmillan Company of Canada, 1970.
Careless, J. M. S., and Brown, R. Craig, eds. *The Canadians, 1867–1967.* Toronto: The Macmillan Company of Canada, 1967.
Carey, Charles. *A General History of Oregon.* Vol. 1. Portland, Ore.: Metropolitan Press, 1935.
Clark, Gerald. *Canada: The Uneasy Neighbor.* Toronto: McClelland & Stewart, 1965.
Clement, Wallace. *The Canadian Corporate Elite: An Analysis of Economic Power.* Toronto: McClelland & Stewart, 1975.

347

Cook, Ramsay, with Saywell, John, and Ricker, John. *Canada: A Modern Study.* Toronto: Clarke, Irwin & Co., 1971.

Creighton, Donald. *John A. Macdonald: The Old Chieftain.* Toronto: The Macmillan Company of Canada, 1955.

Dafoe, J. W. *Laurier: A Study in Canadian Politics.* Toronto: McClelland & Stewart, 1963.

Diefenbaker, John G. *The Years of Achievement, 1956–62. One Canada: Memoirs of the Right Honourable John G. Diefenbaker.* Toronto: The Macmillan Company of Canada, 1976.

Donaldson, Gordon. *Fifteen Men: Canada's Prime Ministers from Macdonald to Trudeau.* Toronto: Doubleday, 1969.

Frankfurter, Glen. *Baneful Domination.* Don Mills, Ontario: Longman Canada Ltd., 1971.

Fullerton, Douglas H. *The Dangerous Delusion: Quebec's Independence Obsession.* Toronto: McClelland & Stewart, 1978.

Graebner, Norman, ed. *Manifest Destiny.* Indianapolis: The Bobbs-Merrill Co. Inc., 1968.

Granatstein, J.L. *Canada's War: The Politics of Mackenzie King Government 1939–45.* London: Oxford University Press, 1976.

Grant, George. *Lament for a Nation: The Defeat of Canadian Nationalism.* Toronto: McClelland & Stewart, 1971.

Greenough, William Parker. *Canadian Folk-Life & Folk-Lore.* Toronto: Coles Publishing Co., 1971.

Gustafson, Ralph. *An Anthology of Canadian Poetry.* Harmondsworth, Middlesex, England: Pelican/Penguin Books, 1942.

Hemon, Louis. *Maria Chapdelaine.* New York: Random House, 1934.

Hertzman, Lewis; Warnock, John W., and Hockin, Thomas. *Alliances and Illusions: Canada and the NATO–NORAD Question.* Edmonton: M. G. Hurtig Ltd. Pub., 1969.

Hutchison, Bruce. *The Far Side of the Street.* Toronto: The Macmillan Company of Canada, 1976.

    The Incredible Canadian: A Candid Portrait of Mackenzie King. Don Mills: Longmans Canada Limited, 1952.

    The Unknown Country. New and Rev. Ed. Toronto: McClelland & Stewart, 1965.

Keenleyside, Hugh L., and Brown, Gerald S. *Canada and the United States.* New York: Alfred Knopf, 1952.

Kilbourn, William, ed. *Canada: A Guide to the Peaceable Kingdom,* an anthology. Toronto: The MacMillan Company of Canada, 1970.

Lower, Arthur, R. M. *Colony to Nation: A History of Canada.* Toronto: Longmans, Green, 1946.

Lower, J.A. *Canada: An Outline of History.* Toronto: Ryerson Press, 1966.

McDonald, Jim, and MacDonald, Jack, eds. *The Canadian Voters' Guidebook.* Don Mills: Fitzhenry & Whiteside, 1972.

MacLennan, Hugh. *Two Solitudes.* Toronto: Popular Library, 1945.

Morton, Desmond. *NDP: The Dream of Power.* Toronto: A. M. Hakkert, 1974.

Mowat, Farley. *Canada North Now.* Toronto: McClelland & Stewart, 1976.

    People of the Deer. New York: Pyramid Books, 1952.

    Tundra. Toronto: McClelland & Stewart, 1973.

Myers, Gustavus. *History of Canadian Wealth.* Vol. I. Toronto: James Lewis & Samuel, 1972.

Newman, Peter C. *The Canadian Establishment.* Vol. I. Toronto: McClelland & Stewart, 1975.

Newman, Peter C., and Fillmore, Stan, eds. *Their Turn to Curtsy—Your Turn To Bow.* Toronto: Maclean-Hunter, 1972.

Patterson, E. Palmer, II. *The Canadian Indian: A History since 1500.* Don Mills: Collier-Macmillan, 1972.

Pearson, Lester B. *Mike.* Toronto: University of Toronto Press. Vol. 1, *1897–1948* (1972). Vol. 2, *1948–1957*, ed. John A. Munro and Alex I. Inglis (1973). Vol. 3, *1957–1968*, ed. John A. Munro and Alex I. Inglis (1975).

Peat, Louisa W. *Canada: New World Power.* New York: Robert McBride, 1945.

Perry, Robert L. *Galt, USA: The "American Presence" in a Canadian City.* Toronto: Maclean-Hunter, 1971.

Pickersgill, J. W. *My Year with St. Laurent.* Toronto: University of Toronto Press, 1975.

Pope, William Henry. *The Elephant and the Mouse.* Toronto: McClelland & Stewart, 1971.

Porter, John. *The Vertical Mosaic: An Analysis of Social Class and Power in Canada.* Toronto: University of Toronto Press, 1972.

Pryde, Duncan. *Nunaga: Ten Years of Eskimo Life.* Toronto: Bantam Books, 1973.

Roberts, Leslie. *Canada: The Golden Hinge.* Toronto: Clarke, Irwin, 1952.

Robins, John D., ed. *A Pocketful of Canada.* Toronto: W. M. Collins & Son, 1948.

Rohmer, Richard. *Ultimatum.* Toronto: Clarke, Irwin, 1973.

Skelton, Oscar D. *Laurier: Life and Letters of Sir Wilfrid Laurier.* Vols. 1, 2. Toronto: McClelland & Stewart, 1965.

Starowicz, Mark, and Murphy, Rae, eds. *Corporate Canada: Fourteen Probes into the Workings of the Branch-Plant Economy.* Toronto: James Lewis and Samuel, 1972.

Stursberg, Peter. *Diefenbaker: Leadership Lost 1962–67.* Toronto: University of Toronto Press, 1976.

Talman, James J. *Basic Documents in Canadian History.* Scarborough, Ont.: D. Van Nostrand Co., 1959.

Telegram-Toronto Canada 70 Team. *The Challenge of Confrontation.* Toronto: McClelland & Stewart, 1969. Vol. 1, *British Columbia: The Great Divide.* Vol. 2, *The Prairies: Alienation and Anger.* Vol. 3, *Ontario: The Linchpin.* Vol. 4, *Quebec: The Threat of Separation.* Vol. 5, *The Atlantic Provinces: The Struggle for Survival.* Vol. 6, *Coast to Coast: Canada 70—Summary.*

Thordarson, Truce. *Trudeau and Foreign Policy: A Study in Decision-Making.* Toronto: Oxford University Press, 1972.

Trudeau, Pierre. *Conversations with Canadians.* Toronto: University of Toronto Press, 1972.

    Trudeau and Federalism: Federalism and the French Canadians. Toronto: The Macmillan Company of Canada, 1968.

Trudel, Marcel, and Jain, Genevieve. *Canadian History Textbooks: A Comparative Study.* Ottawa: The Queen's Printer, 1970.

Vallieres, Pierre. *Choose!* Toronto: New Press, 1971.

Wade, Mason. *The French Canadians: 1760–1967.* Vols. 1, 2. Toronto: The Macmillan Company of Canada, 1968.

Westell, Anthony. *Paradox: Trudeau as Prime Minister.* Scarborough: Prentice-Hall of Canada, 1972.

Whiteford, Andrew H. *Indian Arts: North American.* New York: Golden Press, 1970.

Winn, C., and McMenemy, J. *Political Parties in Canada.* Toronto: McGraw-Hill-Ryerson, 1976.

REFERENCE WORKS

Canada, Parliament, Senate, Standing Senate Committee on Foreign Affairs. *Canada-United States Relations.* Vol. 1. Ottawa: The Queen's Printer, 1975.

Canada 1944: The Official Handbook of Present Conditions and Recent Progress. Ottawa: The King's Printer, 1944.

Canada 1955-56: The Official Handbook of Present Conditions and Recent Progress. Ottawa: The Queen's Printer, 1955.

Canada 1971: The Annual Handbook of Present Conditions and Recent Progress. Ottawa: The Queen's Printer, 1975.

The Canadian Pocket Encyclopedia 1971-72. 27th Annual Edition. Quick Facts, 1971.

The Canadian Pocket Encyclopedia 1971–72. 27th Annual Edition. Quick Fact, 1971.

Facets of French Canada. Ottawa: ACELF (The Canadian Association of French-speaking Educators), 1967.

PAMPHLETS

Canada Weekly. Canada, Department of External Affairs, Canadian Information Service Division.

Canadian Press Comments. Canada, Department of External Affairs, Canadian Embassy, Washington, D.C.

Special Speech Publications. Canada Department of External Affairs, Canadian Embassy, Washington, D.C.

Statements and Speeches. Canada, Department of External Affairs.

NEWSPAPERS AND MAGAZINES

Calgary Herald
Canadian Forum, Toronto
Canadian Review, Ottawa
Citizen, Ottawa
Economist, London
Gazette, Montreal
Globe and Mail, Toronto
International Perspectives, Ottawa
La Presse, Montreal
Le Devoir, Montreal
Maclean's, Toronto
National Geographic, U.S.A.
Newsweek, U.S.A.
New York Times
Oregonian, Portland
Ottawa Journal, Ottawa
Statesman-Journal, Salem
U. S. News & World Report, U.S.A.
Vancouver Sun
Wall Street Journal, New York
Washington Post
Winnipeg Free Press

Index